REBEL ISLAND

Jonathan Clements presented several seasons of *Route Awakening* (National Geographic), an award-winning TV series about Chinese history and culture. He is the author of many acclaimed books, including *Coxinga and the Fall of the Ming Dynasty*, *Confucius: a biography*, and *The Emperor's Feast: a history of China in twelve meals*. He has written histories of both China and Japan, two countries that have, at some point, claimed Taiwan as their own. He was a visiting professor at Xi'an Jiaotong University from 2013 to 2019. He was born in England and lives in Finland.

REBEL ISLAND

THE INCREDIBLE HISTORY OF TAIWAN

Jonathan Clements

SCRIBE

Melbourne | London | Minneapolis

Scribe Publications
18–20 Edward St, Brunswick, Victoria 3056, Australia
2 John St, Clerkenwell, London, WC1N 2ES, United Kingdom
3754 Pleasant Ave, Suite 100, Minneapolis, Minnesota 55409, USA

Published by Scribe 2024

Typeset in Garamond Premier Pro by the publishers

Printed and bound in the UK by CPI Group (UK) Ltd, Croydon CR0 4YY

Scribe is committed to the sustainable use of natural resources and the use of
paper products made responsibly from those resources.

978 1 915590 27 5 (UK edition)
978 1 957363 74 5 (US edition)
978 1 761385 48 3 (ebook)

scribepublications.com.au
scribepublications.co.uk
scribepublications.com

in memory of
David Johnson (1943–2021)

三年一小反，五年一大亂
'Every three years an uprising, every five a rebellion.'
Xu Zonggan (1796–1866), governor of Taiwan

CONTENTS

LIST OF ILLUSTRATIONS

Within the text

Plate section

13. End of Japanese rule
14. Dwight D. Eisenhower's 1960 visit to Taipei
15. 'We shall certainly recapture Taiwan' propaganda poster (IISH / ChinesePosters.net)
16. Chiang Kai-shek Memorial Hall (AngMoKio / Wikimedia Commons)
17. Chiang Kai-shek statues (Chintung Lee / Shutterstock)
18. Chen Shui-bian and Annette Lu (AFP Photo / Robyn Beck / Getty Images)
19. Taipei 101 (Jeffrey Liao / Shutterstock)

Every effort has been made to trace the copyright holders of illustrations and obtain permission for the use of material reproduced in this book. If any inadvertent omissions have been made, these can be rectified and acknowledged in subsequent printings or editions.

PREFACE

At 394 km from north to south, and 144 km at its widest point from east to west, Taiwan has a land area of 35,800 square kilometres — roughly the same size as the Netherlands, Switzerland, or the state of Massachusetts. Some sources give its land area as 36,100 square kilometres, which would encompass not only Taiwan itself, but several dozen outlying islands it still retains as part of the Republic of China, the last remnants of the forerunner to the People's Republic established on the mainland in 1949. These include the Penghu (Pescadores) Islands in the middle of the Taiwan Strait, and the islands of Matsu and the Kinmen archipelago just off the Chinese coast.

For the last couple of millennia, ever since seafaring technology has brought it into range of nearby landmasses, the island has been situated at an important crossroads. It is 160 km to the Chinese mainland across the Taiwan Strait, but it is also a mere 320 km, hopping along the Batanes islands, to the north coast of the Philippines. You'll read in multiple sources that Japan is '1,100 km away', but that is precisely the sort of geographical fudge that the Taiwanese islanders have exploited for centuries. In fact, it is only 162 km from the coast of Taiwan to Yonaguni, the nearest of the Ryukyu Islands — Japan, or some possession of it, is just as close as China. For centuries, the Taiwanese have capitalised on their liminal position, crossing the 'thousand kilometres' to Japan by darting from one little island to the next, rarely out of sight of land, smuggling silk, hides, and tea into Japanese ports, and trading back in China in brocades, ironware, and swords.

These contacts were not so easy in ancient times. The Kuroshio ('Black Stream') current off Taiwan's eastern coast is part of the wider North Pacific Gyre, which was capable of snatching smaller, pre-modern boats in its grasp and propelling them far out to sea. It formed an effective barrier between Taiwan and the southernmost Ryukyu Islands in earlier centuries.[1] Between Taiwan and the Penghu Islands, there is also a north–south trench of significantly deeper water, known to old-time Chinese sailors as the 'Black Ditch' (*Heishui guo*). Even today, the area is subject to challenging phenomena — in storms, the currents can run in unpredictable directions or form sudden whirlpools. Even in the 21st century, Penghu fisherman tell tales of the Black Ditch as a cursed region of the sea, where the spirits of the dead demanded appeasement through human sacrifice once every three years.[2]

The Tropic of Cancer slices through the middle of Taiwan, on a line of latitude between the modern cities of Chiayi and Hualien. North of this line, the climate is temperate. On the south side, it is tropical, with a winter monsoon that blows in from the north-east, and a summer monsoon from the south-west. The far south of the island, particularly the spit of land around Kenting and Eluanbi, is several degrees warmer year-round than the northern parts of the island.

The weather conditions in Taiwan created particular problems for pre-modern agriculture. The rainy season in the north is predictable and evenly spread, lasting from October to March. But south of Chiayi, the same period is dry, with torrential rainstorms arriving to pummel south Taiwan from May to September. This plays havoc with what would usually be the spring–summer growing season for farmers; before the 20th century, it limited rice growers in the south to a single crop per year, of a food that might otherwise be possible to harvest twice or even three times.[3]

Throughout Taiwan's history, this has presented a challenge to settlers — on multiple occasions in the record, there are mentions of would-be colonists defeated by its savage climate, which was also a haven in olden times for malaria and other tropical diseases.

•

If we imagine the whole history of the human habitation of Taiwan, up to the present day, as a single calendar year, then humans first arrive on 1 January — although those ancient people have left behind none of their DNA, only fire sticks and stone axes. The Neolithic period, which saw settlement of the island by the ancestors of today's Formosan indigenous communities, begins around 1 November. The rise on the mainland of the First Emperor, Qin Shihuang, his Terracotta Army, and the very concept of there being a China that Taiwan could become a part of, happens sometime on 3 December. Prolonged and enduring ties with the Chinese on the mainland are initiated around Christmas. The Ming-dynasty loyalist Koxinga and his men arrive in the small hours of 28 December, and their regime is toppled with a Qing-dynasty retaliation by lunchtime. The Japanese annex Taiwan as a colony around midday on 30 December, and are themselves ousted shortly before dawn on New Year's Eve, making way for the mass arrival of Chiang Kai-shek's Kuomintang (KMT), the Chinese Nationalist Party, in retreat from Mao's Communists on the mainland. Martial law stays in force until just after breakfast, and the entire modern history of a democratic Republic of China on Taiwan occupies the next 18 hours until midnight, when I am telling you this.

In other words, Taiwan's *history* — in a literal sense, the written record of its events and culture — occupies less than 2 per cent of the period that it has been inhabited by human beings. Such a comment would be true about most other parts of the world, but there are some places, and Taiwan is one of them, where a concentration on modern history risks adding to the marginalisation of the voices and experience of the ethnic groups that have lived there the longest. In her recent work on indigenous cultures, the archaeologist Kuo Su-chiu points out just how overwhelming a dispassionate sense of deep time is, and how misleading it is for traditional historiography to focus on the spats between Chinese and Japanese, or nationalists who believe that Taiwan is part of China and separatists who wish it wasn't.

Taiwan's own sense of self is usually understood, if it is understood at all, in vastly simplified terms that have only meant something in the last century. The nature of the source material requires me to gloss over the prehistory of Taiwan in a single chapter, as if the rest of the book is a round-robin letter of the past year from weird cousins who only focus on the Christmas vacation.

I'm sorry *when* I offend you. When identity politics are such a crucial part of a nation's story, and the nature of its identity so open to question, someone is sure to take umbrage at particular perspectives. Taiwan may be the location in which these historical events take place, but the historical actors have wildly shifting ideas of who is the protagonist and who is the antagonist. Events themselves are often subject to retroactive interpretations and emphases — retold by new factions and assigned new meanings.

Almost every chapter of this book finds a different power bloc contesting Taiwan. Our understanding of Taiwanese history is so modular, so beholden to the influences of the observers who chronicled it, that it might even be possible for a reader to choose to enter this book at *any* point, experiencing Taiwan from that point on. Such issues can exert powerful influences on the way that facts are interpreted. Japanese archaeologists, who first scientifically documented Taiwan's past, played up connections to the Philippines, thereby undermining the island's cultural and historical connections to China, and helping to justify their own presence as colonisers. The following generation of Chinese archaeologists working under the ruling KMT instead emphasised pre-modern Taiwan's connections to the Chinese mainland. Conversely, the 21st century has seen a vast increase in archaeology relating to Taiwan's indigenous inhabitants, yet again reflecting changes in the modern political climate.[4]

There are multiple overlapping Venn diagrams at work here — lost indigenous peoples; the extant indigenous peoples, termed 'Formosans' here for clarity's sake; the nativist Chinese (*bensheng*) and their ancestors born on Taiwan in the Ming and Qing eras, themselves split into subethnic factions of Fujianese (Hoklo) and Hakka; the Japanese (*Wansei*) born on Taiwan during its 50 years as a Japanese colony (some of whom stayed, while some returned to Japan); the colonial-era Chinese migrants (*Taigan*) who became nominal Japanese subjects in order to gain extraterritorial advantages on the mainland; the indigenous soldiers (*Takasago*) who, for various reasons, embraced suicidal loyalty to the Japanese; the 20th-century refugees born elsewhere in China (*waisheng*), and their contemporary descendants, whom we might split, in turn, into subgroups of 'Blue' conservatives supporting the notion of Taiwan as a mere province within a Republic of China, 'Greens' favouring an independent Taiwan, and even a scattering of 'Reds' wishing for assimilation into the People's Republic. Both 'Blues' and 'Greens' also have a lighter shade at their edges, that prefers to simply cling to the status quo of Taiwan's current limbo state, regardless of whether they see Taiwan as part of China or separate from it.

In both modern and pre-modern times, Taiwan has enjoyed a unique territorial status. It has been a stronghold of pirates and smugglers, a promised land of coastal emigration from Fujian and Guangdong provinces via the Taiwan Strait, and a secret backdoor to Japan. It was the site of failed settlements for both the Spanish and the Dutch, and a retreat for the last of the Ming resistance, an accidental acquisition by the Qing dynasty, only reluctantly retained amid multiple indigenous uprisings. It was a prime target in the Sino-French War of the late 19th century, and an environment hostile enough to repel several invasions solely on the basis of climate and disease. Handed over as a spoil of war, its 50 years as a Japanese colony continue to have a strong influence on the island's culture and connections. Most famously, in 1949 it became the site of the rump government of the Republic of China, as the mainland fell to the Communists. After 38 years of martial law, the liberalisation of the refugee regime led to free elections, and a new conflict over the meaning of 'independence'.

Over and again, in early discussions of Taiwan as a frontier society, we see references in foreign accounts to the march of 'progress' — to the need to find markets for new products, and sources for new fuels. In terms of what philosophers call an 'integral accident', new demands create new problems. There would be no need to suppress wreckers on the coast if there were not a huge upsurge in passing shipping; no need to secure the port of Keelung if coal were not so important to steamships. The arrival of the musket, high-quality steel, and then the rifle radically transformed the destructive force of hunting expeditions and tribal conflicts that had unfolded with little change for thousands of years.[5] The worldwide demand for smokeless gunpowder in the 19th century turned the island's ancient camphor forests into a hotly contested resource. In the 21st century, camphor has given way to a commodity even more critical to the global economy: computer chips.

Taiwan is a lively subject in academic curriculums, not the least because it is a tantalising 'Other' to the People's Republic of China — a road less travelled, a capitalist alternative, or a vestigial throwback. It has also been, on various occasions in 20th century history, a backdoor for economic investment on the Chinese mainland, particularly in 1980s Fujian, as well as a troublesome rogue province, ever-present in the speeches of mainland politicians ready to rattle their sabres.

A search on Amazon of the upcoming English-language books tagged with 'Taiwan' returns results in which a majority are concerned with future wars and US foreign policy — a disturbing number of them spat out by content mills and wiki-scrubbers determined to cram the sales lists with ominous and threatening concepts. But such a bias is not repeated in other languages. In Japanese, for example, Taiwan is not merely a modern political hot potato, but also a former colony with a 50-year history of its own. That, too, can lead to some violent subjects — of all the books written in post-war Japan on Taiwan history, fully 10 per cent focus on the Musha Incident of 1930, in which an angry indigenous group massacred the Japanese attendees at a school sports day.

When I first arrived in Taiwan in 1991 (as if jumping into this book part-way through Chapter Ten), I was bewildered by the experience of being transported to a 'China' nothing like the People's Republic of my textbooks and teachers. Sometimes it felt like I had phased into an alternate reality, off-kilter from the real world, such as when I looked at a locally printed map and found out that Israel, owing to its early recognition of the People's Republic in Beijing, did not apparently exist (diplomatic relations with Taiwan were established in 1992), while Outer Mongolia was still part of China (Taipei did not recognise its 1911 independence until 2002). When I played the unauthorised local version of Monopoly, one of the Community Chest cards included a reward for shooting down a Communist fighter invading local airspace.

The accent lacked the Beijing burr I had so carefully learned, and now had to unlearn fast, and conversations all around me would often code-switch into speech that was initially only identifiable to me as *not* Chinese. I assumed that it was Taiyu ('Taiwanese Hokkien'), although even that term covers a parcel of languages from across the water in Fujian and Guangdong, including Hokkien and Hakka. Japanese was a secret cant among the elderly, served by a shadowy market in *enka* music sequestered at the rear of the record stores. Twice a week, I got up at dawn to teach English at a major bank, where my adult students slowly revealed themselves as political cynics, mistrustful of both the ruling 'Blue' KMT and the underdog 'Green' Democratic Progressive Party (DPP) that had recently challenged the KMT's four-decade stranglehold on power.

The Mandarin they speak in Taiwan is *very pure*, I was assured by university management as they waved me off to class. They neglected to mention that people don't always speak Mandarin in Taiwan, which is why for many locals, it is a second or third language. The further south you went, the likelier it was that the 73 per cent of the population that were Taiwanese-proficient would use it as their language of choice (see Notes on Names). Nineteen years later, at a political rally for the mayor of Tainan, Hsu Tain-tsair, I listened as he began in soundbite Mandarin for the mass-media cameras, but switched into Taiwanese in order to present himself as a man of the people — a common political tactic since the 1970s.[6] Meanwhile, 12 per cent of today's population speak Hakka. In Taoyuan, Hsinchu, and Miaoli counties, within ten kilometres of metro Taipei, native Hakka speakers are in the majority. Some of the Hakka would be sure to tell you that their Chinese was the purest of all, since it supposedly retains the accents and pronunciations of their medieval ancestors, who fled the nomad invaders of north China.

The 1.7 per cent of the population that today identify as indigenous speak at least one of 16 surviving Austronesian languages; to confound the historian, another dozen indigenous languages have died out in the last couple of centuries.[7] The idea that Taiwan is a 'Mandarin-speaking' island is a *political* decree, issued in the 1940s by the refugee KMT government, and enshrined in 1953 in a strict educational policy. That, in turn, was at least partly designed to stamp out Japanese, the lingua franca of Taiwanese culture and civil life for the first four decades of the 20th century, and still a shibboleth that pops up in local slang.

Such issues even filter down to the words we use. *Taiwan*, the 'terraced bay', derives from the Chinese name for the landfall near what is now Tainan, and hence derives from the period in the island's history when it began to fall under mainland influence. Or rather, that is the official story. The term *Taiwan* may have been used by indigenous people to refer not only to the terraced bay named by Chinese sailors, but also to the unwelcome outlanders who flocked there to trade and settle.[8]

Some separatist advocates prefer to refer to their home island as *Formosa*, using a deliberately non-Chinese term, although that, too, is an identity-politics minefield, as it derives from the name assigned to Taiwan by Portuguese sailors. Among the indigenous tribes of the south, the island is also referred to by another name, *Pekan*, meaning a place of sanctuary found after much wandering and tribulation. This book is an attempt to combine all these contending assumptions and claims into a history of this beautiful, lively, diverse, and rebel island.

INTRODUCTION

THE ROVER INCIDENT

(1867)

On Tuesday 12 March 1867, the trading vessel *Rover* was heading from Shantou on the south Chinese coast, up to the port of Niuzhuang on the coast of Manchuria. The favoured route was to swing out to the western side of Taiwan and then through open sea straight to the north, thereby avoiding the troubled coastal waters of the Chinese mainland.

Captain Joseph Hunt was not prepared for the risk presented by the reefs and shoals in Taiwanese waters. The area had been mapped some years earlier, but the crew of the survey ship had given up early in the face of a gale. Hunt therefore had little to go on but the hand-waving apologies to be found in *The China Pilot*:

> the sea was observed breaking very heavily over the Vele Rete rocks and heavy tide ripples extended nearly the whole distance across to them from the South Cape ... [A] reef is said to project from this cape, for high breakers, projecting to a considerable distance from the cape were observed ...[1]

There was no lighthouse on the south of Taiwan at the time, nor was the area even regarded by outsiders as 'civilised', since only occasional Chinese traders ventured along the black, forbidding cliffs into the lands claimed by multiple indigenous tribes. In hindsight, *The China Pilot's* warning, that there might be up to 15 km of uncharted reefs ahead of the *Rover*, should have been sufficient, but Hunt's ship sailed right into the rocks, tearing a hole in its side.

The *Rover* foundered, flooded, and began to tip over. As its death throes slowly played out, its crew scrambled to get to the lifeboats. Soaked to the skin, and clutching a mere handful of personal items, they hauled away from the capsizing wreck, dragging on the oars for 17 long hours until they finally reached land.

Captain Hunt's wife, Mercy, was one of the first people ashore. With her long Victorian skirts waterlogged in the escape from the ship, she was clad in hand-me-downs from the sailors — a man's breeches and shirt. Seeing an indigenous woman near the shore, Mercy Hunt gingerly approached her, proffering some money, and trying to explain, via sign language, that the party needed a guide to get them to civilisation.

Instead, the woman returned with a party of warriors, targeting Mrs Hunt in the belief that as the initiator of the parley, she was the leader of the foreigners. The party killed the Hunts, their white crewmates, and all the Chinese, except two, who escaped to report on their fate.[2]

The luckless crew of the *Rover* had no way of knowing that they were trespassing on land belonging to the Koalut subtribe of the Paiwan. Furthermore, they did so at the start of a rare date in the tribal calendar in which young menfolk of the Koalut Paiwan were expected to take the head of an enemy in order to win a wife. Normally, the coastal Paiwan preferred to avoid all contact with foreign ships, as there were folk memories of similar vessels arriving and carrying off their people. The aversion to foreign ships was so strong that the Paiwan tribes even had a taboo against eating chicken, in place ever since an unspecified ancient time when a cock's crow gave away their location to foreign raiders.[3]

Later that month, a punitive force dispatched 'with chivalrous promptitude' in the *Cormorant* out of Kaohsiung, wisely chose not to pursue armed tribesmen into the forest.[4] We have such detailed accounts of the events, in part, because of the particular interest taken in them by the US consul in Amoy (also known as Xiamen), Charles Le Gendre, who fancied himself as a China expert, and was determined to prove his mettle in resolving the situation.

Le Gendre was a fantastic character. Born in France, he had served in the American Civil War, in which a gunshot to the face had cost him an eye and part of his nose. He had arrived in Amoy a year previously, determined to make his mark on south-east China, and saw the *Rover* incident as the perfect chance for him to interfere on Taiwan, which was technically within his jurisdiction on the other side of the Strait.

'After a cruise of ten days in those quarters,' he wrote, 'we returned to Amoy, fully persuaded that nothing but carefully conducted negotiations with the aborigines, sustained by an imposing force, would ever bring about a change in their manner of dealing with foreigners.'[5]

There was money in it, too. A *China Mail* announcement by Mercy Hunt's wealthy relatives offered $2,500 (a year's salary for a working man at the time) for the return of her remains to receive a Christian burial. Rear Admiral H.H. Bell, commanding the *Hartford* and *Wyoming*, attempted a punitive expedition against Le Gendre's advice, but then retreated, commenting: 'These natives ... are very different from those described by the Chinese imagination, and are really much more formidable than the untamed beasts whom the former consider it to be dangerous to hunt.'[6] Bell had been taken aback by the firepower wielded by the Koaluts, who

US marines and sailors fire into the forest at Koalut tribesmen, 1867.

had primitive muskets bartered from Chinese traders. Using forest cover to repeatedly retreat and reload, tribesmen wielding single-shot muzzle-loaded antiques proved unconquerable by marines with more modern weapons.

When Le Gendre's request to mount an expedition of his own was refused, he arranged one anyway, at Fuzhou commandeering the *Volunteer*, the crew of which had been expressly ordered merely to ferry him across the Strait. Instead, he allowed the Chinese to believe that he was in command of an official American response, and inveigled them into providing him with a force of local Chinese soldiers on Taiwan.

In the hinterland, the intrigues over the victims continued. A local entrepreneur had met some tribesmen and offered them the princely sum of $15 for what was left of Mercy Hunt. In doing so, he scared them with tales of the coming retaliatory force, leading the indigenous people to dump Mrs Hunt's remains under a tree near their village, where local dogs had gnawed on her bones. The Koaluts saw no issue with taking the heads of invaders, but were deeply embarrassed that they had broken a taboo by killing a woman — Mercy Hunt's change of clothes being the unfortunate factor that had sealed her death.[7]

The foreigners were stumbling into a complex situation, and risked leading an army against an innocent indigenous subgroup that had nothing to do with the Koaluts who had murdered the *Rover*'s crew. In fact, noted one tribesman, had the unfortunate Hunts come ashore but 300 yards along the beach, they would have been in the domain of an altogether friendlier clan.[8]

Claiming to have nothing to do with the Koaluts, this new tribal group, from a neighbouring mountain village, had now determined that the size of the response was presumably proportional to the importance of Mrs Hunt, and that they deserved a bigger reward before they helped return her bones.

Le Gendre's account continues for page after page with the haggling over the articles of the *Rover*'s luckless dead, as his agents wandered in search of such trifles as a watch, a pocketbook, and a cameo portrait. Amid all this dickering, it came to light that the 'here-be-dragons' vagueness of foreign mapping had ignored the presence of a coalition of 18 indigenous tribes, the Seqalu. This coalition had an overlord by the name of Cuqicuq

Garuljigulj, who was at war with several other groups, including the group that had attacked the survivors of the *Rover*. The Americans called him Toketok.[9]

Toketok was in his early fifties, and had a commanding air about him. Le Gendre described him as short and stocky, but highly energetic, and with a hybrid hairstyle that echoed that of the Chinese on the coast — his greying hair was shaved at the front in the Chinese fashion, with a 12-inch braid at the back. He was attended by an entourage of warriors, many of them wearing pheasant plumes in their hair, and with earlobes expanded by 'washer'-like earrings. Some carried muskets with highly polished barrels; others bore pikes, 'the heads of which were ornamented with the hair of the unfortunates they had killed'.[10]

Toketok explained to Le Gendre how things were likely to have looked from the Koaluts' perspective, suggesting that the Hunts had blundered into a vendetta stretching back decades, if not centuries.

> A long time ago … white people had all but exterminated the Koalut tribe, leaving only three, who survived to hand down to their posterity the desire for revenge. Having no ships to pursue foreigners, they had taken their revenge as best they could.[11]

The journalist Edward House, in covering this event, found the story plausible, blaming the vendetta on the Dutch who had briefly occupied Taiwan in the 17th century, whose actions were 'stained with misdeeds as gross as any which the Asiatic savages, at this day, have given reason to complain'.

Toketok agreed to talk with Le Gendre on the grounds that he had been impressed by the martial puissance of the Americans aboard the *Hartford* and the *Wyoming*. Their gunboat diplomacy had been enough to spook him into holding a conference, whereas the Chinese had singularly failed to impress him. When the Chinese attempted a similar negotiation, he fobbed them off by sending his daughters to tell them they were not worthy of an audience.

There had been a series of misfortunes among Toketok's subjects. Some wild pigs had eaten a field full of someone's crops, a tribesman had been bitten by a shark, and two local men had killed each other in a fight.

All these events were blamed on evil spirits left behind by the white men, who could not be trusted, and would kidnap indigenous people to take away to their factories, where the tribesmen believed their bodies were chopped up and refined into opium.[12]

There were two vital factors that helped Le Gendre in his negotiations. One was the aforementioned realisation among the Koaluts that they had killed a woman — head-hunting in the Seqalu was a custom of men versus men, and the death of Mercy Hunt had hence been an 'accident' liable to bring a curse. They were also wrong-footed by Le Gendre's own unique negotiating style, which included threatening at one point to pluck out his own eye, and then doing so — the locals were unaware that one side of his face was a reconstruction, and the eye was glass.

We are fortunate to have several accounts of these events — not just Le Gendre's, written in the hope that he would be seen as some sort of conquering hero, but of others, including the British customs official William Pickering. Pickering's account, benefiting from a better appreciation of local politics and languages, notes that Le Gendre had marched into the middle of a standoff between a dozen different tribal organisations, and that Toketok's assent was less of a royal command, than a concession forced through pressure from local Hakka settlers, who were usually not on good terms with the indigenous people, but were frantic to secure some sort of deal in order to prevent further incursions in the area by the Chinese authorities. They had used a powerful negotiating tool, threatening to cut off the locals' supply of ammunition unless they played along.[13]

Le Gendre avoided mentioning much of this, instead reporting that he had successfully negotiated a treaty, including a promise that white sailors would be under Toketok's protection if they were shipwrecked on the Taiwanese coast. This in itself was a moment of some historical dispute. Either the notoriously self-aggrandising Le Gendre was getting a handshake deal with a local strongman to stop murdering shipwrecked sailors, or, if you wanted to look at it another way, a representative of the US government with consular authority was striking a diplomatic agreement with the ruler of a foreign land, granting right of safe passage for US citizens. The former is a footnote in the history books; the latter a legal precedent for the existence of an autonomous, indigenous 'state' in south Taiwan, outside Chinese jurisdiction. Such is the interpretative contention that characterises so much Taiwanese history.[14]

For several years thereafter, sailors on Taiwan's south-east coast were indeed treated with a degree of benevolence. 'But, after all,' notes James Davidson in *Formosa, Past and Present*, 'the territory which Toketok controlled was of a very uncertain extent, and while he kept his own immediate tribesmen in order, he frequently found difficulty in curbing the savage spirit which existed among his neighbors.'[15] One group in particular, the Botan tribe, refused to acknowledge his authority — a fact which would lead to another international incident in 1874. But that is another story, told in Chapter Five. For now, the Americans regarded Taiwan as little more than a marine hazard, mismanaged by its Chinese overlords. The only effective way, argued US officials, 'of rendering the region permanently safe and freeing the waters of that vicinity from their perils would be the dispersal of the aborigines from the shores and the occupation of the coast by a powerful ally'. The Chinese would do, they said, but previous experience suggested that 'the task was beyond both their inclination and their power'.[16]

As for Mercy Hunt, her story, particularly the killing of a woman in contravention of Koalut taboos, and the fervid, gamified quest for her possessions, would drift into local legends and folklore.

In 1931, beachcombers on the coast near Kenting found human bones beneath the sand. The waters off Taiwan had been no stranger to shipwrecks and tragedies, and the remains were put in a pot and taken to a nearby shrine dedicated to the Lords of Ten Thousand Responses, a euphemistic reference to the myriad 'hungry ghosts' lost at sea without families or descendants, who might be prevailed upon to grant wishes, but needed to be appeased with occasional offerings.

A local spirit medium claimed that the bones were that of a foreigner, a 'Red-Haired Princess', which led in 1961 to the addition of a side chapel, dedicated to someone now called the Princess of Eight Treasures.[17]

Over the years, local folklore evolved still further. The 'Red-Haired Princess', it was said, was a woman who had come ashore in southern Taiwan and had been murdered by local tribesmen. Her possessions were divided up among them, and needed to be symbolically reassembled — to this day, the temple contains a pair of modern-day clogs, apparently one of the vital missing items.

And then, in July 2008, a Mrs Ang, an old woman in her eighties, was lost for five days while mushroom-picking in the mountains. When she eventually returned, she claimed that she had run into an exceedingly tall, naked woman, who tried to steal her clothes from her.

A spirit medium got involved again, stating that Mrs Ang was being haunted by the 'Red-Haired Princess', murdered some centuries earlier, who would take the lives of ten locals within the year unless she was appropriately appeased. It so happened that six people in Ang's home village had already passed away by the summer, and three more were seriously ill, implying that Ang herself might be in line to be the tenth.

A hastily arranged ritual called down the spirit of the Goddess of Mercy to smooth things over, but the idea of a local celebrity, albeit tragic in origin, was irresistible to the authorities. In the 21st century, the Red-Haired Princess had gained a highly unlikely backstory, backed by local tourist initiatives and supported by an apocryphal book claiming that she was 'Margaretha', granddaughter of the Prince of Orange, born on the same day, and yet a world away, from the Taiwanese demigod Koxinga in 1624. She had been sailing to join her fiancé, Maarten, at the Dutch Fort Zeelandia in Tainan in the 1640s, when her ship, the *Utrecht*, had run aground in south Taiwan on land claimed by the Koalut, where she met her tragic end.

Today, the shrine of the Princess of the Eight Treasures continues to thrive. Every several years, the spirit of the princess is supposed to communicate with the daughter of the temple caretaker, informing her that it is time for her bones to be removed from their ceramic container and aired in the Taiwanese sun. The locals have come to adopt their Dutch princess less as a malevolent spirit and more as a patron goddess, said to watch over the community.

The story of south Taiwan's Dutch guardian spirit is a wonderful evocation of the island's rich historical clash of cultures. Mercy Hunt was not Dutch, although the term 'Red Hair' (*hongmao*; more colloquially in Hokkien, *angmo*) is a catch-all micro-aggression in the Chinese-speaking world for anyone of European ancestry.[18] She was not a princess, and she was murdered two centuries later than claimed. Nor does she have anything to do with the original Princess of the Eight Treasures, who was a character in a Chinese opera, *Five Tigers Pacify the West*, a nomad warrior said to have come to the aid of the Chinese during the Song-Khitan wars of the Middle Ages. But her story has somehow endured, wrenched out of its original time, buffeted by misunderstandings and retellings between the indigenous peoples of Taiwan and the Hokkien-speaking Chinese, filtered through various influences of the Dutch colonial period that ended long before she was born, and the Japanese colonial period that arose after she died, until it has become a focus of civic pride and tourist clickbait. By 2015, local legend held that the foreign woman haunting the Taiwanese coast had ceased to be a restless spirit, and had ascended to heaven as a newly minted goddess.

CHAPTER ONE

SONGS OF THE DEAD

Prehistoric and Mythical Taiwan (~to 1349)

The Taiwan Strait was once a plain that stretched out from mainland China, with a mountainous outcrop at its midpoint (today's Penghu Islands), and Taiwan itself a mountain range that terminated in sea-cliffs to the east. Archaeology suggests that during the Palaeolithic these lost plains were populated with deer and stegodons, a now-extinct cousin of the elephant, but any sign of the region's human inhabitants has been drowned since the end of the last Ice Age. Our only evidence for the existence of such people stems from the time that they would have moved to the mountains as the waters rose. In 1907, a Japanese archaeologist found two stone axe-heads in a peat bog on the Penghu Islands. If their location was indeed as reported, it would suggest that humans were hunting on the plains at least 30,000 years ago, shortly before people first arrived in what is now Japan.[1] Between 18,000 and 22,000 years ago, a group of early humans huddled in a cave at what is now Baxian on the east coast of Taiwan, rubbing sticks together to make fire — the sticks are all that remain of them.[2]

Those people do not appear to have been the ancestors of the indigenous Formosans, whose words have been dated by historical linguistics as being no more than 4,500 years old, calving off from Proto-Austronesian about 1,500 years before that.[3] Much work still needs to be done in establishing the chronology and population movements of

11

Taiwan's tribes, some of whom are presumably 'original aborigines', while others are later arrivals. In Nan-kuan-li, in the suburbs of Tainan, under a 20th-century sugar-cane plantation, archaeologists uncovered evidence of human habitation dating from around 3000 BC, roughly the time that construction began on faraway Stonehenge. They found a second settlement a few hundred metres to the east, where later occupants began cultivating both rice and millet — possibly out of a need to diversify crops in order not to be left with nothing if one failed.[4] Those same people often relied on marine produce, leaving behind middens containing three tonnes of shells that once contained 49 species of bivalves and gastropods, predominantly oysters and several kinds of snail.[5]

Not far from the Baxian caves on Taiwan's eastern coast, itinerant fisherfolk passed through Changbin around 3000 BC, leaving stone waste and discarded fishing gear made of bone antlers. Around the same time, in Dapenkeng in what is now the Taipei suburbs, Neolithic people began using rounded pottery jars, often cord-marked or pressed with seashell outlines. These coastal arrivals all favoured locations close to fishable waters or streams. Some even experimented with rice cultivation, although some of their descendants seemed to shun rice.[6]

By 2500 BC, there were two ethnic groups on Taiwan's east coast, the Qilin on the Taitung coastal hills, and their neighbours, the Beinan people (ancestors of several modern groups, including today's Puyuma), who left slate megaliths dotted along the rift valley that runs parallel to the sea for 150 km from Taitung up to Hualien.

When the waters of the Strait were at their highest, the mountain range we now know as Taiwan receded out of sight, beyond the horizon, two days from the mainland by sail- or rowboat. When the waters were at their lowest, 'Taiwan' would have been visible across a canyon carved by the antediluvian ancestor of today's Min River, which flowed from what is now the coast of China, around to the east of the Penghu highlands, and emptied into the proto–South China Sea. It is this drowned watercourse, carved by an ancient meltwater torrent, that today forms the undersea trench known to Chinese sailors as the Black Ditch.

The water levels steadily rose from the end of the last Ice Age until roughly a thousand years ago, but there have been several occasions over the millennia where there have been spikes in the sea level, known to

Chinese archaeologists as the 'six sea-invasions and six sea-withdrawals'.[7] On each occasion, the water level on the Fujian and Taiwan coast rose between 20 and 60 metres, forcing locals to flee to higher ground, creating sudden coastal settlements and drowning evidence of intermediate stages in migration and culture.

The treacherous nature of the waters of the Taiwan Strait is a relatively recent development — and man-made. By 3000 BC, inhabitants began to clear areas of forest, burning the vegetation to enrich the soil and create areas to grow crops. The extent of such slash-and-burn agriculture on the island had created scrubland fields that lured more deer out into the open, but also led to a rapid escalation in soil erosion. No longer held in place by trees, the topsoil of the Taiwanese highlands was stripped away by fast-flowing rivers. Former Neolithic coastal sites can now be up to 20 km inland, under seven metres of silt. A similar, seasonal mudslide pushed out into the rising waters of the Strait, transforming the shape of the seabed and the currents above it.

'Navigation along the west coast of Taiwan,' writes Richard Pearson, 'was much easier thousands of years ago in the Early Neolithic ... before the rivers of central and southwestern Taiwan poured alluvium along the shallow coastline, creating flats, ever-changing shoals and shifting islets formed by dangerous currents.'[8] For centuries, these treacherous waters discouraged mainland sailors from venturing further east than the Penghu Islands, creating an intangible barrier to would-be settlers before the early modern period.

These fluctuations were accompanied by changes in the flora and fauna. Sediment analysis of the land around Sun-Moon Lake reveals that, sometime around 8000 BC, a rise in temperatures caused the vegetation to favour subtropical white gourds, scented apples, chestnuts, and water chestnuts, instead of the oak, elm, and willows that had previously flourished there.

Ad hoc anthropology in the 19th century by William Pickering suggested broad and perhaps obvious categories of later arrivals — a south that had assimilated newcomers from the Philippines at some point; a north with stronger connections to the Ryukyu Islands and Japan (some tribes share Ryukyu-style hand tattoos); and a western coast with clear connections to the Chinese mainland, the source of a large migration

around the turn of the Christian era. George Taylor, lighthouse keeper on
the southern tip of Taiwan, similarly observed in the 1880s that:

> There are traces in their lore, games and common sayings of a like
> diversity having at one time prevailed in their language; scraps
> of doggerel and rhyming numerals may be heard repeated by the
> children, and the old people will tell that long ago their ancestors
> spoke this tongue.[9]

Before the coming of the Chinese, and even during the centuries of
early contact, the political landscape of Taiwan looked very different.
At the risk of imposing anachronistic borders or territories on what was
already a series of shifting areas of influence, the divisions of prehistoric
Taiwan are now only dimly appreciated, particularly in the north and west,
where centuries of contacts with foreigners have eroded tribal identities.
Before the arrival of outsiders, before the clearing of farmland and the
destruction of camphor forests, before the establishment of reservations
or the drawing of the 'guardline' (what would be known in the Japanese
era as the 'savage boundary') that separated the civilised west coast from
the barbarian interior, Taiwan comprised multiple tribal lands.

These included the tall Siraya people in the south-west, and the
confederation of the Paiwan in the south-east, the Amis on the east coast,
and the Atayal of the northern hinterland. Some tribes are now extinct,
some barely remembered through a few surviving artefacts and words.
Others strongly assert modern identities or territories, even if such things
might be relatively recent developments in their histories — the result of
migrations, mergers, or even battles. Japanese anthropologists in the 1920s
drew up a map of Taiwan that visualised the Atayal lands not as territories,
but as *directions*, reconstructing the Atayal's slow-but-sure migration over
generations.[10] The coastal Truku speak of their tribe's origins up in the
mountains, at Pusu Qhuni, a sacred stone in what is now Nantou county
in the centre of the island, from which the first man and woman were
said to have emerged in the distant past, conflated in the minds of some
modern-day Atayal Christian converts with the story of the Garden of
Eden.[11] Since then, they have moved slowly to the east, along what is now
Taroko Gorge, until 'they saw the reflection of the sun on the ocean in the

distance for the first time, blinking their eyes because of the bright new sight'. Their local geographical terminology still refers to their ancestral home as Behind the Mountains (*Mqribaq*), and to the coast as what it was in the tribal mindset before they reached it, the Place Where the Sun Rises (*Nklaan hidao*). Generations later, they still largely disregard the sea as it is not part of their forest and mountain-oriented 'life-world', while the neighbouring Amis people swim in, forage by, and sail on it.[12]

The Thao people claim to have once lived in the 'mountains of the ancestors' (*Alit* in several Formosan languages; Alishan to the Chinese), but were led north after their legendary founder, Paidabo, tracked a white deer through the canyons until it jumped into glittering waters. The Thao

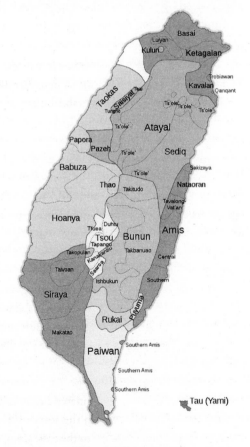

Taiwan's indigenous peoples.

then settled beside what is known today as Sun-Moon Lake, claiming its entire shoreline as their territory, and worshipping their gods in the form of sacred bishop-wood trees. Accounts differ as to when they embarked upon this migration to their promised land — it may have been 1,100 years ago, or it may have been as little as 200.[13]

There is, similarly, a folk-tale alluding to various migrations among the unrelated Tao people of Orchid Island off the shores of Taiwan. At first, there was a great flood, which led the Tao to their island home, which they referred to in their native language as the Place of Human Beings (*Pongso no Tao*), or Facing the Mountains (*Irala*, in reference to the towering cliffs of the east Taiwan coastline). At some point in Tao history, legends claim that the tribe was menaced by a child-eating octopus, which was lured to a fiery death by a vengeful hero, but decomposed so stinkily on the beach that the Tao had to relocate to elsewhere on the island.[14]

Crucially, the various Formosan tribes developed a widespread equilibrium, based on what we would now call sustainability — systems that would be widely disrupted in more recent times by the arrival of outsiders. Among the Thao, this took the form of a folk-tale about the Taqrahaz, a mermaid living in Sun-Moon Lake, who smashes up fish traps and rips netting. Confronted by Numa, a Thao tribesman, she hectors him about the perils of overfishing, and a shamefaced Numa returns to his people to encourage them not only to use fewer nets and traps, but also to start rigging bamboo garden-rafts on the lake. These improve the fishes' access to algae and insects, and provide tribesmen with a fixed site to harvest the marine life drawn to them. These 'floating fields' (*futian*) became a feature of long-term aquaculture sustainability on the lake.[15]

The Rukai people today occupy three counties of forested hills in south Taiwan, to which they migrated at some point in the past from the nearby 'Ghost Lakes' — taboo territories said to hold the spirits of their ancestors. Historically, each adult male had his own hunting territory, into which others were not permitted to stray. The land was his alone because of the careful management required. 'Hunting' was not merely a matter of wandering a patch of land taking occasional pot-shots at deer; it involved the careful maintenance of traps and pits, the long-term topiary of cul-de-sacs and killing grounds, and even the cultivation of clusters of edible plants to lure in his prey. He hunted there under sufferance of his chief, who was considered to be the ultimate owner of all land, water, and resources within the tribal lands, and to whom successful hunters were expected to present 'the best parts, such as the leg, heart and liver' of any animals killed.[16] The Rukai hunting season traditionally extended from October to March — the gap between harvesting and planting for farming men, and out of breeding season for most prey, as well as a period of the year when lower temperatures reduce the chance of meat spoiling in traps before a hunter returns. Rukai lore comes with an array of superstitions and beliefs — it was taboo to hunt a clouded leopard, since a beast of that species legendarily led the Rukai to their new home. Sightings of *masiang* birds could be used to foretell likely good hunting days; sneezing and farting were considered bad luck for hunters. Moreover, the demarcated hunting zones, and the taboo area around the Ghost Lakes, gave space for animals to breed and flourish away from hunters.[17]

Among those tribes that practised farming, early foreign observers recorded a series of intricate taboos and abstinence rituals. The Siraya people had a word in their own language for a 'second rice harvest', but when first observed by foreign chroniclers in the 17th century, only produced one a year with their meagre tools and draft animals. Presumably, they had originally come from a place where a second crop had been possible. Nudity was compulsory for Siraya during the growing season (the warm summer months), because it encouraged the gods to bring rain. When the rice was half-ripe, the Siraya had to abstain from many luxuries — including alcohol, rice, and bananas — for fear that breaking that taboo would bring animals to ravage their crops.[18]

Such oral traditions, of course, can evolve and change with the times; it is all too easy to assume that an indigenous folk-tale is an unadulterated account of ancient times. The musicologist Lin Sin-lai, collecting 'mountain songs' in the 20th century, reported that more than half of the 'traditional' songs he recorded turned out to be either all-new creations or reworkings of older tunes with modern lyrics.[19] In 1981, the political activist Annette Lu entertained an audience at an Amnesty International event in the Netherlands by explaining the lyrics of 'an old Taiwanese folk song' about a local girl pining for a Dutch doctor. The 'old' song, however, was actually younger than she was, composed when she was seven.[20]

Comparing recordings of 'traditional' Atayal songs made at the end of the Japanese colonial period, Wang Ying-fen found that between the years 1920 and 1940, they mutated beyond all recognition, losing their original two-tone, spoken-word elements and transforming instead into songs on a pentatonic scale influenced by the Japanese settlers.[21] Similarly, it is difficult to tell the precise age of traditional chants, such as the Amis 'Elders' Drinking Song', the lyrics of which are timeless, although the modern tune appears to have adopted certain elements of the Japanese musical scale.

My dear friends and relatives who come from far away!
Thanks for coming to see us! Come, let's sit together.
We will sing for you, as you sang for us when we visited you before.
Let's sing while we drink.
How much we sing is how much we drink.

Japanese influences continued to persist after the end of the colonial period, when familiar tunes were retooled as 'local' products. In the case of songs like 'Hometown in Twilight' and 'Mama You Take Care, Too', both alluding to lonely figures in exile from their homeland, anthems of post-war Taiwanese identity were sung to tunes that were originally Japanese.[22]

Another tune, the 'Dutch Song', was supposedly taught to the Paiwan by traders from the Netherlands in the 17th century. It was only in modern times that the nonsense lyrics were deconstructed by anthropologists, to uncover a song that had originally been written in 1887, long after the Dutch era, part of which reads:

Inconstant barbarians, men of Taiwan
Men of Taiwan, unclothed and raw
Men of Taiwan mired in misfortune ...
The people of the Hundred Surnames are your brothers.[23]

The song had drifted from its original Hokkien (the language spoken in the coastal province of Fujian) and into an indigenous variant, and over the course of a century, the Paiwan had forgotten that it was first sung to them by mainland Chinese.

Misrepresentations and misunderstandings led to decades, if not centuries of tensions. George Anson, off Taiwan in 1742 on the lookout for Spanish treasure galleons, was wary of lights on the coastal waters and beaches, assuming that wreckers were trying to lure his crew ashore to murder them. It was another 120 years before Bonham Ward Bax of HMS *Dwarf*, embedded in south Taiwan as a military observer, noted that the indigenous people had a habit of night-fishing with lamps as lures on their catamarans, and that Anson might have been projecting his own privateering ambitions on a bunch of completely innocent fishermen. 'I expect that fisherman of the time,' Bax wrote, 'were merely following their trade in the same manner as they do in the present day, and hardly more anxious for a visit from strangers than they are now.'[24]

The modern narrative of Taiwan's indigenous peoples is one of oppression and suppression, centuries of struggles against colonialism and imperialism, a developing sense of ethnic pride and defiance. But there are shadows to be glimpsed of times when they, too, fought bitterly over resources and territory. History remains a tale told by the winning side.

Every two years, the Saisiyat people hold an autumn 'Ritual to the Short People' (*paSta'ay*), a ceremony in which the tribe begs for forgiveness for a prehistoric genocide. The Honoured Short People (*Koko'ta'ay*), it was said, were of darker skin, and low height, and lived on the other side of 'the river', where they were most remembered for the sounds of their songs and dances. The Saisiyat, newcomers settling in the area, were initially welcomed. The two tribes would meet for joint harvest celebrations, with the Koko'ta'ay crossing the *siboL* river that separated the Saisiyat lands from their own homes among the mountainside caves. The Koko'ta'ay were skilled at spell-casting as well as singing and dancing, and brought vibrant new entertainments to the Saisiyat celebrations.

Over time, the Saisiyat came to be wary of the Koko'ta'ay magic. It was said that a Koko'ta'ay man was able to raise a Saisiyat warrior from the dead, but also that the Koko'ta'ay would sometimes use their powers to bewitch and impregnate Saisiyat women.[25]

The Saisiyat had no proof of these accusations, until an occasion at a harvest festival, when one of the dwarf people was caught in the act of molesting a Saisiyat girl. In one version of the story, vengeful Saisiyat men cut down a Koko'ta'ay sacred tree, only to be cursed by a surviving shaman.

Or a cunning Saisiyat man invited the Koko'ta'ay to a banquet, turning on them and pursuing them back across the rope bridge that connected their lands, only for the fleeing visitors to tumble to their deaths in the ravine below. Whatever the case, it seems that the Koko'ta'ay were all killed due to the actions of the Saisiyat.

It was not long before the curse of the dead Koko'ta'ay began to take effect:

> The skies darkened and blood seeped up from the ground below ... All the wild pigs and other animals fled in fear. The crops of rice and other vegetables withered and died. Finally, a plague of poisonous snakes slithered into the village, randomly exacting a venomous revenge on whoever was in the way.[26]

Shortly thereafter, the Saisiyat lands were wracked with a terrible famine, leading to the first *paSta'ay* in an attempt to appease the angry spirits of the dead.

The multi-part ceremony, in which all the Saisiyat are supposed to participate, involves ritually welcoming, hosting, and then sending the spirits on their way. Anyone who misbehaves at the ceremony will be cursed until the next. The two tribes of the Saisiyat, a northern and southern subgroup, meet two months before the ceremony to practise the songs. Completing the entire song cycle takes between four to five hours, incorporating a series of Saisiyat rituals and a component of songs taught to them by the extinct Koko'ta'ay. Over the course of three nights, the north and south Saisiyat sing to each other at their ceremonial meeting on the riverbank, before commencing a song of invitation, intended to bring back the spirits of the Koko'ta'ay. There are other songs, some with identifiable content, some reduced to doggerel by years of repetition. Some are even golden oldies, apparent remnants of what used to be a harvest festival before it was co-opted for tribal penance, including planting and weeding songs, and the Saisiyat's own recounting of a legend of Wa-an, the 'Thunder Lady' — daughter of the Thunder God, sent down from heaven in order to teach farming to the Saisiyat. Wa-an falls in love with a Saisiyat man, but they are childless on account of her laziness at the hearth, which ends, literally with a clap of thunder, when her first attempt at cookery causes her to be struck by lightning and spirited away back to her father's realm, leaving only a banana tree behind. Ever since, Saisiyat women have worn swastikas on their dresses, in memory of the daughter of the lightning — this ancient representation of the thunderbolt does not have the same Nazi associations as it does in Europe.[27]

Eventually, they sing the *Wawaon*, the 'song of the enemy', the last surviving relic of the extinct Koko'ta'ay, sung in their memory by the descendants of the men who slew them, and the *kiSkorkoroy*, the 'song of exorcism'. They dance wearing sacred dance hats or 'moonlight flags' (*kilakil*), and 'buttock bells' (*tapangaSan*), chimes that dangle behind the dancer's belt, decorated with Wa-an's swastika — it is taboo for strangers or members of other families to touch them. The southern Saisiyat also carry a sacred snake whip (*paputol*) to dispel evil spirits. Once every ten years, there is an augmented version of the ceremony, in which members of one particular tribal family are authorised to dance with their 'big festival flag' (*sinadun*).[28]

On the final night, the Saisiyat sing songs of reconciliation, as well as a song of 'sending home', and a song of the 'road home', dispatching the spirits back to their resting places, and buying the tribe another two years free of bad luck.[29]

There is much for a historian to unpack in the *paSta'ay*, starting with its 'historicity' — its location in historical time. It was once an *annual* event, but became 'every two years' after Japanese colonial authorities intervened at the turn of the 20th century. In modern times, like many other ethnic festivals, it has become not merely a special occasion in its own right, but a rare opportunity for the village elders to instil a bit of tradition and native culture on their increasingly absent descendants, for whom it may be the only event in the calendar that lures them home. In 1986, after the ceremony had to be held amid heavy rains, family members were admonished for not showing up or for turning to Christianity, with claims that the Koko'ta'ay spirits were angry, and needed to be shown more respect on the occasion of the next traditional festival. But what is the tradition being retold?

Even the Saisiyat themselves cannot agree on the precise details of the legend, but its broad plot points — a conflict over resources, with a rival whose own name for themselves has been erased from the record —

resonates with many similar legends from all around the world. The word *Koko* appears to be a later addition — an honorific prefix for the departed Ta'ay people, added within living memory. Amid the garbled variants of the story, there is one that suggests that the Saisiyat themselves were reduced to but a single man, who made his peace with the surviving shaman, and repopulated his clan with the help of seven daughters 'gifted' to him by yet another tribe. However, my first suspicion is that the 'curse' came first, and what is being remembered is the regrettable aftermath of a battle for survival in the midst of a famine or natural disaster.

There are some ready to believe that the ritual re-enacts a historical moment from thousands of years in the past, a position that has gained traction in recent times, after a skeleton unearthed at the Xiaoma caves near Taitung several decades ago was ferreted out of the vaults, subjected to contemporary analysis, and determined to be that of a 'negrito' female — a pygmy type of hominid also found in the Philippines. She had been buried there roughly 6,000 years ago, several centuries before the arrival of the ancestors of today's surviving tribes, at a time when the waters were so high that there was no such thing as the plains, only what is now the mountains.[30]

Early-20th-century photograph from *National Geographic*
of Saisiyat tribesmen and their hunting dogs.

But at the time that the *paSta'ay* was first recorded by Japanese anthropologists in 1915, it was said to refer to events that occurred a mere four centuries earlier. Were the Koko'ta'ay wiped out some time in the 1500s, shortly before Europeans first arrived? Or is 'four centuries' one of those vaguely large numbers, like Arabic's 'forty thieves' or Mandarin's 'hundred demons', not intended to denote a real number? And how would that tally with claims made elsewhere that the Saisiyat's current territory only dates from the 1680s, when they fled there to avoid corvée labour for the Kingdom of Dongning (see Chapter Three)?[31]

Could the *paSta'ay* refer to an ancient tribal memory of prehistoric conflict? Or could it be something far more recent? Consider, for example, the possibility that the term 'little black people' is a direct translation of the Spanish *negrito*, and might even refer not to ancient hominids, but to fugitive slaves from Taiwan's Spanish or Dutch colonies. To add an extra level of confusion, the Saisiyat are not even the only Taiwanese tribe to have legends of 'little black people'. In fact, 14 other Taiwanese tribes have a total of 258 folk-tales referencing something like the Koko'ta'ay in their own traditions, such as the fairy folk celebrated in Paiwan folklore in the south, one of whom admonishes lost travellers with the song:

You think I am fatherless, motherless, small,
Devoid of that wisdom which parents install;
Yet I was when fathers and mothers were not,
And will be when mankind as such is forgot.[32]

Among the tribes of the north of Taiwan, including the Saisiyat, the 'little black people' are referred to as enemies and rivals. Among the southern tribes, including the Paiwan, Puyuma, Rukai, and Hla'lua, they are mentioned as allies or even ancestors.[33] As late as 1685, Lin Jianguang's *Sketch of Taiwan*, written shortly after the island came under the control of the Qing emperors, could state:

Going deeper into the mountains, the people there look like monkeys, less than three feet tall. When they see someone, they climb to the tops of the trees ... there are some who live in holes that they have burrowed out, like people in prehistoric times.'[34]

Could it be that some sort of dwarf hominid, akin to the Koko'ta'ay of Saisiyat folklore, did indeed survive into the early 17th century?

This is a recurring issue with discussing 'prehistory' in a literal sense. It brings along with it the risk that observers like those Japanese anthropologists might be imposing their own expectations or ideas upon the events they witnessed. Throughout the Japanese colonial period, when the earliest academic accounts of Taiwanese indigenous peoples were written, there is evidence, from both sides, of indigenous locals and colonial Japanese ready to seize upon apparent links between both cultures' mythologies. In particular, there is the matter of the similarities between the origin myths of several tribes, here recounted in the variant found among the Amis.

The brother and sister, Pilukalau and Marokirok, are the sole survivors of a great flood, washed away from their homeland of Karara in a makeshift boat, and marooned on Taiwan. After they grow up, Marokirok deceives Pilukalau by disguising herself with animal hides, and gives birth to their 12 children, who themselves become the ancestors of four different indigenous clans. Another brother and sister, Lutsi and Lalakan, are also washed ashore, but give birth to snakes and frogs, which they lock in a chest until the goddess Sauliyau sends her son Tatakosan down to Earth to deal with their problems, and teach them how to farm millet and rice.

There are remarkable, and possibly overly hopeful, parallels here with the origin stories of the Japanese themselves, as recorded in the eighth-century *Record of Ancient Matters* (*Kojiki*) — a brother and sister haphazardly siring the ancestors of the storyteller. There are even more Japanese echoes in the tale of Tejamatsan, the goddess who cannot hide the radiance of her own body, who must decide between two suitors, one of whom is the Thunder God. The question, which thus far seems unanswerable, is to what extent these stories are mangled myths appropriated from the Japanese, or whether *both* Japanese and Taiwanese legends are descended from a compendium of beliefs stretching all the way from the south Chinese coast and up the Ryukyu archipelago.[35]

Even then, all that they can agree on was that there was a Great Flood. The Atayal say it was *because* a brother married his sister, and that the heavy rains fell for seven days and seven nights. Various sacrifices were tried to appease the gods, including a dog, an ugly girl, and then an attractive one

— shades here of ancient Chinese flood myths about the Yellow River. Other tribes suggest that sibling marriages were necessary *because* of the flood, with the population so depleted.

The Bunun people have their own version of the legend, but theirs concentrates more on the efforts to save their livestock and pets. Sacrifice, for the Bunun, takes on a different form — the flood is caused by a snake-monster trapped in the river, and the kindly Bunun people are eventually forced, by depleted supplies in their mountain retreat, to become hunters in order to stay alive. The story is also used to explain later animal taboos among the Bunun, who refuse to kill *kapisi* birds, on the grounds that one such animal faithfully brought them fire after they lost their kindling.[36]

Certainly, it is possible that modern observers, and indeed modern indigenous peoples, can make what historians call the 'error of tradition', assuming that contemporary practices are ancient ways that have somehow survived, and not relatively recent habits. Among the Bunun tribe, anthropologist Janet McGovern noted a tradition that the sacred fire had to be maintained at all costs or risk a curse — an ancient belief of dwindling relevance ever since the Dutch had sold the tribesmen tinderboxes that could easily rekindle the flames.[37] The use of tinderboxes is an obvious modern shift, as is the fact that the 20th-century Atayal used clusters of needles to tattoo themselves, whereas before the coming of foreign traders they had relied on thorns and soot.[38]

Other developments are less easily noticeable, particularly if they are not a presence but an absence. In 1918, during an island-wide drought and cold spell, the red quinoa (*djulis*) favoured by some southern tribes flourished, maintaining their food supply, while other tribes were forced to lean on state assistance.[39] The archaeologist is apt to wonder, what foodstuff did the *extinct* tribes rely upon during some unrecorded prehistoric famine, in which a formerly widespread food item died out shortly before its cultivators?

The archaeological record tells us that Taiwan's prehistoric inhabitants lived on a diet of wild animal proteins — deer, boar, rats, goats, and in a delicacy that is a step too far even for modern-day Taipei indigenous restaurants, bat entrails. Travelling among the indigenous peoples in the 1860s, William Pickering reported being offered a raw honeycomb in which 'the larvae predominated', and that his hosts appeared to think that he was being given the best helping, with the honey only of secondary consideration.[40] Pickering and his fellow Victorians, in fact, present a wonderful snapshot of whatever passed for daily life in the 1860s and 1870s — enthusiastic consumption of almost-raw meat, with barbecuing reserved only for those cuts that were already going off, plump rats as a special treat, and acceptance of agriculture in any form only as a very last resort. For the tribes as late as the 1870s, the ideal way of life was one of hunting and gathering — indeed, the local sense of masculinity often depended on it, with prowess at the amassing of resources and the taking of heads being the main means of demonstrating one's appeal to women.[41] We can *assume* that the way of those tribes was unchanged from centuries past ... but millennia, too?

In 1916, Ishii Shinji was astonished to see the Paiwan people exhibiting the same characteristics and culture in the 20th century that had been described in the Chinese *Book of Sui* 1,300 years earlier, but such claims are fraught with possible misunderstandings, not only of what is still there to be seen, but also of what may have faded away.[42] In the early years of the seventh century, Emperor Yang of China's short-lived Sui dynasty sent three expeditions across the sea to 'Liuqiu' (i.e. Ryukyu), which *may* have been to the Ryukyu Islands themselves, but is more likely to have been to 'Great Ryukyu', the island of Taiwan.[43]

The land they reported was a territory under dispute, where previous years of benign and low-level contacts across the Strait had been thrown into chaos by new arrivals, not from China, but from somewhere to the south — 'bands of fierce marauders who conquered the west coast of the island and drove the aboriginal inhabitants into the central mountains'.[44] It was these people, not the *original* aborigines, who were subject to an imperious visit by mainland representatives, and who reacted with fierce resistance when the Emperor's envoy demanded they pay tribute. A punitive Chinese expedition not only burned the village of these tribes — presumed to be ancestors of the Paiwan peoples — but added insult to injury by using the blood of the slain to caulk the hulls of their ships.

Among the Paiwan, there were 'three sacred treasures' — bronze knives, ceramic pots, and the 'tears of the sun', comma-shaped glass beads. Tribal tradition holds that they fell when the heat of a woman's cooking pot pushed the sun away, or that Paiwan ancestors first fashioned them from the eyes of dragonflies. Like the bronze knives, glass beads in general appear to have been a popular trading item in the prehistoric marine coastal routes — the Paiwan themselves being likely to have arrived from elsewhere in South-East Asia sometime after the third century AD. Although today they are fashioned locally, historic relics show some of these objects to have originated from the Chinese mainland during the Warring States Period (475–221 BC).[45] Evidence points to glass beads being one of the items of new material culture arriving in Taiwan, brought by settlers from the northern Philippines, whose descendants began making and distributing them locally.[46]

It is also worth pointing out that the most visible tribes today are not necessarily a reflection of their footprint in historical time. The Amis, Atayal, Bunun, and Paiwan benefit today from having ancestral lands on the eastern side of the former 'guardline' or 'savage boundary' drawn from north to south through the island by the Chinese authorities and maintained by the Japanese. Those tribes who dwelt on the more hospitable plains were the first in the firing line of colonists, and hence represent the most recent die-off of linguistic and cultural diversity — the right of the descendants of these plains tribes to be recognised as indigenous people was only legally acknowledged in 2022, and has yet to be enshrined in law.[47] The Siraya, for example, who were the original inhabitants of the Tainan region, were so thoroughly overrun by migrants from the mainland that they faded into the general population. Their DNA thrives, invisibly, among many an old Tainan family, but the last native speaker of the Sirayan language died in the early 20th century. While their contemporary cultural association prefers to describe Sirayan as 'dormant' rather than extinct, it has only been preserved through scholarship and archival research.[48] Much of what we know today about the Sirayan language, including attempts to resurrect it, has been gleaned from 17th-century Dutch missionary texts, including a bilingual edition of the Gospel of Matthew by Daniel Gravius.

Historical linguistics offers a window into the world of the Siraya, often through what they *don't* say. Gravius claimed to be unable to find the words in Sirayan for 'gambling', 'servant', or 'slave', while the absence of a term for 'stealing' or 'robbery' has been taken by some researchers to suggest a communal society. Or it might reflect taboos on certain terms, kept from the nosy missionary — we genuinely don't know, forcing us into a process not of deduction, but of 'abduction', filling in the information implied by absences in data.[49]

Predictably, a similar extinction occurred in the area of what is now Taipei, where the evidence of the original Ketagalan and Basai inhabitants can now only be found in a few scattered relics. Amid political reversals in 1996, the road in front of the Taipei Presidential Office Building was renamed from Long Live Chiang Kai-shek Road to Ketagalan Boulevard, tardily acknowledging the people who had lived there long before Chiang Kai-shek. The Basai people were a particularly interesting group, a sort of wandering fix-it tribe that eschewed head-hunting and agricultural cultivation in favour of handicrafts and trade, performing numerous artisanal functions. Beyond the Basai homeland in the north of the island, there were scattered Basai settlements throughout the lands of other tribes, offering weaving, carving, and smithing skills. The Basai language hence evolved into a sort of pidgin, and was often the default form of intertribal communication, even among non-Basai.[50]

Even then, researchers note that they were salvaging snippets of a culture that was already ailing and contaminated by cross-pollination, their interviewees often proving to be doubtfully 'pure' resources.

Multiple accounts of the indigenous peoples, for example, refer to the custom most abhorrent to foreign visitors — head-hunting. But head-hunting itself meant different things to different tribes. Among the Koalut it was part of a manhood ritual, but among certain Tsou groups, for example, it was usually pursued only in revenge for a perceived grievance. In an aside from the Japanese administrative records in 1930, an interpreter comments that only the mountain people are habitual head-hunters. The *plains* dwellers only beheaded *mountain* dwellers for the bounty available to them from the Japanese authorities, suggesting either that the plains people are, or had become, more 'civilised' over the previous century, or that they had been 'ensavaged' by their new colonial masters, encouraged to pursue a method of warfare that was previously alien to them.[51]

Beyond such major issues, there are thousands of tiny micro-nuances that can also change the story that people tell about themselves. A group of Paiwan visited London for the Japanese Exhibition in 1910. They brought back with them several foreign habits, including saying 'Thank you' and 'Good day', and hailing each other by shaking hands.[52] Similarly, among the Puyuma and Saisiyat tribes, a custom arose of worshipping their ancestors in the form of ancestral tablets, a practice picked up after living close by to Hakka Chinese from the mainland. This was, as a result, a local appropriation, which bore no relation to previous Puyuma and Saisiyat culture.[53]

Ishii Shinji wrote in 1916 that the Formosans were 'great smokers', but such a habit cannot have existed before the coming of Europeans, since tobacco was a New World crop.[54] Tobacco has nevertheless sneaked its way into tribal folklore, as if it has always been a feature of Formosan life. In all cases, the stories cannot possibly be more than a few centuries old. In some cases, it seems that the tobacco legend has been adapted from a pre-existing folk-tale about the origins of betel-nut chewing.[55] Among the Amis, for example, there is a legend that the tobacco plant first grew from the grave of a heartbroken girl, who either took her own life after her fiancé died, or did so because she was unable to find a man who would marry her. Meanwhile, in Kiwit village, the plant is said to have grown from the graves of a brother and sister who killed themselves when their incestuous love was forbidden. Such stories are undoubtedly part of indigenous culture, but not of ancient traditions.

Hence, many aspects of indigenous material culture *might* be relics of the Stone Age, but are far more likely to have been born from more recent innovations or contacts with newcomers. Even the tribal 'homelands' are a matter of conflicted historicity — some groups were shunted into new areas by Dutch settlement, or Chinese colonists, or Japanese plantations.

Archaeology of indigenous sites must, by necessity, include the excavation not only of ancient settlements, but of homes abandoned within living memory. In this book, I adopt an authorial equivalent, moving in the chapters that follow into recorded history, but returning periodically to those moments where it bumps once more into indigenous prehistory, presenting new perspectives and evidence on the culture and traditions that existed on Taiwan before literal history was feasible.

CHAPTER TWO

THE BEAUTIFUL ISLAND

New Arrivals (1349–1644)

'It is a vast land,' wrote Wang Dayuan of the island he called Liuqiu, 'with forests of huge trees.' Climbing a mountain that rose up from the shore, he gazed back out to sea, and watched the waves swell in the Taiwan Strait. 'At midnight [sic], I saw the Valley from which the Sun emerges; the red rays lit up the sky and made the tops of the mountains all bright.'[1]

Wang's *Brief Account of the Island Barbarians* (*Daoyi Zhilue*, 1349) is the earliest verifiable Chinese report of the island of Taiwan. In it, he describes the people of the Penghu Islands in the Taiwan Strait, whom he regards as Chinese subjects, before moving on to chilling stories about the apparently cannibal inhabitants of the larger, tree-covered island further to the east. Wang alludes to mainland magistrates collecting a salt tax from the Penghu Islanders, but regards Taiwan itself as the nearest of the 'foreign' countries, beyond Chinese authority.

> The land is rich, the fields fertile; it is suitable for farming ... They do not have boats and oars, but cross the water by means of rafts. The men and women bind up their hair. They make their garments from coloured cloth. They boil seawater to get salt, and ferment sugarcane juice to make liquor ... Should a person from another country offend them, they cut off his raw flesh and eat it, and they take his head and hang it on a wooden pole.[2]

Despite such dangers, Wang alludes to an ongoing trade between Taiwan and the mainland already in existence, with ships from Quanzhou, just across the Strait, unloading pottery, 'precious pearls', and 'coarse dishware', for which the Formosans exchange 'gold nuggets, yellow beans, millet, sulphur, beeswax, the hides of deer, leopards and moose'. Boatmen from the mainland had been drawn to Taiwanese waters as early as the 13th century, at first as fishermen tracking the seasonal migration of mullet.[3]

Wang's account distinguishes between the friendlier locals with whom he had some interaction and a different tribe from an area where it was 'twice as hot', alluding to the far south of the island, where subtropical becomes tropical — the realm of the Paiwan.

> The people are accustomed to esteem raiding and plundering. The men and women twist their hair into tufts, and tattoo their bodies with black juice, clear up to the neck. They choose red silk or yellow cloth to wrap about their heads.

> The country has no chief. [The warriors] frequently pack up their rations and row out in their small boats, crossing over to foreign lands. There they hide in the wild mountains and solitary valleys where there are no inhabitants. When they encounter a fisherman and a woodcutter, they at once take him alive and then return.[4]

Wang describes the habit of these people of selling their captives to other tribes for two ounces of gold per head, and claims that other tribes in the area have similarly adopted this practice.

Already in this early account we can see the growing diversity of Taiwan — there are Chinese goat herders and fisherman on the Penghu Islands, and allusions to several different Formosan tribes. By the second half of the 15th century, there were more contenders for territory on the island. Taiwan is not mentioned, but heavily implied as the likely offshore base for numerous incursions of 'pirates' on the Fujian coast in the 1540s.[5] In 1549, the Ming Emperor renewed coastal prohibitions and a ban on all trade between China and Japan, effectively turning any voyager between the two areas into an outlaw, and criminalising all traders in a formerly lucrative business as 'smugglers'.

This, in turn, propelled Taiwan into a new role as a secret trading post — a handy location, just beyond the horizon, within reach of the Penghu Islands and the Fujian coast, but outside the jurisdiction of the Ming Emperor. Smugglers, pirates, and illegal migrants are not the sort of people to keep written records, but reading between the lines of later accounts, we can see ample evidence of more-enduring contacts between Taiwan and the mainland. Contacts were long-term enough for some of the Chinese fishermen to become proficient in indigenous languages, allowing them to function as interpreters for other newcomers. The seasonal fishermen had also set up small plantations for their own use, seeding certain areas of the coast with apple and orange trees, and ready sources for bananas and melons.[6]

At some time around this point, the island also gained a new name, courtesy of a group of new arrivals. Portuguese traders, in search of opportunities in China but rebuffed by the authorities, poked around the coastlines of nearby islands, possibly even circumnavigating Taiwan on the homeward journey. Although they did not have any lasting presence in the region, they did leave some enduring place names. Passing the Penghu Islands, they observed a number of Chinese fishermen at anchor, and conferred the name Pescadores ('The Fishermen'). Their breathless enthusiasm for the lush green west coast of Taiwan, viewed from a distance, led to the entry on subsequent European maps of the name *Ilha Formosa* ('Beautiful Island').[7]

Ong Iok-tek's fantastically irascible *Taiwan: A History of Agonies* notes that 'Portuguese seamen, in fact, had a habit of screaming "Ilha Formosa" at the sight of every island they spotted', resulting in at least a dozen other 'Formosas' dotted around the modern world map.[8] But he appears to be the lone cynic, and the concept of Taiwan as a 'beautiful island' has formed part of its inhabitants' sense of self for many centuries since.

The first Portuguese ship to make actual landfall in 1582 had a far from beautiful experience. Running aground part-way through a trip from Macau to Japan, 300 survivors of a nameless shipwreck spent a miserable three months on the beach, slowly assembling a smaller escape vessel from the debris. They subsisted on meagre supplies of rice, and a few items of local game trapped and hunted by their more intrepid members.

The wrecked Europeans initially enjoyed a cordial, if guarded, relationship with the local Siraya people, after a crewmember from the Philippines, a young boy who spoke Tagalog, was somehow able to barter for food. The Portuguese might have looked exotic to the locals, but were by no means the first outsiders to come ashore.

It was only after a few days, when the European guests started to outstay their welcome, that the relationship turned sour, possibly through the arrival of an entirely different and more hostile group. The Portuguese were unaware that they were not the first outsiders in the area, and that certain clans had discovered after looting the silk from an earlier Chinese shipwreck that crews might barter for the return of their cargo.[9]

> Later, some natives, armed with bows and quivers, fell on us and with great spirit and determination, without hesitating and without hurting anyone, divested us of everything we had. They came every day, and more often at night, killing some and wounding many with their arrows, to the point that we had to defend ourselves the best we could.[10]

Not all of the visitors returned home. At least one stayed, who introduced himself to Dutch travellers 30 years later as that same boy from the Philippines, now a middle-aged man with a local wife and children.[11]

The site of the beach confrontation was a long, calm lagoon separated from the sea by a series of sandbanks and shoals that ran for five miles parallel to the coast. It would eventually be known as Luermen, the 'Deer's Ear', and provided a reasonable harbour for small ships sheltering from the swells of the Taiwan Strait.

In the more immediate area, the 'Beautiful Island' was enjoying its new role as a haven for smugglers. Musket-wielding Japanese men arrived on ships and occupied the coastline near the Luermen lagoon, chasing the nearby Formosans into the forests. They did not stay for long, but presented enough of a threat that when a new nest of Japanese pirates sprang up 'again' near what is now Tainan, the Chinese were prepared to authorise a taskforce to evict them in 1603. Or, rather, *some* Chinese. Higher levels of government regarded the Japanese as a geopolitical and criminal threat, whereas their underlings at a local level saw them as an issue out of their jurisdiction, best ignored in order to conserve resources, manpower, and the peace. Before their fleet left the Kinmen islands off the Fujian coast, the leaders of the taskforce were repeatedly quizzed by local officials about the perceived wisdom of leading an assault on a place that was 'not our territory'.[12]

The scholar Chen Di, a veteran of earlier wars against Japanese pirates on the Chinese coast, accompanied the force as a military adviser and diarist, determined to chronicle a trip beyond the bounds of China, into an unknown land. Chen's *Zhu-fan-zhi* (*Record of the Barbarians*) became the primary source for most subsequent Chinese writings about Taiwan for the next century, and exhaustively reported his observations about the local Formosans, whom he found grateful to the Chinese for liberating them from the Japanese invaders.

'Strange indeed are the Eastern Barbarians,' he wrote, although part of the strangeness for him was how close their supposedly distant land proved to be. With a good northerly wind, it was only a day and a half's sail to the Penghu Islands, and then the same again to reach Luermen, whereupon a wide-eyed Chen chronicled the huge difference between himself and the Formosans — 'inbred savages' who mystifyingly didn't fish despite living beside the sea, and walked about naked or half-naked. Chen regarded the Formosans as illiterate and barely numerate, rarely able to state their own age with any surety. The womenfolk wore grass skirts, and lacked eyeteeth, which were ritually knocked out in their mid-teens as part of their ceremony of womanhood. The men had pierced ears — later writers would note that the ear lobes were sometimes stretched by iron weights.

Chen reported some slash-and-burn agriculture among the unnamed tribe, but that it came accompanied with strange traditions, including a virtual vow of silence among the villagers, who would till their fields without speaking and only acknowledge each other with glances out of some taboo thought to be imposed by the god of harvests.

Another taboo was attached to deer-hunting, which was only permissible at particular times of the year.

In winter, when the deer come out in herds, then some hundreds or tens of men will go after them, run them down until exhausted, and surround them. The spears find their marks and the catch is piled as high as a hill; every village has its fill of deer meat.[13]

Chen was impressed at the vast venison feasts, but also by the careful drying of excess deer meat to make jerky, and the preservation of deer horn, penis, and tongue, presumably for sale to Chinese merchants. The hides, too, were 'piled as high as the rafters'. Deer-hunting was so integral to some Taiwanese tribes that their languages reflected intricate nuances in terminology — the Favorlang people, for example, had at least four words for deer.[14]

Chen was, however, repulsed by the Formosans' habit of eating the contents of the deers' intestines, which they prized as a delicacy.

They lay open the intestines, and the recently swallowed grass ... called 'hundred grasses ointment' — this they will eat by itself without satiation. When Chinese see it, they retch. [The barbarians] eat pig but not chicken ... they only pluck their tail [feathers] to decorate their flags ... When they see Chinese eating chicken and pheasant, *they* retch. So who can say what is right or wrong when it comes to taste?[15]

Many of the local customs seemed to have analogues among the ethnic minorities of South China. Even today among the Kam people of Guizhou, for example, the locals also prize half-digested intestinal grass as a delicacy, wringing it out into their dishes to add an acrid, burning heat to the taste — a pre-modern alternative to the chilli, which was still a new arrival in China when Chen was writing.[16]

There are other analogues to be found today, for example, among the pheasant-worshipping Miao of South China, whose courtship traditions of serenades and moonlight trysts also seem oddly similar to the customs that Chen goes on to describe, as well as the division of labour between men and women, and the counting of each new year from each autumn harvest.

With some grasp of the ritualised nature of some tribal conflicts, Chen observed:

If something causes a quarrel between neighbouring villages, they mobilize their warriors and at an agreed-upon date, go to war. They kill and wound each other with the utmost of their strength, but the following day they make peace, and thereafter have the same relations as the first, without hating each other. Having cut off the heads, they strip the flesh from the skulls and hang them at their doors. Those who have many skeletons hanging at their doors are called braves.[17]

Despite the victory of the Chinese force that Chen accompanied, Japanese ships continued to show up in Taiwanese waters, particularly as the unification of Japan under the Tokugawa shogunate left the outlying feudal lords with spare manpower to put to work on new projects. In 1609, for instance, the king of the Ryukyu Islands sent a letter to the Chinese emperor, complaining about samurai interference in his country, and claiming that he had recently refused a Japanese request for soldiers to help them in a putative invasion of Taiwan.[18] In 1616, the king sent another letter, warning the Chinese that the lord of Nagasaki was planning to send a fleet of 13 ships to establish a trading base on Taiwan. Only three of them reached Taiwan, where they were soon shooed away.[19]

A far more dangerous presence in the area was that of the Dutch East India Company (often abbreviated VOC, from the original *Verenigde Oostindische Compagnie*), founded in 1602 as a result of European tensions, as a new front in the war of the Netherlands against Spain. Within two years, the first documented Dutch vessel had reached Taiwan, with captain Wybrand van Warwyck dropping anchor at the Penghu Islands, before being chased away by a Chinese fleet.[20] His colleague Cornelis Reijersen returned to Penghu, initially under the impression that the Chinese had agreed to trade with him there, but instead found only frightened fishermen. Eventually, an envoy arrived from the Ming Emperor, instructing him that he was not welcome on Chinese territory, but that he was welcome to ply his trade beyond the Emperor's jurisdiction: 'if we wished to go to the island of Formosa, and to fortify ourselves there, the king would have no objection ...'[21]

It would be another decade before the Dutch took the offer seriously. The VOC had first set its heart on seizing Macau, a Portuguese colony on the south coast of China, on which VOC ships made several raids. The last, and biggest, the Battle of Macau in 1622, ended in a resounding defeat for the Dutch and the loss of several hundred men, after which Reijersen retreated, firstly to Penghu. There, he was reminded of the earlier directive about illegal settlements on Chinese territory, and he finally crossed the Strait to build a more permanent Dutch presence, at the 'Terraced Bay' (*Tai wan* to the Chinese) — a name which ultimately came to be applied to the entire island.

Reijersen's base, Fort Zeelandia, was on the coastline at what today is known as the city of Tainan, formerly a seasonal campsite for Japanese smugglers. Better harbours could be found to the north, at what are now Keelung and Tamsui, but Fort Zeelandia was built on a site selected for its proximity to the sea-road to the Penghu Islands and the mainland — handy not only for trade, but for the simple logistics of shipping men and materials to build the fort in the first place.

The harbour at Tainan was frankly outmoded, suitable for smaller ships from a century earlier, but straining to accommodate the galleons and junks of the 17th century. This, however, was also a strategic advantage for defence. The channel for larger ships through Luermen was a complex zigzag, a narrow trench two fathoms deep that forced any ship approaching Tainan to snake along a sea-road three times as long as a direct route. A later poet wrote of it:

Iron sand piled firm in seven mounds
Like a whale striking the water, waves abound
Any ship is hard to come,
This is what heaven has created as Luermen.[22]

Once inside the lagoon, a ship would have to anchor some distance from the shoreline and disembark its passengers and cargo into smaller boats. These, too, could only make it halfway to shore before their keels struck the sandy bottom. It was feasible to wade through calf-deep water for another few hundred yards, but travellers who didn't want to get their feet wet had to hail ox-drivers from the shoreline who would trundle their carts out to ferry them ashore.[23]

There were other disadvantages to Fort Zeelandia's location, namely the absence of any decent wells, requiring fresh water to be brought over from the landward side.

The establishment of Fort Zeelandia is a major point in the history of Taiwan, marking, in the words of the historian Chiu Hsin-hui, 'the first profound foreign interactions' and inaugurating 'a historical sequence of colonial domination' that extends until the present day. The Dutch usually get the blame for this, although their era was preceded by several decades of increasingly large-scale contact with Chinese ships since the 1560s, which had already exerted a substantial influence on the indigenous territory, culture, and economy. Regardless, the combination of the Dutch East India Company and the many thousands of its Chinese minions (and subsequent rivals) would change Taiwan forever.

> In the course of [the next] four hundred years, the island of Taiwan changed from an island populated exclusively by Austronesians into the homeland of some 23 million ethnic Chinese with a small minority of 475,000 indigenous people, making up less than 2 per cent of the population.[24]

Or, to put it another way, what was once Austronesian Taiwan was now a culture in 'a protracted process of retreat', shrinking physically away from its old territories, but also culturally transforming under the influences of three new, powerful influences: capitalism, the Christian religion, and the very notion of statehood.[25]

The introduction of exotic commodities — bells, gems, tools, and other trifles — overturned a tribal culture that had kept everybody equal. Some of the first Dutch arrivals presented gifts to the first tribesmen they encountered.

'They are extremely envious and jealous of each other,' wrote one Dutchman, 'for, if you give something to one of them in the presence of another, you immediately sow discord among them.'[26] This was not merely a matter of personal interactions, but of diplomacy, as the VOC discovered to its cost when it leased land from one village, Sincan, for the price of 15 bolts of cloth. As VOC labourers began harvesting bamboo to build houses, they were approached by the inhabitants of the neighbouring village, Mattauw, who demanded to know what they were doing. When the enquiring villagers were told that the labourers were building a settlement, they returned in an angry mob of over 300 armed men, exacting revenge for a perceived slight, since a 'gift' had been made to one village, but not another.

Before long, the Dutch presence at Fort Zeelandia was dividing the nearby tribes. In 1626, the VOC meddled in an indigenous dispute, by demanding the villagers of Mattauw return items stolen in a raid from the village of Sincan, along with some pigs by way of apology. This only served to make the Sincan villagers bolder in their dealings with Mattauw, leading to a further conflict in which the VOC interceded, again on Sincan's side, by sending a party of musketeers.

Yet another group on the shores of Taiwan was the Japanese — traders from Nagasaki, led by one Hamada Yahei, who refused to pay the new Dutch tolls and tariffs. Instead, Hamada attempted to involve the Japanese government militarily, kidnapping 15 Sincandian head-hunters and spiriting them away to Nagasaki, where they were dressed up as a Formosan 'delegation' and brought to the Shogun's headquarters in Edo. Here, Nagasaki's chief official hoped to persuade his lord that Sincan was a 'nation' ready to proclaim its loyalty to the Shogun and was requesting the assistance of a samurai armada. Instead, the fake delegation failed to even gain an audience, and returned empty-handed in 1628, whereupon the VOC governor Pieter Nuijts imprisoned its members on the grounds of suspicious behaviour.[27]

The standoff would fester for several months, with Nuijts convinced that the Sincan headman, Dika, had been a willing participant in the Japanese ruse, and the Sincandians increasingly resentful at the sight of their menfolk in captivity. Increasingly strident protests led Nuijts to send a party into Sincan to arrest Dika, demand reparations from the Sincandians, and to destroy the houses of the 'delegation' members.

By the summer of 1629, indigenous resentment had reached a boiling point. A party of 60 Dutch musketeers, sent to watch for Chinese smugglers at the Mattauw river, were the victims of a new alliance between Mattauw and Sincan, massacred in a surprise attack as Mattauw men helped them across the river. Inevitably, there were further Dutch reprisals, and further impositions on the Formosans. The ineffectual Governor Nuijts was eventually sent home in disgrace, replaced by a far more belligerent leader, Hans Putmans.

Historians favour the Dutch version of history because Fort Zeelandia and its masters in the VOC kept detailed written records, turning the indigenous people into nameless background characters, rebels to be suppressed or clients to be swindled. For more than half of the 40 years that the Dutch were the supposed masters of Taiwan, they also had to contend with the presence of a Spanish colony on the north of the island, at what is now Keelung and Tamsui, briefly known as the forts of Santisima Trinidad and Santo Domingo. The tensions between Fort Zeelandia and its rival harbours in the north fluctuated in line with international politics beyond the scope of this book, revolving around the Spanish interests in trade between China, Japan, the Spanish Philippines, and the New World. At the local level, in terms of the Spanish role in the history of Taiwan itself, their brief reign in the north was characterised by events very similar to those experienced by the Dutch.

Although the Spanish dealt with different indigenous peoples — the Basai, Kulun, and Kavalan in their immediate vicinity — their reports of unrest mirror those of the Dutch. When discussing whether or not the 'Indians' were owed reparations for Spanish acts by men under the leader Bartolome Martinez, including the burning of their villages, one Spanish authority wrote:

> The entry to Isla Hermosa ... was justified even if individual soldiers committed some violations. [Martinez] promised the natives compensation for the abuses and for the land that the Spaniards seized. However, the Indians did not abide by this [arrangement] and instead perpetrated treason and theft, provoking [us] to wage war against them, and to withdraw the right to restitution.[28]

It was not long before the Spanish noted some of the rare values of their new colony, in particular the nearby access to 'sulphur deposits in large quantities'.[29] Crucially, the Spanish expected the locals to heel to their order, and for their colony to succeed with a relatively small complement of European and Filipino soldiery. The Dutch vastly augmented their own manpower with wave upon wave of Chinese settlers, ensuring that their own colony enjoyed far greater success.

The Dutch records both preserved and suppressed indigenous traditions — they are often the first surviving writings on many Formosan matters, but filtered through misunderstandings and lack of nuance. Even so, there are some remarkable observations made by the new arrivals, not the least by David Wright, a Scotsman working for the VOC (the 'Dutch' East India Company employed many nationalities) particularly regarding the diversity of the nearby tribes. The Dutch already understood that most of the villages they encountered were autonomous territories under larger linguistic or cultural umbrellas, such as the 11 sites around the Dutch settlement, which occasionally warred with one another but were all tribally Siraya. Further afield, there were clusters of villages with single overlords, such as Cardeman, a polity of five villages with a female ruler known as the Good Woman for her friendliness towards Dutch missionaries. On the coast north of Dutch territory, a man called Kamachat Aslamies controlled the lands around several river systems, leading the Dutch to proclaim him to be the King of Middag — the name of his realm deriving from the Dutch translation of his headquarter-village, Darida Suyt (literally 'Midday'). Kamachat refused to allow Christians on his territory, although he soon found his lands under attack in a Dutch campaign that at first detached several villages from his command, and eventually secured his allegiance as a Dutch vassal.[30]

David Wright was unimpressed with 'King' Kamachat, noting: 'He keeps up no great state, and only has one or two attendants accompanying him when going abroad.'[31] In her landmark account of the Dutch colonial era, Chiu Hsin-hui offers a vital additional suggestion: Kamachat's dominion was a relatively recent development, occasioned by the rise of Chinese traders on the coast only a few years earlier, and the resultant consolidation of power among the inland tribes. Far from being the hereditary king of a Taiwanese nation, he was more of a grand entrepreneur, presiding over scattered villages that had suddenly fallen under the influence of the potential wealth to be gained by selling food, resources, and trading goods to coastal visitors.[32]

There were other clues to the impact that the Chinese presence had already made. Dutch missionaries were horrified at a local indigenous custom that refused a woman any children until she was in her late thirties.

... for, when she is with child, the fruit of her womb is destroyed ... They call one of their priestesses, and, on her arrival, the woman lies down on a couch or on the floor, and is then pushed, pinched and roughly handled till abortion follows, which occasions more pain than if the child had been brought living into the world.[33]

It was not, perhaps, the woman's age that was important, but that of her husband, since a couple was not expected to *create* life until the man had fulfilled his youthful obligation of *taking it* as a head-hunter. The practice of abortion, sometimes up to a dozen or more times in a woman's reproductive life, not only kept down numbers, but ensured that the loss of a man to other head-hunters would not leave his children fatherless.[34]

This, too, appeared to be a relatively recent development. Chen's otherwise reliable account from 1603 made no mention of abortion among the Siraya, which could mean that the custom observed 20 years later by the Dutch had only evolved in living memory. Indeed, the missionary Georgius Candidius was told by an old man that there had been many radical changes to Siraya culture since the 1560s, suggesting that many elements of Sirayan 'tradition', including the harsh rules on childbirth, had developed in reaction to the coastal presence of Chinese pirates and traders, and the need for head-hunters to operate in a more military fashion.[35]

There were, undoubtedly, many hundreds of Chinese visitors to Taiwanese shores before the coming of the Dutch, but this, too, is a historical fact subject to political interference. Tonio Andrade notes that there have been attempts by Chinese scholars to play up the importance of these pre-Dutch contacts, in order to suggest that the Chinese pirate organisations amounted to the establishment of 'political authority'. He is ready to concede that they might have amounted to warlords of the Penghu Islands, but not with any enduring sway over Taiwan itself, which required the mass migrations of Chinese sponsored by the Dutch.[36]

It is possible that the arguments of those Chinese scholars, intended to establish a longer Chinese *political* presence on Taiwan than currently accepted, may indeed get their day in the sun, in the light of more recent scholarship that is prepared to reconceptualise marine power bases as seaborne communities.[37] The 'pirates' that the Dutch ran into in the Taiwan Strait were not a mere handful of ships preying on passing traders. They were members of a powerful, widespread organisation, comprising hundreds of vessels, land-based families and associates, forts, and harbours. Forced to operate off-the-books by Chinese law, this entity did not see itself as made up of pirates and smugglers, but of entrepreneurs struggling for mastery of the waters of the Taiwan Strait and the sea-roads as far afield as Siam and Japan.

Both the Dutch of the VOC and the mainland authorities of China's Ming dynasty meddled in the affairs of this powerful maritime force, sometimes leaning on it for trading assistance, sometimes fighting with it over jurisdiction, and sometimes backing some of its internal factions in the hope it might destroy itself.

Ultimately, the most prominent figure in this organisation was a charismatic man from Fujian that the Dutch called Nicholas Iquan, known to the Chinese as Zheng Zhilong — in the interests of clarity, we shall refer to the pirate network hereafter as the Zheng organisation, partly because of his habit of selling licences to other ship-owners, for which they were able to fly the Zheng emblem on their masts to avoid attack by other ships. 'No vessel can show itself on the coast of China,' wrote Pieter Nuijts, 'or Iquan has it in his power.'[38] Iquan was not the founder of the organisation, but he had worked his way up in it since the 1620s, cementing alliances with the earlier generation of captains, and marrying into the organisation's management. The historical record lists him as having an impressive number of 'brothers', many of whom had animal sobriquets — Zheng Zhilong was technically 'Dragon Zheng', but in the records of his forces there is also a Panther Zheng, a Phoenix Zheng, a Leopard Zheng, and a Tiger Zheng, along with a menagerie of a dozen lesser animals. Some of them were blood relatives, although others were more likely to be 'brothers' in the sense that the Zheng organisation was a fraternity like many a later Chinese secret society.

Nicholas Iquan was a major power player in southern China, and liable to have been an instrumental force in the Dutch colonisation of Taiwan. He first crops up in Dutch records as an interpreter for the pirates, irritating Cornelis Reijersen with the way he handled negotiations.

By 1628, Iquan had been bought off by the ailing Ming dynasty, assigned an official government role as an 'admiral'. In fact, both he and his bitterest rival had received the same cunning government offer of a pardon and commission for *ending the pirate problem*, but Iquan had been the victor in their subsequent war. In a path to power that would be mirrored in 20th-century Taiwan by many a gangster seeking legitimacy (see Chapter Ten), Iquan became a leading political figure in the administration of Fujian, continuing to run his trading operations while also gaining influence on land. He can even be found in Chinese records earnestly suggesting that one of the solutions to a Fujian drought would be a mass exodus of the victims to Taiwan, setting them up as farmers with 'three taels of silver and an ox', implying that he was intimately connected to the Dutch colonisation plan.[39]

News that Taiwan's indigenous unruliness, as well as the Chinese pirate presence, had been quelled in some areas, led to an increased interest in migration, particularly from the famine-hit region of Fujian. Nicholas Iquan had removed the 'pirate problem' by destroying his rivals, while his sometime Dutch allies were determined to pacify the island of Taiwan. Keen to fast-track their Taiwan colony into a powerful regional force, the Dutch not only enticed Chinese settlers from the mainland, but kidnapped them. A thriving market in slaves fed at least some of the Dutch military adventures in the Taiwanese hinterland, and one VOC governor even suggested that the company try to tie Chinese settlers to their new island home by shipping in some slave-wives from South-East Asia.[40]

Some Chinese plantation workers came of their own accord, fleeing poverty in Fujian province and forming a new caste of nativist settlers. Tonio Andrade characterises Taiwan before the Dutch as merely a place of chance encounters and occasional trading between the Chinese and the Formosans, and that on the occasion of the Dutch arrival, there were probably barely a thousand Chinese to be found on Taiwan. It is only after the establishment of the Dutch colony, and its need for rapid expansion, labour services, and, most importantly, stable agricultural supplies, that the Chinese population increased by any significant amount, effectively becoming 'a Chinese colony under Dutch management'.[41]

In the case of the Siraya people, on whose tribal lands the Dutch had settled, the local population amounted to something like 20,000 on the day that Reijersen arrived. The locals were imposing — early accounts report that the Sirayan tribesmen towered 'a head and a neck' above the Dutch.[42] Within a generation, by the year 1650, the number of Chinese migrants brought over to serve the Dutch had ballooned to 15,000, threatening to outnumber the indigenous population. Such migrants also represented an aggressive colonial force of their own, often advancing into Formosan territory ahead of any official Dutch ventures, to the extent that some Dutch expeditions to supposedly unexplored lands found Chinese settlers already living there.

The Dutch missionary Georgius Candidius observed that the Chinese had severely disrupted tribal traditions among the indigenous people, who now hunted not for their own requirements, but to satisfy demands from foreign traders.

> The flesh of the animals killed is bartered for wood, articles of dress, and other things, to the Chinese. The natives seldom keep a carcass for themselves, but they keep the entrails, which they eat with all the filth attached.[43]

Centuries of careful adherence to codes of sustainability among the indigenous peoples were now threatened by the demands of these foreign markets. In the case of the Formosan sika deer, reported in centuries past as being ridiculously plentiful, the coming of the Dutch saw a predatory and invasive over-hunting. Hides of the sika deer comprised a major part of Taiwan's export market, not only to the Chinese mainland, but up to Japan, where they formed a vital component in samurai armour and saddles — a commodity more lucrative than silk for its traders. The deer population was fated to decline over the following centuries, at first through the culls of up to 200,000 a year during the Dutch colonial era, and through the subsequent appropriation of many deer runs as agricultural land during the Qing administration and the Japanese colonial era. The last sika deer seen in the wild was killed in 1969, and today they can only be found in captivity and on the NT$500 banknote.

The arrival of the foreigners also transformed the nature of tribal violence. When many tribal conflicts had once been settled in ritualised combat, with victory conceded to the first side to take a human head, a dispute could be resolved by a single death, followed by a three-day celebration in which the killers invited the spirit of their victim to join their tribe and dwell among them in friendship. It did not take long observing the new arrivals for the Siraya to favour a more drastic style of killing as many of the enemy as possible.[44]

Although the Dutch are today generally remembered fondly on the mainland, this is what historians call an 'error of nescience' — those who had cause to be less appreciative of the Dutch presence were killed off. The Dutch undertook a number of military campaigns against the local tribes, bringing them under the authority of the VOC, and thereby forcing them to pay tributes and tithes, and to apply for hunting and fishing licences like the Chinese, in order to continue their previous traditions.[45]

In 1633, under the command of Governor Hans Putmans, who was considerably more proactive than his predecessor, the Dutch on Taiwan launched a series of expeditions to pacify their rivals. This included a surprise attack on Nicholas Iquan's fleet in Quanzhou Bay and a blockade on Amoy Harbour. Although the action cost Iquan dearly, he retaliated two months later, routing the Dutch shipping and forcing them into a humiliating compromise: he would permit them a 'trading post' on the mainland, but insisted that his own ships be the sole freight carriers to serve it.[46]

In the same year, the Dutch undertook a raid on Lamey Island just off the south-western coast of Taiwan, 'as an example for their murderous actions against our people'. A landing party of 200 Dutch, 40 Chinese 'pirates', and 250 Formosans inadvisably split up, only for the ships' surgeon and some of his Formosan porters to be surprised in the forest and beheaded by local warriors.

As the rest of the landing party proceeded through the island, they uncovered numerous relics of a lost ship. Some of the coins found by the Dutch had been minted in 1628, leading the captain, Claes Bruijn, to deduct that the Dutch artefacts on Lamey had been plundered from the VOC yacht *Beverwijck*, presumed lost at sea two years earlier. It would eventually be revealed that 50 crewmen had survived the wreck of the *Beverwijck*, only to stumble ashore to be massacred by the Lamey Islanders.[47]

A retaliatory strike in 1636 comprised 100 VOC soldiers and 'a large contingency' of Formosans, led by the Dutchman Jan van Lingga. The

Lamey Island menfolk took to the hills and the forest to mount their traditional warfare of attrition, but the Dutch made a beeline straight for the caves where the women and children were hiding. Sealing off all but two points, van Lingga burned sulphur and pitch at the entrances. Forty-two of the Lamey Islanders crawled out and surrendered. Several hundred more could be heard weeping and screaming inside the caves for the next few days, until they finally succumbed to thirst or the fumes. Several further missions rounded up the surviving men and women on the island, which was eventually depopulated of its indigenous inhabitants — 'cleansed and liberated', wrote Governor Putmans without a shred of irony, 'from these murderous people'.[48] After many years of further raids, the last 13 inhabitants of Lamey were spirited away in 1645, by a Chinese merchant who had rented the island from its new Dutch 'owners'.

The Dutch mounted another campaign against the Favorlang to their north in 1637, in an effort to suppress the area, but also to protect Chinese lime-burners and deer-hunters, who complained they had been attacked by locals. The indigenous people said quite the opposite, that the Chinese wandering into their territory were blatantly ignoring the terms of the licences granted to them by hunting out of season, in contravention of the deal that the Dutch had made with the Favorlang to police such actions.[49]

A revised deal was eventually struck to the great disadvantage of the Favorlang, who were 'granted' the right to a third of the land that was once all theirs. By 1638, when the Favorlang had pushed back against further Chinese encroachments, Dutch reprisals deprived them of all their lands. A series of tit-for-tat murders and assaults ensued, until 1642, when a Favorlang chief arrived at Fort Zeelandia to return the skulls of several Dutchmen. It was supposed to have been a gesture of reconciliation, but only led to further fighting. By 1644, Dutch power had extended to the south and north, culminating in a campaign against the Kingdom of Middag that saw its ruler accepting official status as a Dutch vassal. As a symbol of his admission to the fold of civilisation, he was given a free stick.[50]

Of the several hundred Lamey Islanders who survived the depopulation of their island, the men were put to work in chain gangs in Batavia on Java and in Tainan, while the women and children were placed in servitude with Dutch families, and at least one would end his days in Europe. One of the infant survivors of the cave massacre is known to have grown up to become a sailor with the VOC — he is recorded in the town records of Amsterdam, marrying a local girl in 1656, with the name Jacob Lamay van Taywan. In 1668, as 'Jacob Lamij', he is recorded in the Westerkerk baptismal records as the father of Neeltje, the daughter of his second wife, Clara.[51]

Jacob at least managed to escape the fate of the rest of his tribe. Those remaining on Taiwan, indigenous, Chinese, and Dutch alike, would soon find themselves in the firing line of an all-new threat, caused by events a thousand miles away.

CHAPTER THREE

REBEL BASE

Koxinga and the Kingdom of Dongning (1644–1683)

The year 1644 marks a new chapter because of events that happened on the mainland, when the enfeebled Ming dynasty fell to an invasion by the armies of the Manchus, from the north side of the Great Wall. The Manchus proclaimed themselves to be a new order, the Qing dynasty, savagely suppressing all mention of their Ming predecessors, and imposing themselves on the Chinese as a new aristocracy.

Even the Manchus were taken aback by the speed of their conquest, bolstered by successive waves of turncoats, so that by the time the 'Manchu' army reached the southern provinces, it was largely composed of Chinese soldiers, fighting other Chinese soldiers. The first two years saw rapid advances over all of north and western China. The southern provinces took longer to fall and were not declared pacified until 1659. In an accident of military history, one last outpost of Ming loyalists would hold out until 1683, spurring the Manchus to tardily send a final force, led by ageing warriors dragged out of retirement, to shut down this bastion of resistance. The occupation of this territory, its two decades as the so-called Kingdom of Dongning, and its ultimate fall, is what makes this story part of the history of Taiwan.

The hold-out provinces of the south were all protected to some extent by the geography — Fujian in particular was ringed by a defensive semicircle of mountains, its coastline a series of jutting promontories separated by estuaries. Although the last Ming Emperor had killed himself as Beijing fell to Chinese rebels, themselves shortly afterwards ousted by the Manchus, the provinces still in the hands of Ming loyalists gained a rump government, the 'Southern Ming', which would proclaim a series of imperial family pretenders as figureheads for the loyalist cause. One such would-be ruler, the 'Longwu Emperor', arrived in Fujian in 1646 with his entourage, throwing himself on the mercy of the most powerful local warlord, the Ming 'admiral' Nicholas Iquan, whom we last saw acquiring his position after the imperial authorities were unable to stop his massive smuggling franchise. With little to hand out but promises and honours, the Longwu Emperor thanked his rescuers by granting a series of noble titles. Nicholas Iquan was proclaimed a marquis and put in charge of the counter-offensive. His various brothers and nephews were made counts and captains, and a special honour was reserved for his eldest son.

The teenage Zheng Chenggong had lived at his father's fortress at Anhai on the Fujian coast for almost a decade, having arrived with his mother, Miss Tagawa, a woman from the port of Hirado in Japan, who had been Iquan's lover in his days as an itinerant smuggler. Hoping to butter up his rescuers, lest they turn into captors or kidnappers, the childless Longwu Emperor conferred his own imperial surname, Zhu, upon the half-Japanese boy. It was not quite an official adoption, but spoke volumes about the degree to which Longwu was relying upon the support of a maritime community that, until only a few years previously, his predecessors had dismissed as pirates. The boy hence gained the sobriquet 'Knight of the National Name', *Guoxingye* in Mandarin, but remembered in posterity by its Hokkien pronunciation: Koxinga.

Koxinga was a very different man from his wily father. Whereas Iquan had schemed and stabbed his way to a position of paramount authority, Koxinga had been raised as the son of a millionaire. He had received the best education that money could buy, and was understandably starstruck by the Emperor's attention, proclaiming: 'I will be faithful to you even unto death.'[1]

Unfortunately, such youthful idealism was beneath Nicholas Iquan and many other members of the Zheng organisation, who were masters at telling which way the political wind was blowing. Repeatedly in the campaigns further north, the Manchus had guaranteed that Ming officials who defected to the Qing would be able to continue in their posts in the new order — this was part of the reason for the incredible speed of the advance. By the time the Manchu armies were approaching the mountain passes around Fujian, Iquan had already resolved to defect, offering his loyalty to the Manchus' new Qing dynasty, which thanked him by making him a duke. He seems to have genuinely expected the rest of his family to follow suit, as many did, although Koxinga was swift to warn his father of the risks of leaving one's base: 'The tiger that leaves the mountain has no power; fish are trapped out of the ocean.'[2]

Koxinga refused to give up on the Ming dynasty, a resolve that hardened when the Qing armies took the Zheng fortress at Anhai, killing Koxinga's Japanese mother in the process. Famously burning the robes he had worn as a Confucian scholar, Koxinga became the leader of the Ming resistance, much to the embarrassment of his father, who was soon under house arrest in Beijing for failing to deliver the rest of his fleet to the Manchus. Over the years that followed, father and son would exchange increasingly snippy letters about the nature of duty, as Iquan tried to persuade Koxinga to relent. Meanwhile, Koxinga led a series of campaigns, at first against the members of the Zheng organisation that had defected, taking several offshore islands in 1647, then taking Amoy itself in 1650. In that year, as an indicator of his power at sea as far afield as Japan, one observer noted that of 'seventy Chinese ships recorded in the harbour at Nagasaki, 59 were identified [as] Zheng's ships'.[3]

Now ennobled as a duke by yet another Ming pretender, Koxinga continued to harry the Fujian coasts, making substantial gains within sight of the sea, but unable to assert quite as much authority on land.

These distant events made their impact felt on Taiwan, where the disruptions of Fujian trade and population affected the Dutch East India Company's bottom line. It also led to tensions among the Chinese — their numbers swelled by refugees, their attitude towards the Dutch who had fought the Zheng organisation becoming increasingly hostile.

In 1652, Pauw, a Chinese man who lived near Fort Zeelandia, burst into the presence of the latest governor, Nicolaas Verburg, to warn him of a plot underway. Pauw revealed that his brother Fayet (known in Mandarin as Guo Huaiyi), a village leader, was planning to massacre the Dutch leaders at an upcoming banquet, and then to lead a rebel force to seize the castle. Governor Verburg sent a platoon to the village and found 'the Chinese all astir'. Fayet had already marshalled substantial forces, with a rallying call that asserted the Dutch had no right to rule over the Chinese:

> My friends, we have long been exploited to the bones by the red-haired barbarians and we are bound to vanish at their hands before long. Why do we sit and wait for death? We should rise and fight. If we win, Taiwan would be ours to keep.[4]

Deprived of his planned surprise attack, Fayet led 16,000 men in a riotous assault on the neighbourhood near Fort Zeelandia. The stable master, Nicholas Marinus, and three grooms hacked their way on horseback through the crowd, and reported immediately to Verburg at Zeelandia. Verburg sent out the troops, in a mismatched battle between Fayet's rebels, armed with sticks and bamboo stakes, and a combined force of 120 Dutch musketeers and 2,000 'Christian Formosans'.

It is only *after* a discussion of the revolt that the Dutch reports shiftily mention that they had recently imposed a poll tax on the Chinese residents. An off-handed account of the aftermath reveals that the entire sorry episode lasted for 15 days, and saw considerable atrocities on both sides:

> Fayet and one thousand eight hundred of his men were slain; besides which many women and children, and Lonegua, the second in command of the enemy's army, were captured. The last-named was roasted alive before a fire in [Tainan], dragged behind a horse through the town, and his head was then stuck on a pole. Two of his chieftains, who had ripped up a pregnant native woman and torn the child from her body, were broken upon the wheel and quartered.[5]

The poll tax may have only been a catalyst. There were remarkably few ships arriving from the mainland — later revealed as a deliberate policy from Koxinga to prevent the Dutch from learning of his plans to run for Taiwan in the event of a military setback in his war of resistance against the invading Manchus. 'There was very good reason,' wrote François

Valentyn, 'for believing that the uprising on 8 September 1652 was not undertaken without his knowledge.'[6] A letter arrived from the VOC's masters in distant Batavia, informing the governor of Taiwan that these suspicions were not without merit:

> numerous rumours are now current in China concerning the son of Iquan called Koxin, who, pressed hard by the Tartars [Manchus], can no longer hold out in China, nor find himself safe there. He has therefore gone to sea with a great force, and adopted a course of piracy, intending to keep an eye on Formosa, with the view of ultimately settling down in that territory.[7]

For now, Koxinga was clinging to the idea of a counter-attack on the mainland. He only turned his attentions to Taiwan after his enemies made his tenure on the mainland impractical. In 1656, the Manchus fought back by forbidding human habitation within 50 km of the sea along 1,500 km of south Chinese coastline, the provincial waters of Guangdong and Fujian. The ban was designed to cut off Koxinga from every possible means of support — financial, material, and personal.[8]

In the late 1650s, Koxinga mounted the largest campaign of his military career to date, a thrust at Nanjing, 300 km inland. If that seems like a foolhardy operation for a leader with a primarily maritime power base, it helped that Nanjing sat on the wide Yangtze River. Nonetheless, the Manchus made life as difficult as possible for Koxinga's men by seeding the river with a network of chained-together floating fortresses, the 'Boiling River Dragon'. Despite initial gains, by 1659 Koxinga was on the retreat. It had been 15 years since the initial Manchu invasion, and his Nanjing campaign was a last-ditch attempt to whip up support among a younger generation that did not even remember the previous dynasty.[9]

Defeated, he returned to his Fujian base, known as Think Ming (*Siming*), forced to plot a drastic, long-term solution to restore his dwindling power base. The rumours, in circulation for a decade, that he would seek to make Taiwan his new headquarters, finally came to be true. He was aided in this by coming into possession of a marine chart, smuggled out to him by a Chinese settler, that would allow him to navigate Luermen.[10]

The last VOC governor of Fort Zeelandia, a Swede named Frederick Coyett, had repeatedly warned his masters in Batavia about the likelihood of an attack by Koxinga, begging them to send him reinforcements. A messenger from Amoy in 1660 reported that he had found the entire city preparing for a large-scale naval assault on somewhere, but when the man asked about the likely target, Koxinga had archly noted that he 'was not in the habit of publishing his designs'.[11]

In a private conference with his generals, Koxinga revealed his true intentions for a generation-spanning project to prepare a counter-attack from Taiwan:

> [We were told] of the bounty of Taiwan, that it possessed ten thousand acres of fields and gardens, a thousand miles of undeveloped arable land, and revenues of several hundred thousand taels. Our artisans would have ample opportunity there for shipbuilding and arms manufacture. Of late, it has been occupied by the red-haired barbarians, but they number barely a thousand. We need but lift our hands to capture it. I wish to secure Taiwan as a base ...[12]

His plan did not meet with unanimous assent: many of his officers rightly believed that it was fated to drag them away from their remaining strongholds on the mainland.

Even as the VOC council in Batavia authorised the removal of Coyett for his supposedly unjustified paranoia about a Chinese attack, in spring 1661 Koxinga set sail with 25,000 men, against a Dutch military presence of only 905 soldiers, defending a community of another 800 Dutch women, children, and male non-combatants.

The Dutch initially tried to tough it out, counting to some extent on the unknown allegiances of their Formosan vassals, but also on a misguided assumption that a Dutch soldier was easily worth 25 Chinese, and that the odds were consequently still in their favour.

The overconfident musketeer Captain Pedel assured his men that: 'The Chinese had no liking for the smell of powder or the noise of muskets; and that after the first charge, in which only a few of them might be shot, they would immediately take flight and become disorganised.'[13]

He based his belief, which turned out to be fatal for him and 117 other soldiers, on the VOC's experience of the 1652 uprising, not an encounter with battle-hardened veterans of a decade of warfare. In the naval battle around Fort Zeelandia, the Dutch warship *Hector* was hit in its powder magazine and blown to smithereens. Powder also turned out to be a sore point at Fort Provintia, which was severely undersupplied. Its commander was accused of skimming most of the gunpowder and selling it to Siamese traders only a few weeks earlier, although by the time he was accused, with Fort Provintia already cut off and surrounded by the Chinese, he was too dead to defend himself.[14]

Fort Zeelandia was large enough and equipped enough to withstand a long siege. It was, in fact, better supplied than the people besieging it. Outside its walls, Koxinga's men threw themselves into intensive agriculture, to grow enough food for themselves.

'There was scarcely a corner of these lands that hadn't been enclosed or planted,' commented the interpreter Philip Meij of the thousands of potato allotments, 'and we were amazed by these heathens' industriousness and zeal.'[15]

By starting an agricultural revolution on Taiwan, Koxinga would inadvertently commence a centuries-long process of further attrition against the indigenous peoples. Particularly in the 18th and 19th centuries, the opening of new agricultural lands would have a long-term, multi-generational effect caused by the sheer forces of newcomer numbers generated by such prosperity. Since prehistoric times, the indigenous custom of slash-and-burn cultivation, leavened with hunting and gathering, had been enough to support between 15 and 25 people per hectare of land. The advent of 'dry' farming, such as fields of wheat, millet, or potatoes, took the supportable number little higher, to 25–30. But 'wet' farming, in flooded paddy fields growing rice, took the numbers of supportable humans per hectare to 600–700.[16]

The early agricultural boom was a matter of desperation. The 25,000 men Koxinga had arrived with would eventually grow in number to 40,000, effectively doubling the Chinese population of Taiwan.[17] Unknown to the Dutch at Fort Zeelandia, his soldiers were attempting to secure larger areas of supplies but running into indigenous resistance. In the north, the commander who had so swiftly trounced Captain Pedel lost

1,500 men trying to take on the surly Kingdom of Middag. In the south, the Chinese forces lost another 800 in a similar war against the locals. Part of Koxinga's problem was that he was cut off from his own supply lines by bad weather, a fact mourned in a contemporary song:

> The windstorm blows, rolling the ocean
> Churning the clouds like cotton
> The huge ships, filled with thousands of tons of rice
> Are turned back by towering waves and can't go east
>
> The officers and men on the Eastern Expedition are starving,
> Nearly at the point of death
> They look westward, but the rice ships never arrive.[18]

Over the following 11 months, as the Dutch waited in vain for the sight of a relief fleet of their own from Batavia, Governor Coyett wrote bitterly of the puissance of the Chinese soldiers, and of the annoyingly multi-ethnic nature of Koxinga's army. In particular, he was affronted that Koxinga had 'two companies of "Black-boys," many of whom had been Dutch slaves and had learned the use of the rifle and musket-arms. These caused much harm during the war in Formosa.'[19] His wording implies that they had defected during the siege, but in fact Koxinga's personal entourage, the 'Black Guard' of African and Indian soldiers, had been inherited from Nicholas Iquan, who had begun recruiting such men a generation earlier.

A topic of greater annoyance to the Dutch was the speed with which the local indigenous people went over to Koxinga's side. Promised amnesty and good terms, the villagers of the communities around Fort Provintia sent a delegation to Koxinga to announce their allegiance, although their new master soon put their loyalty to a series of severe tests. Formosan tribesmen with Christian names were forced to stop using them, and the leaders of the Sincan village, once regarded by the Dutch as their most 'beloved children', were drafted by Koxinga as his new executioners.[20]

Coyett blamed a German soldier, Hans Radis, for breaking the siege. Defecting to Koxinga's army, the traitorous Radis told them of Fort Zeelandia's Achilles heel — the fact that its designers had originally overlooked an area of high ground from which an enemy could fire down on the interior of the fort. This weak spot had been tardily reinforced with a small watchtower, called Utrecht, but had apparently escaped the notice of the Chinese. Poring over the evidence, historian Tonio Andrade observes that it is unlikely that the Chinese 'needed a drunk German' to tell them about it.[21] Regardless, shortly after Radis gave himself up to the Chinese, Koxinga's sappers and artillery focused the bulk of their resources on destroying Utrecht, the brickwork of which was pounded by so many cannons that it 'quickly lost the whiteness of its mortar and showed itself very red'.[22]

The Dutch abandoned Utrecht, although they did leave a booby trap behind — a slow fuse on the remaining gunpowder in the magazine, which blew the place apart, along with several of its enthusiastic Chinese occupiers. Koxinga himself came within a hair's breadth of being killed in the explosion — he had been warned by Hans Radis that the Dutch might leave a surprise, but had been determined to be 'first' in the fort.

The loss of Utrecht spelled the end for Fort Zeelandia, and Koxinga is remembered by Chinese posterity as the hero who expelled the Dutch from Taiwan. A 1955 propaganda print shows him pointing imperiously out to sea as the shamefaced Dutch scamper to their ships. Behind him stands a crowd of allied Formosans, including a bunch who appear to have wandered several hundred kilometres from their homelands. For his service in ridding China of foreigners, he was eventually celebrated even by the Manchus he so bitterly opposed, although he did not live long enough to see that day.

Even as Koxinga's men were taking stock of the meagre pickings from Fort Zeelandia's remaining food supply, he was plunged into a dispute with his relative Zheng Tai back on the mainland. Zheng Tai was at least partly responsible for the lack of supply ships during the siege. The news that Koxinga had recently become a grandfather at 38 was tempered by the revelation that his son, Zheng Jing, had impregnated the wet nurse of one of Koxinga's other children, which technically made it an act of incest. One of Koxinga's last acts, as he descended into a madness that may have been part malaria, part syphilis, was to order Zheng Jing's execution, although he was ignored.

Koxinga died in the summer of 1662, heartbroken at the news of the demise of the last Ming pretender on the mainland, and apoplectic about Zheng Jing's activities. He left a weary poetic summation of his progress:

> Thickets hewn and barbarians dispelled.
> It took a decade to finally recover ancestral glories.[23]

His successors on Taiwan re-evaluated this progress and placed it at the start of a new Thirty-Year Plan: 'Grow in the first ten, enlighten for the next, mature in the last ten years to vie with the mainland.'[24] After some jockeying for power among various factions of the Zheng clan, Zheng Jing took over from his father, often remaining on the clan's island strongholds off the mainland, while his underlings tried to hammer the newly acquired Taiwan into a suitable rebel base, beginning by sending a notification to the Ming pretender that Zheng Jing was assuming his father's titles. Since the Ming pretender was already dead, they did so by writing a proclamation and then burning it so it could reach him in the afterlife. He continued to rule from the grave for some time, with Zheng Jing insisting on using his calendar and year-numbering as late as 1670, and annually paying his respects at Fort Provintia to an empty throne.[25] Other zombie-Ming measures included the institution of a shadow Ming government, civil-service exams as if running the entire Chinese empire, and outreach programmes among the indigenous population, to teach them Chinese and further reduce the influence of the Dutch era. The Dutch, however, were busily trying to come back from the grave, offering to help the Manchus oust Zheng Jing's resistance regime, and had to be shooed away from a new foothold in north Taiwan in 1664. More welcome arrivals, at least to Zheng's administration, were another 30,000 Chinese refugees, fleeing the Manchus across the Strait, and lured by Zheng's promise of three tax-free years for new settlers.[26]

Zheng Jing is often overlooked by Taiwan historians — Koxinga's life and legend often seem to overwrite his son's achievements.[27] Koxinga retains a huge footprint in Taiwan's local folklore, and the island is speckled with tourist spots where he is alleged to have bested an opponent or dispelled a magical haunting, even though his own reign on Taiwan was so short that he cannot possibly have been everywhere. A ghostly red light in the river at Jiantan, near Keelung, was said to be the treasured sword hurled by Koxinga at a river monster. Confounded by a poisonous fog at Yingge, he turned his artillery on the cursed Eagle Brother Stone, which emitted its black miasma no more.[28] When the lower waters of the Tamsui River turned to run back upstream during an earthquake, he again trained his artillery against the supernatural phenomenon, bombarding Turtle Mountain and pacifying its spirit. Curiously, these locations are all within the environs of modern-day metropolitan Taipei, whereas Koxinga himself arrived far to the south in Tainan, and surely died before he could visit.[29]

Instead, in tales like these we may be seeing the garbled memories of later military advances in those areas by Zheng Jing's forces — there are a surprising number of once-majestic features that were cannoned into oblivion by new arrivals. One doubts, for example, that Koxinga personally had the time in his few remaining days of life to march all the way to the village of Meinong outside Kaohsiung, where he is supposed to have carved a memorial to his mother on a 'woman-shaped rock', now on the grounds of the Stone Mother Temple (*Shimu Gong*).[30] Today, the temple is a focus of local worship, favoured particularly by expectant and young mothers, who believe that tea fed to their children after being poured over the rock's nipple-like extrusion will bring health and obedience. But the stories about the sacred rock only arose after the 1730s, when the area gained more Chinese colonists, and the temple itself was built around a series of natural rock features only in the 1980s. Such tales seem, to me at least, to muddle pre-colonial tribal beliefs about a 'mother stone' with Chinese worship of a number of mother goddesses, and a smattering of Japanese colonial-era tales about Koxinga's mother.

In 1664, Zheng Jing authorised a series of military expeditions to establish farms, pushing the boundaries of his territory north from the Tainan area towards what is now Taichung. This led to conflicts with the indigenous inhabitants, with Zheng himself leading an army of 3,000 men in 1671 against a group liable to have been Atayal:

> Not content with tattooing their bodies all over, they also tattoo their faces. They look utterly weird, like devils. They frequently sally forth to burn and loot and kill people. When the local barbarians hear they are on the warpath they weep and wail, and flee far away to escape them.[31]

The army marched through ominously silent forests, before taking a break at midday amid a patch of sugar cane. There, they were ambushed by several hundred Formosans, leading to a fight with heavy casualties on both sides. Zheng Jing, however, was determined to establish new colonies, particularly in the forested hills, where timber to replace his dilapidated warships was a crucial commodity.[32]

Many other parts of the island date folklore to the coming of 'Koxinga's' (i.e. Zheng Jing's) men. In the farms around Chiayi, locals tell stories of a phantom ox that can sometimes be seen wandering among their own herds. It is, supposedly, the spirit of the eight oxen brought to Chiayi by farmer-soldiers led by Koxinga's officer Ye Jinmei, which died tilling the fields but were buried by farmers rather than eaten for their meat. This, in itself, reflects the agricultural traditions of southern Chinese farmers and ethnic minorities such as the Miao of Guangxi, who treat their oxen with similar reverence, and is likely to be a tale that grew up in opposition to beef-eating practices among later colonists.[33]

One enduring feature of the Zheng era was occasioned by soldiers' habit of hanging their shields and swords on their doors. There may have been an element of feng shui symbolism in warding off evil, although the truth may have been more prosaic, and the presence of military-grade weapons outside someone's house may have been intended as a deterrent to thieves. Whatever the original reason, the appearance of a lion-faced shield, appearing to clutch a sword in its mouth, became a common icon on Tainan residences, and these 'sword-lions' (*jian-shi*) have been resurrected in modern times as tourist attractions — on buildings, postboxes, and in Tainan's Sword-Lion Square, a public space near what was once Fort Zeelandia.[34]

Fort Zeelandia itself was renamed by its new Chinese masters, as Anping (a mash-up of two different terms for 'peace').[35] In a flurry of other changes, the old Dutch sites were rebranded as strongholds of a defiant Ming dynasty. The settlement on the coast of Taiwan was now Dongdu ('the Eastern Capital'), and Taiwan itself was now the Kingdom of Dongning ('the Pacified East').[36]

Zheng Jing's most influential adviser was Chen Yonghua, his former tutor, and the author of the aforementioned Thirty-Year Plan to retake the mainland, although he was soon announcing that maybe the Zheng

'Sword-lions' have become emblematic of Tainan, this one appearing in Haishan Hall,
built in the early days of Qing rule.

clan was better off not bothering: 'We resolve to stay here, and have no
intention towards the west [the mainland].'[37] There was certainly no love
lost between Chen and the Manchus, who had forced his father's suicide
during the invasion, but tantalisingly little remains of him in material
record. On a trip to his mansion in Tainan, built soon after the removal
of the Dutch, I was intrigued to find that his roof beams were held up by
little Dutch gargoyles, bending under the symbolic weight of working for
the Chinese. Over time, Chen came to envisage the Zheng family's destiny
as creating a 'Great Ming among the waves, that administers a separate
territory from the Qing'.[38] There were even indicators that this might
be achievable, particularly after a Zheng fleet successfully pushed the
Dutch out of Cambodia in 1670, and American silver began pouring into
Taiwan via the Philippines. Zheng ships did brisk business not only on the
Mekong Delta and in the harbours of Siam, but also beneath the noses of
the Manchus. The freshly appointed Chinese governor of Fujian happily
looked the other way as many of his subjects indulged in a lucrative trade
across the Taiwan Strait with the Qing dynasty's supposed enemy. Zheng

raiding parties would frequently be 'surprised' by Fujian coastguards, who would then 'pursue' them until they were out of sight of the Manchus, and then feverishly trade their goods with each other.[39]

It was Chen who pushed for Zheng Jing to enter into trade agreements, with his former Dutch enemies, with the Japanese, with the English, and with anyone else who would offer him money. Staying alive was only part of the mission of the Kingdom of Dongning; Chen's Thirty-Year Plan for retaking the mainland would require huge wealth, best generated through trading in sugar, camphor, gold, and deerskins. Although this might seem innocent to modern readers, to a regime that was supposed to comprise the last Ming loyalists, it amounted to a humiliating climbdown — proclaiming themselves as the last true-hearted Chinese, but treating foreign powers and corporations as trading equals, rather than submissive vassals.[40]

Zheng's own surviving writings show him flip-flopping between life as an island king or a Ming rebel, and even perhaps the possibility that he might found some new outpost of China *beyond* China. He made repeated allusions to China's Bronze Age, when many areas now regarded as inalienable provinces were once regarded as foreign lands.

> Thousands of mountains and hundreds of valleys stretch far into the horizon. Fragrant forests twist and turn unto the edges of the blue clouds, while water turns green in the creeks. The people and houses on both shores welcome the dawn, and fishing boats throughout the rivers sail with morning winds. The ancient sages may find the place a bit difficult to describe, but the gowns and caps of the Han country are the same as all antiquity.[41]

In such a vein, it is worth noting that while the term 'King' (*wang*) in Chinese did once denote the title of an independent ruler, it had been a mere administrative post in China for at least 1,800 years, ever since there was an Emperor to overrule him. In calling himself the 'King' of Dongning, Zheng Jing was not necessarily proclaiming independence, but assigning himself a leading rank in what he claimed to be the continued administration of the not-quite-dead Ming dynasty.[42]

Messages from the Manchus on the mainland, or at least from their local representatives flailing for a compromise, became increasingly conciliatory, suggesting that if Zheng Jing continued to pursue this trade-focused organisation, he would be left alone, or even accepted as a vassal to be held at arm's length. Zheng himself clung to his father's focus on an eventual Ming restoration, and benefited from the support such rhetoric brought him among committed Ming loyalists, who joined his regime and participated in the Sinification of what had been Dutch Taiwan. Despite his claims to be the king of an independent island, Zheng Jing continued to write of his grim determination to lead a counter-attack:

> The Ming fate is faint on the mainland
> But its spirit endures on the island
> It is my strong intent never to fall
> Day and night, I prepare for war.[43]

Such a stance left him permanently unable to agree to the Manchus' demands that he give up the pretence of there being a lost Ming dynasty worth restoring. In 1667, rejecting their overtures yet again, he boasted that he had 'opened another universe at Dongning, outside the imperial map'.[44] In 1670, the crew of a Zheng ship detained and massacred the crew of an ambassador's vessel heading to the mainland from the Ryukyu Islands. They were, Zheng Jing curtly announced, carrying 'tribute to barbarians on barbarian soil'.[45]

Zheng allowed such bellicosity to win out, disastrously committing himself to a campaign on the mainland, a decade ahead of his own officials' timetable. China's far south was less under Manchu suzerainty than it was divided between several powerful warlords, whose allegiance to the Manchus had begun to waver. When the rulers of Fujian, Guangdong, and Yunnan rose up in the 'Revolt of the Three Feudatories' in 1673, Zheng threw in his own forces.

Retaking the former Ming stronghold of Amoy in 1674, Zheng bragged of his resurgent rebels, enjoying a meteoric success on the Fujian coast because of his familiarity with the people there. Many of the older generation were former Zheng associates, left behind when Koxinga launched his attack on Taiwan. Others were *current* Zheng associates, part of the smuggling network that had never quite gone away. Still more were Hokkien-speaking Chinese like Zheng Jing himself, who saw him as a kindred spirit. His support in Fujian, in fact, proved to be so strong that one of his *allies*, the rebellious governor of Fujian, sent a force back to attack him, fearful that he might suddenly turn on him and cut off his supply lines as he advanced on Manchu territory. An allied general was obliged to send mediators to calm them both down, lest they look like a laughing stock to the Manchus.

The rebellion faltered within three years. Zheng was only prevented from quitting Amoy in 1677 after a boldly contrary display by the city's residents, who kneeled en masse before his entourage and refused to budge.[46]

Zheng's allies were defeated, and his involvement in the war made him a far more prominent target for Manchu reprisals. Even then, the Manchus were prepared to offer (or at least pretend to offer) Zheng Jing almost everything he wanted in 1679, as long as he gave up his coastal holdings and moved out of sight and out of mind, over the Strait to Taiwan. In a major concession, they did not even demand that he shave the front of his head and braid the rest of his hair into a queue down his back, which was the symbol of submission to the Manchus.

> If your Excellency should choose to retreat to Taiwan, this court will cease fire. Never again attempt to invade China. Your Excellency need not wear a queue. Whether or not to submit to pay tribute is entirely your choice. The court wishes Taiwan to be another Korea, another Japan.[47]

Zheng continued to refuse, and was forced to evacuate Amoy in 1680, returning to Taiwan, where his own mother berated him for his 'lack of talent'.[48] He died in 1681, leaving his heirs locked in a bitter argument over which of his two contradictory policies they should follow. Should they pursue independence for their island, or knuckle under to the mainland regime?

Zheng Jing's departure for war had masked a power struggle by factions at his Taiwan court. The influential Chen Yonghua had married his own daughter to Zheng Jing's eldest son, Kezang, who was left in charge as regent when Zheng Jing went off to fight on the mainland. At the time,

Kezang was only 12 years old, affording his father-in-law a position of considerable authority, and leading to numerous proclamations and purges in Kezang's name, designed to protect his father-in-law against other factions.

After Zheng Jing's death in 1681, a new faction rose in opposition to Chen Yonghua. Feng Xifan, Zheng Jing's former bodyguard, forged an alliance with other disaffected courtiers, and argued with Koxinga's widow, the Queen Dowager Dong, that Kezang was not really Zheng Jing's son at all. Rather, he was allegedly the son of a butcher, passed off as Zheng's heir by a wily concubine. Such a story would never have held water while Zheng Jing was alive, as he had witnessed Kezang being born. But with Zheng Jing gone, there was nobody to stand up for Kezang, and the Queen Dowager was evidently persuaded — there were whispers that she regarded the circumstances of Kezang's birth as the final stroke that had killed her husband, a resentment harboured for an entire generation.

In his grandmother's presence, the hapless Kezang was murdered by some surviving members of Koxinga's Black Guard — in the words of one chronicler, 'by the black slaves barbarously strangled', although I personally find it suspicious that the Queen Dowager herself should suddenly die soon afterwards. The new ruler of the Kingdom of Dongning was now Kezang's younger brother, Keshuang, an 11-year-old boy who was also, conveniently, the son-in-law of Feng Xifan. When Keshuang's official regent, his uncle, also died soon after, Feng Xifan was free to take over.[49]

Chen Yonghua's faction believed that the Kingdom of Dongning should fight to the death; Feng Xifan's faction counselled that the time had come to surrender. Even as they bickered, a taskforce was underway from China, led by the one man who might be trusted to secure victory: Admiral Shi Lang, a former Zheng captain who had defected to the Manchus a generation earlier. He arrived leading a navy and marines armoured with an edict from an emperor who had tired of all the politicking over Taiwan's status, and had a new, impatient policy concerning its inhabitants. The Manchu ruler, known as the Kangxi Emperor after his reign title, had proclaimed that people on Taiwan 'were all Fujianese. They cannot be compared to Ryukyu or Korea.'[50]

In other words, merely because they had left Fujian, they did not cease to be subjects of the Emperor. Accordingly, they were not to be afforded the same concessions available to 'barbarians' further afield in acknowledged foreign kingdoms.

On Taiwan itself, Zheng Jing's six-year investment in the Revolt of the Three Feudatories had caused a severe depletion in agricultural manpower, exacerbated by a drought. Shi Lang's navy soon cut off the links to the mainland, while the increasingly harsh famine conditions on Taiwan led to several uprisings by aggrieved indigenous people.

In July 1683, a massive Qing fleet overwhelmed the Penghu Islands. Liu Guoxuan, a commander in charge of a garrison that had not received a ration resupply for over a month, prayed to heaven for a last-minute storm, but did not get his wish. Instead, his forces were routed by Shi Lang, who would later claim that he had a vision of Mazu, the Goddess of the Sea, fighting by his side. In the subsequent Battle of the Penghu Islands, Shi Lang lost only 329 men, and the Zheng forces up to 12,000.

Back on Taiwan, as reports drifted in of successive garrison commanders offering their allegiance to the approaching Shi Lang, young Keshuang followed his father-in-law's advice, and agreed to make the battle on the Penghu Islands the last. When Shi Lang came ashore, it was not to fight, but to accept the surrender of the last King of Dongning.[51]

There are comments by the Qing officials of the last of the men of Dongning 'jumping for joy' at the realisation that they would be keeping their lives. But not all of them made it out alive. In a sad footnote to the downfall of Dongning, servants found the bodies of five women hanging in a palace hall. They were the concubines of Zhu Shugui, the highest-ranking survivor from the Ming imperial family, who had been living under the protection of the Zheng clan since 1662. Zhu took his own life shortly after the loss of the Penghu Islands, when it became clear that the days of Dongning were over.[52]

On shore, Shi Lang's entourage rode to the temple where Koxinga was enshrined, where the admiral knelt in thanks, weeping, as if Kezang and Keshuang's own semi-divine grandfather had somehow also switched sides in the afterlife.[53]

CHAPTER FOUR

BEYOND THE SEA

Taiwan as a Qing Prefecture (1683–1840)

The Kangxi Emperor ruled from the Forbidden City, a fortress complex at the heart of Beijing, designed to impress upon visitors that it was the dwelling place of the ruler of All Under Heaven. His audience chamber was reached only after a long journey through multiple defensive gates, crossing huge courtyards, and climbing towering stone staircases to ornate palaces. The architecture was designed to awe his subjects, but also left its powerful resident with a somewhat imperial sense of proportion.

'Taiwan is merely a ball of mud beyond the sea,' he commented, 'unworthy of development by China. It is full of naked and tattooed savages, who are not worth defending. It is a daily waste of imperial money for no benefit.'[1]

The Kangxi Emperor was reluctant to hang on to the newly acquired island, which he called 'a desolate place'. His advisers piled in, agreeing that it was better to 'empty the land and leave it to the barbarians', meaning the indigenous people, or even to rent it back to the Dutch and make it someone else's problem.[2] Certainly, in the short term, that was what the Qing authorities tried to do, deporting many thousands of settlers back to the mainland. Zheng troops were granted an amnesty, on the condition they served the Manchus. Many were shipped up to the northern border of the Chinese empire, where they fought as 'Manchu' soldiers in battles on the Russian frontier at Albazin. Feng Xifan was made a count, as was

Liu Guoxuan, the defender of the Penghu Islands, who ended his days as the commander of one of Beijing's fortified city gates. As for Keshuang, the grandson of Koxinga, he was taken to Beijing, where the Kangxi Emperor conferred him with a dukedom, and a rank in the Manchu Plain Yellow Banner. He would die in 1707, in his late thirties.

Having fought so hard to capture Taiwan, Admiral Shi Lang was the greatest advocate for hanging on to it. He was fully aware that if left untouched, Taiwan would revert to being a strongpoint for the Japanese, or the Dutch, or the English, who were already pestering him to put in a good word with the Emperor. This, in turn, would only create problems for him on the mainland. Besides, having seen the island for himself, he regarded it as a land rich in resources, there for the taking.

> I have personally travelled through Taiwan and seen first-hand the fertility of its wild lands and the abundance of its natural resources. Both mulberry and field crops can be cultivated; fish and salt sprout forth from the sea; the mountains are filled with dense forests of tall trees and thick bamboo; there are sulphur, rattan, sugarcane, deerskins, and all that is needed for daily living. Nothing is lacking ... This is truly a bountifully fertile piece of land and a strategic territory.[3]

By 1684, Shi Lang had won the Emperor over. Taiwan was incorporated within the Qing empire, inadvertently destabilising the traditional assumption that China was a territory defined by its natural geographical limits. Formerly, China had stretched from the northern snows to the southern mountains and jungle, from the eastern coast to the Central Asian desert. Now, China had a new appendage 'beyond the sea' (*haiwai*), pushing out its sense of its own geography into new areas.

In a sense, the annexation of Taiwan began a process that led not only to Taiwan's incorporation as a full Chinese province in 1887, but to the various spats and flag-plantings of the 21st century over Beijing's interest in possessions in the South China Sea. It also marked the first phase in a new period of imperialist expansion — in the 80 years after taking Taiwan, the Qing dynasty would go on to extend China's borders at a furious pace, doubling the empire's land area by pushing westwards into Tibet, Mongolia, and Xinjiang. Some of the troops involved in these advances were former loyalists of the Zheng regime, resettled on China's northern and western borders, thrown into the front line on the new conquests. This, too, would have long-term effects, confronting the Manchu overlords and their Chinese subjects with the fact that their realm was now truly multi-ethnic — attempts to manage an empire with dozens of non-Han minorities would also have an impact back on already-multicultural Taiwan. Under the Qing in the 18th century, China would achieve its largest ever territorial area. It is this high-water mark of Chinese expansion that has come to define modern China's sense of its sphere of influence.

A common saying in the period was: 'Of every ten who reached Taiwan, just three remain; six are dead and one has returned home.' This may be an accurate reflection of the migrant experience, although the possibility remains that it was Qing government propaganda, designed to make the move to Taiwan as unattractive as possible for the disaffected coastal poor — barriers to would-be migrants came and went, but would not be fully lifted until 1875.[4]

The first Chinese who went to Taiwan to make their fortunes were Hokkien-speaking people from Fujian, often termed Hoklo by Taiwanese custom.[5] Hokkien drifted so far from standard Mandarin pronunciation that one might even call it a separate language. I certainly think of it as one, but saying so is a political act not worth getting into here. Although the historical record in our own age is written in standard Mandarin, most of the events that happened on Taiwan in the course of this chapter and the next were first narrated in Hokkien.[6]

Also arriving was a new group that endures as a powerful presence in modern Chinese society, the Hakka. The Hakka had been present on Taiwan since the time of the Dutch, but it was only after the Dutch departed that their settlements grew to significant size.[7] Originating in north China over a thousand years ago, the Hakka are descended from the refugees who fled south during the periods of nomad invasion. Pushed southwards by the Jurchens and Mongols who overran the Tang and Song dynasties, their ancestors struggled to find empty land on which to settle in a south that was already packed with locals. Instead, they were often forced onto tough-to-farm scrubland, or steep mountain slopes, giving them a reputation for hard work and constant poverty. Their cuisine reflects the need to have large stocks of salted food to defend against famine, and the higher-fat requirements of constant labour to maintain hillside rice terraces.

The name Hakka derives from the Mandarin for 'Guest Families' (*Ke jia*), a passive-aggressive term that accepts them as visitors but implies that they should not outstay their welcome. Uniquely, they have always resisted any attempts to classify them as an ethnic group, on the grounds that they are not an aboriginal tribe, but are in fact the *original* Chinese of the north, clinging to their language and traditions over centuries of enforced population movement. After the fall of Taiwan to Qing forces, the Hakka were some of the major beneficiaries of the relaxation of the coastal settlement prohibitions, accepting Qing government incentives and subsidies to come out of the mountains and resettle the abandoned thousand-mile strip of coastline facing the Taiwan Strait. When they arrived, they found that many Cantonese and Fujianese had beat them to the prime lands, forcing them into a repeat of their age-long struggles to farm on substandard plots, and into rivalries with other peasants. In frustration, many of them joined the quiet exodus across the Strait to Taiwan itself, forming a substantial part of the Chinese settlers of Qing-era Taiwan.

In 1696, in the midst of a drought, a fire at the Fuzhou government warehouses destroyed over 200 tonnes of sulphur nitrate. Worried about the implication for both taxation and gunpowder stores, local officials sent a team across the Taiwan Strait, where indigenous people were known to be able to extract sulphur 'from Taiwanese dirt'. Sulphur had also been one of the export items cited by Wang Dayuan in his Ming-dynasty *Brief Account of the Island Barbarians*.

One of the Fuzhou team members, Yu Yonghe, left a written record of his journey, *The Small Sea Travel Diary* (*Bihai Jiyou*), which survives as an invaluable glimpse of Taiwan a generation after its incorporation within the Qing empire. Wading ashore at Luermen, and drawn in an ox-cart through the neighbourhood, he was at first impressed with the conditions in the four villages that had flourished under the Zheng regime, reporting that 'the houses were spotlessly clean, in no way inferior to villages on the mainland'. His guide told him that they were the beneficiaries of incentive schemes from the Zheng era, to both educate them and increase food supply:

Those of their young men who were able to go and study in the village schools were exempted from corvée [labour], so that they were gradually civilized. The barbarians of these four villages also know to work hard at their farming and to lay up savings, so every household is prosperous.[8]

In a mirror of the Chinese understanding of civilisation as something that fades the further one travels from the imperial centre, Yu was warned that the barbarians became progressively more savage as one travelled away from Tainan. Yu himself already had a sense of thinning, noting that even in these four model villages, he saw 'men and women, with their hair unkept down their backs, and trouserless, still keeping to their old ways'.[9]

The barbarian carters we saw were all covered with tattoos: on their backs birdwings were outspread; from shoulder to navel fishing nets were wound around in diagonal tapering [strokes]; on both arms were likenesses of human heads, severed at the throat, repulsive and frightening. From wrist to elbow they wore several tens of iron bracelets, and there were some who wore them to make their ears large.[10]

Yu did not mention a striking image by his contemporary Lin Jianguang, who noticed that decades of Dutch rule had brought a noticeable evolution in tribal tattooing:

Their bodies are tattooed, and eccentrics will tattoo themselves all over with their writing, which is the characters of the Redheads [i.e. the Dutch].[11]

Even though the Dutch were gone by 1662, and the Zhengs by 1683, the Peipohuan people in the Taichung area would continue to use the writing system they had learned from Dutch missionaries, clinging to Roman letters through 150 years of Chinese rule.[12]

Yu was less impressed with the womenfolk, whom he occasionally found pretty from a distance. Closer up, he recoiled at the sight of their hair riddled with lice, and the stench of deer fat used as ointment.

The island's eventful previous century had left its mark. Yu saw several villages in ruins, where he was told the inhabitants had made the mistake of standing up to the Dutch or the Zhengs, only for entire populations to be wiped out in retribution. Elsewhere, locals flattered him by speaking in breathless tones about the power of the Qing empire. After all, he was told, the red-haired Dutch had conquered the island, but they had been ousted by the Zheng family, and the Zheng family had been defeated by the Qing, who must then, surely, be the most powerful masters of all.

Yu believed that the barbarians had little understanding of money or how to use it, requiring the Chinese officials to adopt a more complex process for collecting tax. The right to collect tax was auctioned to the highest bidder, whose representatives were then placed in direct attendance at each village, to monitor local production and assess the size of each tax burden. This, in turn, was paid through barter, in produce at harvest time, or in various articles known to have a resale value — deer hides sure to still find a ready market in Japan, or dried venison prized in Fujian.

As Yu saw it, the Chinese had two problems. One was the brevity of official postings, with administrators rotating back to the mainland after only three years. Yu found this to be counterproductive, with inexperienced new arrivals cluelessly continuing their predecessors' policies, and not residing in their post 'long enough to warm the mat'.[13]

Yu was even more scandalised by the kind of Chinese he saw in the hinterland and had no qualms about describing many of the 'village merchants' (*she-shang*) as conmen, spivs, and bullies. The Qing authorities had operated a 'frontier guard system' (*ai yong zhi*), initially staffed by assimilated plains people, but increasingly after 1720 by Chinese volunteers.[14] Yu was arriving 60 years into this system, where the initial concept of a solid frontier had been replaced over the decades by a sense that it was the frontiersmen's duty to 'civilise' the people on the far side of the line. Chinese scoundrels were pushing low-quality goods and hand-me-downs on the Formosans, using the island as a dumping ground for unsellable items from the mainland. But Yu reserved most of his ire for the henchmen of the tax-farmers, many of whom he regarded as little more than outlaws fleeing mainland justice. He was scandalised by the attitude of the Chinese representatives in many a village, who abused their positions to become de facto headmen, repeatedly swindled their charges, and betrayed them by misrepresenting communiqués and messages from the Chinese authorities. Yu was particularly irritated by the way in which headmen would abuse their roles as interpreters, to the extent that even if a Formosan sought legal recourse against a local tough, the same strongman was likely to be the translator of any dealings with the Chinese magistrate, and sure to twist testimonies to his own advantage.[15]

Yu's comments reflect the observations of a Chinese folksong, lampooning Taiwan's status as a last-ditch refuge for the indigent, desperate, or criminal elements of Fujian. It is unlikely to form part of a Taiwanese tourist advert any time soon:

Nothing to do at home — Argue with wife
'Why not go to Taiwan?'
Straight to the shore you rush
Beat down the boat fare to smuggle your way to Taiwan ...

Dried potatoes and dried radishes is all you've got to eat
Nine out of ten greens are sure to [make you] vomit ...

Made it to Taiwan. Landed under cover of darkness
Lost in darkness, can't tell east from west
Alas! Held up by bandits and
Robbed of all you've got.[16]

As his wagon train trundled northwards across the island, Yu's eyes were drawn to the sight of the mountains, which he characterised as a forbidden wilderness. The people he met on the coast, in his terms, were *tu fan* — 'local barbarians'. But the higher ground was the realm of the *ye fan* — the 'wild barbarians'.

The wild barbarians are in the mountain fastnesses which rise, range upon range like screens, peak upon peak jutting up to the Milky Way, with dense forests and thickets of bamboo; where looking up one cannot see the sky; where brambles and creepers obstruct the feet; where never an axe has entered since primeval time.[17]

By his own admission, Yu had not actually seen any wild barbarians, but his local contacts were eager to volunteer horror stories about them.

> When they kill a person they immediately take his head back with them. They cook it upon their return, strip the flesh off the skull, daub it with red plaster, and set it at the door. One whose fellows see many skulls at his house is esteemed as brave. As if in a dream, as if drunk, they do not know how to become civilized — they are really no more than beasts.[18]

Yu Yonghe's opinion was in line with the beliefs of the Chinese settlers and the Qing authorities, and the Japanese colonial authorities after them, that the mountain tribes should be left to their own devices:

> For instance if one encounters a tiger or leopard one gets bitten, and if one runs across a poisonous snake one is [likewise] bitten; but if one does not go near their lairs they will not have any thought of harming one; so then one need only let them alone to live and die in the rain and dew.[19]

But throughout human history, there has been a disconnection between colonists' sense of leaving natives well alone, and their interactions in that liminal area that both sides end up regarding as their own. In particular, it becomes an issue when the colonists covet something that they had previously disregarded. Once seized from the indigenous people, hunting lands were ever-after turned into agricultural holdings, with demarcated fences and owners. Camphor trees were destroyed in the extraction of their contents, causing Chinese merchants to venture deeper and deeper into indigenous territory in search of untapped sources.

Government pressures became increasingly severe. In 1720 alone, more than 200 Chinese were beheaded for cutting down camphor trees without official sanction, and in the aftermath of a large-scale earthquake, there was no sign of any reduction in tax demands.

One of the largest insurrections during the Qing period arose in 1721, among settlers angry at predatory tax measures. The leader was Zhu Yigui, a man in his thirties who had arrived from Fujian a decade earlier, and having failed at several other ventures, turned to duck farming on the outskirts of Kaohsiung.

> According to their fashion, these feathered creatures marched out daily in regular rows like files of soldiers, and returned in the evening in the same manner. This circumstance appears to have suggested to our hero his first idea of military tactics, and he was not slow to improve the occasion.[20]

Zhu presented himself as the ideal figurehead for a revolt, in part because his surname was coincidentally that of the Ming imperial family, making him a 'knight of the national name' in the style of Koxinga — he allowed it to be inferred that he was a lost imperial heir. Wining and dining other disaffected local leaders, he became a pivotal figure in a multi-factional revolt that was soon joined by Hakka militia under Du Jongying.

This unlikely alliance of Hokkien and Hakka was testament to the aggrieved conditions under which the settlers were struggling. Unable to marshal enough troops to hold off rebel forces numbering in the tens of thousands, Qing officials turned to the plains people, offering them a bounty for rebel heads. Unfortunately, this proved to be a scheme open to abuse, leading to multiple tribal raids on innocent villagers, and causing many more supporters to flock to Zhu's anti-governmental cause. Briefly repelled on the outskirts of Tainan, the sheer numbers of Zhu's combined Hokkien-Hakka forces overwhelmed government troops, particularly after the leader of the government military forces was conveniently assassinated.[21]

As the Qing administrators fled in 40 ships, Zhu's rebels overran Tainan, where the former duck farmer was proclaimed king of a nation he called Great Ming (*Da Ming*), with the reign title of Eternal Peace (*Yonghe*). With nothing else to hand, his men purloined theatrical costumes to use as his ceremonial robes.

Fearful that history might repeat itself, and that Taiwan would again become a Ming stronghold, the Qing authorities dispatched Admiral Shi Lang's son, Shi Shibiao, to lead a counter-attack from the Penghu Islands. By the time he arrived in Tainan, the Hokkien-Hakka forces had started

to squabble with each other about the nature of Zhu's grand new order —
Du Jongying, whose men had done much of the real fighting, chafed at
being made a duke in the new government, alongside a number of fellow
nobles he regarded as little more than Zhu's cronies and rural chums. He
also thought that his own son should be nominated as heir, initiating
another power struggle.

The rape of a civilian girl proved to be the flashpoint, in which Zhu
demanded a clean-up of military discipline, whipping up other Hokkien
leaders to turn on Du's Hakkas in a battle at the old Fort Provintia, from
which the Hakkas fled. Du and his son subsequently surrendered to
the Qing army under the mistaken impression that they would not be
beheaded. They were taken off to Beijing to be executed, along with Zhu
himself, who had been betrayed by the headman of the village where he
was taking refuge.[22]

Zhu Yigui's revolt was merely the most successful, and hence the
one that thrived long enough to show its true colours, as an outgrowth
of a prolonged, simmering underground opposition to the Qing dynasty,
sustained in secret fraternities. The degree to which there was a genuine
'Ming resistance' is debatable, but the accoutrements of a bygone era, those
halcyon days before the coming of the Manchus, were a commonplace
element of the rituals and inner-circle cant of many a secret society.[23]

The brevity of Zhu's reign, coupled with the military dividend of not
having time to collect taxes or enact practical civil policies, allowed later
generations to regard it with a degree of nostalgia. Zhu Yigui, it was later
claimed:

> treated his subjects as he formerly had his ducks, with due
> consideration. Plunder was forbidden, and property as well as lives
> protected. If any one of his soldiers failed to pay sufficient regard
> to his injunctions, the culprit was beheaded then and there. Such
> discipline naturally had its effect, and the whole populace was
> inspired with confidence in its new master.[24]

Except that obviously wasn't true. Zhu's golden regime had tottered
after barely a fortnight, brought down by internal squabbles among his
own troops — the first obvious signs of the long-term 'subethnic rivalry'

between two groups of Chinese, the Hokkien-speakers and Hakka-speakers.[25]

It also demonstrated to the Qing authorities that their power in Taiwan was feeble enough to be toppled in mere days by the right kind of mob. Thereafter, the Manchus sent annual censors to audit tax collection and other infrastructural issues. Watchmen patrolled the towns and countryside, reporting any suspicious activity, such as a pair of Ming restorationist battle flags, found planted in the middle of a rice paddy outside Zhuluo in 1734 — the catalyst for a futile five-month witch hunt in search of rebels or brigands.[26]

They also relaxed some of the cross-prefectural restrictions on Hakka migration from the mainland, on the grounds that a change of heart among numerous Hakka warriors had proved critical in turning the tide against Zhu Yigui.[27] Over the next few decades, this would increase the Hakka component of the Chinese population of Taiwan to 30 per cent.[28] Qing authorities, previously reluctant to authorise the building of city walls on Taiwan, now acknowledged that it was time to fortify certain government locations, all the better to resist the immediate force of another uprising.

Expansion continued in an uneasy tension between Chinese settlers crowding each other on the coasts or advancing illegally into the tribal hinterland. In 1731, tempers boiled over in the north of the island, after settlers and allied tribes pushed a little too hard to get the people of Middag to perform corvée labour — unpaid work in lieu of tax payments. Middag had been technically a vassal of the Dutch, and left to its own devices by the Zheng regime, but the settlers and farmers encroaching on its borders, and demanding its menfolk help carry the grain that would feed the troops that would oppress them even further, would prove to be the final straw.

Below the surface, the incident was a matter of tribe-on-tribe violence. The initial revolt was liable to have been set off by tribal work-masters accusing Middag labourers of shirking or embezzling. The Qing retaliation involved a collaboration between soldiers from the mainland and 'barbarians to catch barbarians' — indigenous militia with an interest in seizing the possessions, livestock, and land of their rivals. By the time the brutal suppression was completed, the Middag men had been scattered, their lands re-assigned, and half their women widowed.

Chinese foresters began to intrude upon the shores of Sun-Moon Lake, long held to be the territory of the Thao people. Local legends claim that the Thao people under their chief Guzong ('Bone Altar') held back the Chinese settlers, until one realised that an ancient bishop-wood tree on the shoreline was the source of Guzong's authority. Bishop-wood trees, also known as java-wood or *urian* trees, are indeed sacred to several Formosan tribes, prized for their fruits (which can be used to make wine), bark, seeds, and sap (which is used to make a vibrant red dye).

The leader of the Chinese sneaked into the forest by night, but was defeated by the inability of his axe to penetrate the wood of the sacred tree. He returned instead with a 'blade with fangs' and sawed the tree down, hammering a copper nail into the stump to kill it off. 'The blood of the tree,' it was said, 'painted the whole of Sun-Moon Lake red, and the power of the Thao people was greatly diminished'.[29]

But the Chinese were not supposed to be entering Formosan territories at all, by Manchu command.

> For the offence of entering the territory of the aborigines, 100 blows shall be inflicted; and the same penalty, with three years banishment added, for engaging in such occupations as gathering rattans, snaring deer, felling timber, and collecting coya-fibre in proximity to the savages.[30]

This did not reflect the reality of prolonged contacts and trade between the Chinese and the tribes, the origins of a folk-tale that became part of the fabric of the Chinese education system for nearly a hundred years, until it was abruptly cancelled in the late 20th century. At the centre of this legend was Wu Feng (1700–1769), a figure celebrated by the Qing authorities, the later Japanese colonists, *and* the Kuomintang as a 'fearless frontiersman'.

The story of Wu Feng is difficult to narrate in historical time, because it means different things in different contexts. At its most basic level, a Chinese man spent many years trading with the Tsou tribe, but was eventually murdered. Before long, it came studded with embellishments, such as a dramatic claim that he had, in fact, given his life to save two other Chinese.

Over successive retellings, the story became far more convoluted, and involved the deeds of a trader and liaison officer between the authorities in what is now Chiayi and the nearby Tsou people. First visiting them as a young man in his twenties, Wu Feng had spent the next 40 years teaching them the rudiments of agriculture and housebuilding. Under the gentle stewardship of Wu Feng, it was said, the Tsou soon learned the value of iron, setting aside their old flint weapons — the implication is that they were little better than cavemen until he arrived. Having taught them how to farm, he was on hand to sell them metal farming implements, and building materials sufficient to upgrade their rickety rope bridges. Wu also achieved a certain fame as a healer of the sick, challenging the former authority of the Tsou priestesses, who regarded all sicknesses as divine and magical punishments. Instead, Wu sold them kaolin for the relief of dysentery — curing a Tsou chief in the process — along with numerous Chinese herbal remedies.

A cynic might already be wondering if this Wu Feng was less the evangelist for civilisation than one of the 'village merchants' who so annoyed Yu Yonghe, pushing samples and new-fangled gadgets onto the Tsou, creating new demands and problems, and then selling new solutions. He was, it was said, widely liked and appreciated by the Tsou, although his various attempts to discourage them from head-hunting caused friction. He eventually achieved some success with the chief whom he had cured, leading to a ban on head-hunting that lasted for as long as the tribe believed that their good fortune persisted.

In 1767, the Tsou's crops failed. If we are to believe the claim that Wu Feng *taught* them how to farm, then we need also consider that he had steered them over the years into relying far too heavily on a new food source. There was another bad harvest the following year, leading the Tsou leaders to revert to old beliefs:

the ancestral spirits were angry with the way things were going, especially the lapse of the head-hunt. The ritual of the returning warriors at the time of the harvest had been forgotten. The tribe feasted and danced, but neglected the ancestral spirits. Now had come the day of recompense.[31]

Wu's years of trading with the Tsou had created a cascade of disasters. The deer and wild pigs in the forests, which had once been plentiful enough to support the tribe, were now dwindling through over-hunting. The tribe itself was facing a crisis, as the younger generation of Tsou women refused to marry husbands they regarded as substandard, the warriors-turned-farmers having failed to prove themselves as men. There are suggestions, too, of eroding traditions. Once the priestesses of the Tsou had celebrated the head-hunt by journeying to a valley in the Alishan mountains, where their chanting voices were magnified by a powerful natural echo. Now they had no reason to sing their songs.

A crestfallen Wu Feng offered the Tsou leaders a compromise — one last head-hunt to appease their ancestors and mark the beginning of a new era. He told them to await the arrival of a man clad in red, riding on a white horse, to become their final sacrifice. The Tsou obeyed, and on the arrival of the foretold victim, seized him and cut off his head, only to discover to their horror that they had killed Wu Feng himself.

'The story,' comments W.G. Goddard in *The Makers of Taiwan*, 'has grown with the telling,' which is an understatement. He alludes to later embellishments, such as the shamefaced suicide of the tribesman who murdered Wu Feng, but seems to regard the story itself as true, and not a Qing-era folk-tale that, if it has any truth in it at all, merely recounts the death of a Chinese trader in the tribal hinterland.

•

There is a sense, in the history of Taiwan under the Qing dynasty, of a recurring cycle. Landless men seek their fortune on the outlaw frontier, and the successful ones become settlers and landlords on territory newly seized from the indigenous people. The 'militia' that suddenly seem to spring up like weeds in many a Qing-era chronicle were actually a constant presence — bands of guardsmen assembled to protect the landlords from reprisals by indigenous peoples or attacks by *other* Chinese, including those arising from subethnic rivalries such as between the Hokkien-speakers and Hakka-speakers.

There were parts of Taiwan settled solely by Hakkas, but also parts settled just by people from the areas around the cities of Fuzhou, or

Quanzhou, Chaozhou, or Zhangzhou. Along with their families, they imported local loyalties and rivalries that could erupt into sectarian violence in hard times.[32]

Sometimes these communities were able to find common ground with each other through membership of organisations set at odds with the Qing authorities. Crucial to understanding these fraught local politics is an awareness of the social groupings formed by these bands of single male fortune-seekers. How one wishes to describe them — as 'gangs', 'fraternities', or 'mutual societies' — really depends on where one stands on informal, unsanctioned societies. They flocked to communities or corporations that tended to operate outside the feeble Qing legal presence. These societies have many names, although the most commonly known are the Three Harmonies Society (*Sanhehui*, known to posterity as the 'Triads'), the Vast Family (*Hongmen*), and the Heaven and Earth Society (*Tiandihui*). At the lowest level, they were little more than off-the-books mutual funds and social clubs, martial-arts schools, lion-dance troupes, or gangs of street toughs contending over the turf for noodle-sellers and pedlars. At their highest level, as they grew over time through mergers and acquisitions, they became mega-societies — illegal corporations with access to the wealth of nations, of sufficient authority to command political parties and even run revolutions.[33]

The Qing dynasty was first alerted to the existence of the Triads in 1786. Depending on whom one asked, the Triads were formed by either refugees from the Shaolin Temple, erstwhile Qing supporters betrayed by the dynasty after coming to its aid in a mainland conflict, or a secret movement of Ming loyalists, swearing an oath at the fall of the Kingdom of Dongning to one day overthrow the Manchus — their slogan: 'Resist the Qing, Restore the Ming' (*fan Qing fu Ming*). Membership was for life, and signified by secret gestures, the recitation of coded poems, and participation in a blood ritual that seemed to involve the sacrifice of a rooster, standing in for the traitors who had betrayed the Shaolin Temple.[34]

We know all this because of the attempt in 1787 to clamp down upon the Triads. Taiwan's Qing governor ordered a series of arrests of dissidents, provoking a sudden upwelling of protests. When his uncle was rounded up with the usual suspects, the local Triad leader Lin Shuangwen became the ringleader of a group of Triad cells, escalating their actions from a prison break to the murder of the governor and several other officials, and the seizure of strategic points by 50,000 men. Much of the violence cloaked the settling of scores between Lin's Triads and rivals from Quanzhou or the Hakkas. His public face, however, was interpreted as just and upstanding resistance to the Manchus, even though one could read it as a factional proclamation:

> In order to save *our people*, we have especially raised righteous soldiers, and we have taken an oath before Heaven that if we are not benevolent and righteous, we shall die under ten thousand swords.[35] [My emphasis]

The quoted text is from a rebel decree, issued not as some sort of anti-Manchu announcement, but as a prolonged apology and warning to Hakkas and other parties who had been attacked by rebel soldiers. It pleaded for patience in the investigation of the crimes and for a united spirit of 'people from Fujian and Guangdong' (the latter being a common term used at the time for the Hakkas).

It took a year for a Qing taskforce to round up the rebels and quell the unrest. Lin Shuangwen was executed, and his men and their families suffered multiple reprisals, including death by torture, the desecration of their family tombs, and the castration of their sons, who were taken to Beijing to work as eunuch slaves. The nature of these punishments reflects a desire of the Manchus to stamp out resistance both in this generation and the next, inflicting cruelties on families in the afterlife. The Qing response was also characterised by an increased eagerness to manipulate local rivalries — they were aided in their counter-attack by the plains people, as well as the aggrieved and vengeful Hakkas. In thanks for their support, the site of one of the revolt's main battles was renamed 'Righteousness Commended' (Chiayi).

In an attempt to commemorate the area as a Qing stronghold, and not the location of former Ming loyalists, the Manchus erected nine three-metre stone slabs, praising their troops for putting down the rebellion. These can still be seen today, lined up in front of Fort Provintia in Tainan. The Manchus also began dismantling or rebranding some of the local memorials. Koxinga's body had formerly been entombed at Zhouziwei on the outskirts of Tainan, at a site reached by a traditional Chinese 'spirit road', evoking the mainland burials of princes and emperors, flanked by statues of guardian animals and loyal ministers. His son Zheng Jing was buried nearby, as was his ill-fated grandson Zheng Kezang. However, a generation after the fall of Taiwan, the Qing emperor ordered for Koxinga's remains to be removed to the mainland, and interred in Fujian — liable to have been an attempt to not only appease him in the afterlife, but also remove him from potentially rebellious associations in Taiwan.

This left the countryside outside Tainan with a high-profile grave that was deprived of its most famous resident. In the wake of the Lin Shuangwen rebellion, the authorities settled on the site as the ideal location to inter the fallen hero Zheng Qiren, a local strongman who had led one of the anti-rebel forces, only to be killed by Lin's rebels at a roadside ambush.

This was a matter of annoyance to the rebels' surviving relatives and sympathisers. The fields around Zhouziwei, it was said, were plagued by ghostly manifestations of a 'white horse' that trampled crops and caused mischief. This was the excuse for the vandalising of some of the statues near Zheng Qiren's grave, with locals claiming that the only way to stop the equine hauntings was to break the legs of the nearby stone horses, which were believed to be coming alive at night and terrorising the village. It is more likely that the vandalism came first, from secret sympathisers with the defeated Triads, and that the supernatural explanations were concocted to weasel out of reprisals from the authorities.[36]

Periodic uprisings continued, gathering meaning and iconography from their failed forerunners. Effigies of the 'duck king' Zhu Yigui, for example, would enter the pantheon of certain secret societies — there are accounts over a century later of certain Triad rituals treating him like some kind of revolutionary saint.[37] In 1795, he was cited as an inspirational figure for yet another uprising, centring around his old home near Kaohsiung. Soon after this was quashed, he was cited yet again, in a revolt for which the rebels had been promised assistance from over the seas by a 'lost Ming prince', whose much-awaited reinforcements of horsemen and soldiers never arrived. For a few days, his Ming-alike surname was

Zhu Yigui, the former duck farmer who led a revolt in 1721,
celebrated in a modern statue outside Xing'an Palace, with ducks.

brandished on a banner of doomed revolt: 'Great Alliance Zhu' (*Da Mengzhu Zhu*).[38]

Throughout the 18th century, Taiwan remained a prefecture that the Qing authorities would have preferred to keep at arm's length, an unloved appendage to Fujian province, which was already a long way from Beijing's notice or interest. Occasional good-hearted officials achieved some semblance of order there, but much of the island's frontier reputation was well-deserved, along with constant arguments about the extent to which certain 'criminal' activities were worthy of the name — some, indeed, were theft and banditry, but others amounted to the enforcement by local strongmen of laws that the government itself failed to implement.

Sometimes the officials managed to fail even more spectacularly. Fear of foreign incursions led one governor to take the drastic step of filling in the sea-roads through the Luermen sandbanks that shielded Tainan. It would prove to be an environmental disaster, as torrential rains in 1823 swept down the mountains and into the blocked lagoon. Apocalyptic quantities of silt reduced the lagoon, which had once provided a safe harbour for hundreds of ships, to a quarter of its former size. Entrepreneurial fishermen and farmers soon settled on the newly created lands, and further storms reduced the harbour further. Within a generation, the lagoon had gone, and Luermen, the famous 'Deer's Ear', had become nothing more than the name of a beach on the outskirts of Tainan. It was, truly, a place built on shifting sands.[39]

CHAPTER FIVE

WARLIKE ENTERPRISE

Foreign Incursions (1840–1895)

The so-called 'red-haired' foreigners never quite went away. By the 1830s, in fact, they were back in sizeable numbers, pushing on the gates of China, particularly around the Pearl River delta, where their merchantmen were prepared to do anything to make good on the trade in tea, the English name for which derives from its pronunciation in Hokkien.

The Chinese emperor had famously told foreign merchants that China wanted nothing from them: 'As your Ambassador can see for himself, we possess all things. I set no value on objects strange or ingenious, and have no use for your country's manufactures.'[1] Rather than throw away silver to quench the demand for tea back in Britain, traders instead pushed addictive and illegal opium on the Chinese. The drug was farmed in Bengal by labourers under the British Raj, shipped to China and either exchanged for tea or sold to local smugglers, who paid in silver that could be used to buy the tea itself.

As China succumbed to a drug-addiction crisis, attempts to restrict the trade escalated into all-out Opium War. After the Chinese official Lin Zexu seized and destroyed foreign opium supplies in Hong Kong, a British expeditionary force arrived in the Far East in 1840, engaging the outclassed Chinese military on the Pearl and Yangtze rivers. With all China's coastline a possible target, the Qing authorities on Taiwan did their best to prepare for an attack.

Their prospects were not good. The government censor Guo Baiyin was unimpressed with the conditions of the Taiwan garrison, the soldiers of which he found little different from the people they were supposed to be holding in line: 'After crossing to Taiwan, they gamble with prostitutes, form gangs to seek revenge, blackmail civilians, and hold officials to ransom.'[2]

Nevertheless, the Taiwanese coastal fortresses watched for trouble, which arrived in September 1841, when the British transport *Nerbudda* foundered on the nearby rocks. *Nerbudda* had been carrying Indian workers, 240 of whom were left to their fates after the white officers and a few lucky assistants took to the lifeboats. The *Nerbudda* failed to sink, eventually dislodging from its position and drifting mastless for five days. The Indians found themselves in calm waters mockingly close to the coastline, which they eventually managed to reach by fashioning rafts and flotation devices from onboard materials.

The 150 who did not drown while evacuating the ship, or were not killed by Chinese on the shoreline, were imprisoned for the next 11 months in dreadful conditions. The Qing authorities talked up their victory, claiming not to have rounded up starving men on the shore, but to have engaged a warship in battle with their coastal cannons. This they eventually did, but only in October, when the Royal Navy's *Nimrod* arrived, offering $100 per captive for the return of the hostages. When the Chinese refused, *Nimrod* bombarded the Keelung forts, taking out 27 Chinese cannons.[3]

The following spring, a second British ship got into trouble. The brig *Anne*, loaded with coins from an opium deal at the mouth of the Yangtze River, also ran aground off the coast of Taiwan. Her captain pleaded with passing junks to ship him and his crew to safety in Amoy, but eventually threw himself on the mercy of the Taiwanese authorities, who similarly imprisoned the men of the *Anne*.

By the time the news reached Taiwan of the signing of the Treaty of Nanjing, ending the first Opium War, handing Hong Kong to the British, and supposedly guaranteeing the safety of British subjects in China, 187 of the men of the *Nerbudda* and the *Anne* had already been beheaded. John Ouchterlony, in his narrative of the Opium War, records his horror at the mistreatment of the crews, but reserves particular ire for the fate of non-combatants:

It was the fortune of war that they should so perish ... but it will appear a peculiarly hard and cruel one, when it is remembered that these unfortunates had been brought out from their native country, not as regularly enlisted fighting men, bound to obey the call of duty ... but poor washers, sweepers, hospital-assistants and palanquin-bearers ...[4]

Years later, the customs official William Pickering would notice some of their names etched into the wall of the granary where they had been held prisoner, along with tallies 'to show the progress of time, such as schoolboys make to show how many days have to elapse before the holidays'.[5]

In the wake of the Treaty of Nanjing, Britain's ambassador demanded that someone on Taiwan face the consequences. The Daoguang Emperor agreed, but despite calls from the British for heads to roll, he limited himself to incarcerating two officials for a few days for 'exaggerating' their report of a naval victory. Had the news got out, it would have probably reignited the conflict all over again, but the outcome was carefully suppressed. Three years later, when a British official discovered the nature of the officials' punishment — a slap on the wrist and an inland posting away from trouble — his report back to London was not made public.[6]

'Thus did China escape the consequences,' fumed James Davidson, 'of a crime of such magnitude that, had it been committed by any other nation, it would at once have been taken as a *casus belli*, and full and complete retribution exacted.'[7]

The European powers were already finding ample causes for military action elsewhere. In particular, they were animated by the constant failure of the Chinese to guarantee the safety of shipwreck-survivors, resulting in, for example, the grim fate of the sailors of the *Larpent*, en route from Hong Kong to Shanghai in 1850. The *Larpent* ran aground in south-east Taiwan, where unspecified 'natives' killed 23 crewmen and sold three others into slavery.

Much like the repeated encroachments of Chinese settlers into the Taiwanese hinterlands, concessions made to European powers only led to further pressures. Now that Britain had Hong Kong, and treaty-port footholds along the coast, it needed ships to reach them, and guarantees that those ships would be safe. In the Age of Steam, those ships also required coal. The commencement of a second Opium War, combined with demands from traders and missionaries to access China, wrested more concessions out of the weakened government of the Qing dynasty. Beijing had already been protesting for some years at patrols of British warships in the Taiwan Strait, and repeated attempts by British captains to purchase coal in Keelung, where the local variety had been unreliably pronounced 'equal to Newcastle's best'.[8] Taiwanese coal, in fact, became a vital commodity for the British in East Asian waters, particularly after the awarding of a contract to the P&O company in 1854 to run steam-powered mail ships between Hong Kong and the other treaty ports. The United States of America, too, was poking around East Asian waters in search of coaling supplies for its Pacific whalers. In the midst of the more famous mission by Commodore Matthew Perry that opened Japan to foreign ships in 1854, the *Macedonian* and the *Supply* peeled away to conduct a cursory search for missing sailors along the coast of China. Their main interest was the potential presented by Keelung as a coaling port, for which they optimistically reported that Keelung coal would be ideal for use by American shipping.[9] In the same year, a British ship from Hong Kong swapped opium in Tamsui in exchange for camphor — an illegal visitor offloading an illegal cargo to law-breaking locals, while complaining about the need for better protection from Chinese 'pirates' on the way home.[10]

With the signature of the Treaty of Tianjin and the Convention of Peking in 1860, a number of new treaty ports were *officially* opened to foreign ships, including several on Taiwan. To a certain extent, it is likely that the Qing authorities were handing Taiwanese concessions to the foreigners *because* it was not on the mainland coast, but Taiwan was also valued by the Europeans and later Americans as a prize in itself. Accordingly, among the new treaty ports in 'China' opened by the deal, foreigners were now permitted access to Keelung, with its attractive harbour and all that lovely coal, as well as nearby Tamsui, handy for sulphur and the tea plantations, Kaohsiung in the south, and Anping harbour, close to Tainan, the seat of Taiwan's Qing government. Along with these concessions came a re-affirmation of their extraterritoriality, which is to say, exemption from local laws; the 'most favoured nation status' that increasingly and automatically granted rights agreed with one foreign power to all the others; and the foreigners' right to travel safely within the Chinese empire.

This 'right to travel' was a loaded phrase where Taiwan was concerned, since it was never quite established where Beijing's control over the island ended. On paper, all of Taiwan was Chinese territory. In reality, the entire eastern coast was beyond the 'guardline' and beyond Chinese authority. Foreign ships were ever on the increase, and so were their chances of wrecking on a hostile coast. From 1861 to 1867 alone, 28 European or American vessels sank in Taiwanese waters, further escalating the workload of local consuls, and increasing the chances of local responses creating an international incident.[11]

Britain's consulate in Tamsui came to represent most foreign interests, among a local population so fractious that its officials repeatedly asked London to authorise at least one Royal Navy gunboat in Taiwanese waters 'at all times'. The list of their activities in those waters in the 1860s is a litany of arguments over cargoes, panhandling officials removed under threat of violence, dodgy deals, anti-missionary agitation, and general shenanigans.

Specific vessels included the *Vindex*, from which armed Indian soldiers landed to disperse a mob that objected to the building of a corporation house in Tamsui in 1862; two British warships sent to twist the arm of a camphor merchant in the same year; the gunboat *Staunch*, sent to Tamsui to protect the staff of Dent and Co. from angry dockers; and the *Grasshopper*, dispatched in 1866 to escort two cargo ships defying a local embargo and carrying rice out of Taiwan.[12]

In 1865, annoyed at a substantial clump of brushwood that was blocking a navigational aid at Tamsui, the commander of the *Bustard* ordered his men to go ashore and prune it back. While doing so, they were attacked by a bunch of Chinese wielding spears and rocks — the tone of the report, and the eventual $1,000 compensation wrung out of the Chinese authorities, suggests that the locals had deliberately allowed the vegetation to get out of hand, while awaiting a bribe to clear it away themselves.[13]

On land, the Chinese and the indigenous peoples faced a series of tempting prizes in the form of wrecked or indisposed ships. The *Martha and Emily* ran aground in 1862, and was abandoned by her crew after Chinese looters shot her captain. Americans aboard the *Lucky Star* in 1863 foundered on the west Taiwan coast, and had to be ransomed from the local officials. The British tea-ship *Netherby* ran aground on the Penghu Islands in 1864, and was relieved of so much of her cargo by scavengers that she was able to float free again. The crew of the *Abeona*, aground on the Taiwanese coast in 1865, were swarmed by 'two thousand' Chinese, who even relieved them of their clothes and then charged them a ransom to be returned to the authorities.[14]

The *Peking Gazette* would observe that local authorities were often powerless in the hinterland to protect Chinese and foreign visitors alike:

> More than 1,000 cases of murder are committed by these aborigines every year, and brigands take advantage of the asylum offered by this belt of country to make organised expeditions therefrom for the purpose of pillage, while local bullies of the lettered class make defensive operations against the savages a pretext for the levy of money for the support of troops, and set the authorities so completely at defiance that they cannot give effect to their commands ...[15]

This is where we came in, with the wreck of the *Rover* in 1867, not in Chinese territory, where its crew might have been merely robbed and manhandled, but in the Seqalu lands of south Taiwan, where they were beheaded by indigenous tribesmen. Charles Le Gendre's 'treaty' with the chieftain Toketok, as related in the Introduction, is part of this long historical context, as one more attempt by the ever-multiplying foreigners in Chinese waters to secure the safety of their own people. Beyond the human cost of incidents like the wreck of the *Rover*, foreign corporations were arguably even more interested in the value of their cargoes, which were often stripped by entrepreneurial locals, or 'squeezed' by grasping officials. This was particularly prevalent in the opium trade, where the commodity was illegal, but the foreign sellers were practically untouchable under the clause of extraterritoriality. 'Apologists for Britain's gunboat diplomacy,' writes Shih-Shan Henry Tsai, 'claim that deploying warships to Taiwan's ports was not aggression but self-defense.'

This raison d'etre seems reasonable, but the history of British-Taiwanese relations leads one to the conclusion that English diplomats and naval officers served primarily as tools to enable English capitalists and business adventurers to enrich themselves ... British diplomats and customs officers rarely complained to the London government about the violent and illegal conduct of the British subjects living on the island, assaulting mandarin officials or violating customs laws, for example.[16]

At the time of the *Rover* incident, agents for Jardine, Matheson & Co. were in the north offloading cases of opium in exchange for Keelung coal — at a dollar value of $860, a single chest of illegal opium was valued at 57 times the reward offered to Paiwan tribesmen for the return of the body of Mercy Hunt. The value, but also the risk, was even higher in those unopened ports that Jardine ships habitually visited anyway, despite being forbidden from doing so.[17]

The historiography of trade in the Far East tends to emphasise the commonplace exchange of tea for opium, but Taiwan offered plenty of other opportunities for the business entrepreneur. Enumerating the local exports in addition to tea, William Pickering noted sugar, coal, sulphur, petroleum, castor oil, sesame seeds, hardwoods, indigo, turmeric, and even gold.[18] The most lucrative was camphor, a flammable waxy substance that had previously been used as an embalming ingredient or a topical medication. As the 19th century wore on, it became increasingly in demand overseas, as it was crucial in the manufacture of, among other things, celluloid, gun-cotton explosive, and smokeless gunpowder. The camphor trade was not prohibited in and of itself, but acquiring it often involved crossing several legal lines.

To obtain camphor, one needed to go deep into the Taiwanese forests, often into indigenous territory, where the best groves of unspoilt, ancient trees could be found. These trees then had to be felled, their lumber turned into piles of wood chips, which were roasted to extract the rich camphor crystals. A legislative loophole meant that camphor extraction was still classified as a 'lumber' operation, leaving it under the sole jurisdiction of the Chinese government — the only organisation permitted to enter the tribal forests in search of lumber for naval purposes. By the 1860s, the camphor trade had become so lucrative for Taiwan that most of its naval shipyards were converted into camphor-processing plants, much to the annoyance of the British, who were forced to deal with Chinese middlemen, usually Hakkas, to obtain the much-desired resource. In 1867, the year of the *Rover* incident, Britain's ambassador to Beijing complained that this camphor monopoly was a violation of the free-trade agreements that China had struck in the aftermath of the Opium Wars.

William Pickering himself tried to muscle in on the camphor trade, striking a deal with the Tsai tribe of the hinterland to supply him with it directly. He was frustrated by the Chinese authorities, who confiscated his supplies on the grounds that he was breaching the lumber laws. When summoned by the local mandarin to explain himself, he arrived armed with a rifle and a pistol, as well as copy of the Treaty of Tianjin as a more 'pacific weapon'. Despite being from Nottingham, England, Pickering also liked to dress in an aggressively Scottish manner — kilt, sporran, tam-o'-shanter bonnet, and all — possibly an even more terrifying sight for the Chinese.[19]

In 1868, the British gunboats *Bustard* and *Algerine* steamed into Anping harbour, Tainan, and anchored so that their guns were in range of the entire town. They were there to back the demands of Britain's acting consul, John Gibson, who had become frustrated with the camphor politics, as well as an arson attack on a missionary church and the stabbing of a British trader by Chinese security guards. Even as negotiations proceeded, according to William Pickering, the Chinese provoked the British by firing on boats from the *Algerine* —although if the boats were already in the water, we might presume that it was the *Algerine* that was doing the provoking.

'Her commander, Lieutenant Gurdon,' writes Pickering, 'forced to action by this daring insult, landed with a few blue-jackets in the night and attacked the fort, which speedily surrendered.' He neglects to mention that the *Algerine* had also bombarded the town seven times that afternoon.[20] The naval presence would remain in Tainan until early 1869, when the Chinese finally relented and agreed to Britain's demands. Or rather, to Gibson's demands — a sternly worded communiqué from Gibson's bosses advised him that gunboats were not the preferred method of settling disputes, and he advanced no further in British diplomatic service.

Such tussles took on a new dimension in 1871, on the occasion of what might at first appear to have been just another of the many dozens of shipwrecks on the Taiwanese coast. A vessel crewed by fishermen from the Ryukyu Islands ran aground in a storm on the south-eastern coast of Taiwan, and had the misfortune to come ashore not in the realm of the benevolent chieftain Toketok, but in that of the fearsome Botan tribe on the edges of his Seqalu confederacy.

The Botan tribe derived their name from the word for the peony (*mudan* in standard Mandarin), a gentle flower analogy belying their fierce nature. It is not clear that they understood who the Ryukyuans were — diplomatic correspondence has, for reasons that will become obvious, concentrated on the concept that the Ryukyuans were Japanese subjects, whereas as least one source claimed that the Botans had mistaken them for Chinese, and killed them in retaliation for the intrusion of Chinese settlers elsewhere in their territory.[21]

The incident turned into an international flashpoint, seized upon by Japan as an excuse to pressure China over the limits of its territory. A diplomatic mission arrived in Beijing, demanding reparations for the fishermen's deaths, but also manoeuvring with ever more predatory intent over the implications of Chinese responses.

The Chinese negotiator, Li Hongzhang, was outraged when the Japanese envoy showed up with his strategic adviser, a one-eyed American who claimed to have been the only man to have ever struck a deal with Toketok: Charles Le Gendre. Reprimanded and sidelined over his actions as the consul for Amoy, Le Gendre had cashed in his reputation in a spectacularly bold move, writing a book called *How to Deal with China*, couched as (unwanted and unsolicited) advice to the US Secretary of State on Far Eastern geopolitics. His counsel rejected by his countrymen, he sold it instead to the Japanese. On his way back to America, his diplomatic career in tatters, he had stopped off in Tokyo, where he was hired as an adviser to Japan's newly established Taiwanese Aborigines Land Affairs Bureau on the basis of comments like this:

Formosa [i.e. Taiwan] must change hands in the interest of civilization and humanity, no nation would be better qualified than Japan to step in and take the place of China ... Unless the Formosan tribes

are reconciled or else subdued and exterminated either by China or
Japan, the impending evil cannot be averted; and therefore, if China
neglects the task, Japan, in self-protection, must perform it herself.[22]

Le Gendre was auditing the negotiations in search of a 'gotcha!'
moment that he was sure would come. The Chinese obliged him
by offering the excuse that while the massacre of the fishermen was
regrettable, it had occurred on the eastern coast of Taiwan, which was
technically beyond Chinese jurisdiction. When pressed, they admitted
that only the western coast was under imperial control; the eastern side
was practically lawless. The British commander Bonham Ward Bax wrote
that the Chinese had not only disavowed any responsibility for the eastern
part of Taiwan, but in a heated exchange with the Japanese, 'further told
their ambassador that if they wished for redress they had better go and
punish the savages themselves'.[23]

This was what Le Gendre had been waiting for. It would take several
years for the Japanese military response to get underway, while Japan and
the other foreign powers continued to pick at the borders of Chinese
sovereignty — the Japanese in Korea, the British in Shanghai, the French
in Yunnan, each of them snatching deals on which the others would then
capitalise. In 1873, when British merchants started agitating about the
'unfairness' of camphor trading again, an exasperated Li Hongzhang even
suggested that Taiwan was much more trouble than it was worth, and that
the ideal solution was to make it someone else's problem.

> I earnestly memorialised the throne to offer Taiwan to the English
> government to do with the wretched island as they saw fit ... If the
> great island could not be sold, I advocated that it may be made a
> present to England. I told the Council that as England had been so
> ready to grab Hong Kong we might in a measure get even with her by
> making a gift of Formosa.[24]

Li's modest proposal fell on deaf ears, which left the Chinese
authorities watching, helpless, as the Japanese military response
got underway in 1874, led by Saigō Tsugumichi.[25] In fact, the Qing
government was paying so little attention to the Japanese, or was so

disbelieving that an expedition would be arranged, that they had not even bothered to order the Taiwanese authorities to offer any obstruction. Steaming out of Nagasaki during a suspiciously convenient break in telegraph communications that prevented more cautious Tokyo officials from ordering the ships to stay, Saigō's expedition put in at Keelung to resupply, taking onboard Taiwanese coal to allow them to conduct their Taiwanese invasion fully fuelled.

The Japanese expedition followed a similar course to that employed by Le Gendre and the Americans seven years earlier — not by coincidence, since Saigō had several foreign military advisers, including a lieutenant-commander on secondment from the US Navy, and a former US engineer, handed a colonel's rank in the Japanese army. Nor were foreign powers necessarily ignorant of the action — among the 'Japanese' transport ships were the British *Yorkshire* and the American *New York*, on loan from Pacific Mail.

It took a while for the implications to sink in, with a US envoy suddenly announcing to the Japanese government that he could not authorise the participation of American ships or personnel unless the Japanese were undertaking their mission *with the cooperation and consent of China*. Otherwise, it might look like an invasion. Letters from the United States authorities, forbidding the seconded men from participating, only arrived after they had already left.[26]

Unwilling to risk a landing in the choppy and treacherous waters beneath the cliffs on the east coast of Taiwan, the expedition force dropped anchor on the west coast and marched through the hinterland in search of the right tribe. The additional distance was a mere eight miles, but the sight of the Japanese landing on the west coast added to the sense among the Chinese that punishing the tribesmen was a mere pretext. In fact, the Japanese pitched their tents on land that was undeniably Chinese — crowds of local 'Chinese' (probably Hakka) being then employed to build a more permanent settlement, along with huts, gardens, and roads. The Japanese were welcomed locally as a necessary group of enforcers, by settlers who had hitherto been forced to farm their fields with sidearms and muskets close to hand, for fear of an indigenous ambush.[27]

Seasoned strategists might have expected the Japanese mission to be a necessarily short campaign, to be executed before the onset of summer and the dangerous south-western monsoon. But as was soon becoming plain to all observers, the 'expedition' was taking on the appearance of a *colony*, while a flotilla of warships and support vessels kept steaming northwards again to bring in more supplies and manpower.

The Japanese did seize a Botan village, although this was of little use in pacifying the remaining tribespeople, who took to the forests, and maintained an ongoing guerrilla campaign. Saigō's American officers warned him that the Japanese soldiers were far too incautious:

> It seems that these men were allowed to straggle in rather a loose manner considering that they were in the presence of an enemy only too glad to take advantage of an opportunity to surprise any small party which he could hope to overpower easily ... [The indigenous people's] mode of fighting, like that of all savages is to skulk under cover and wait for a moment when they can surprise an enemy or take him at some disadvantage.[28]

They did establish friendly contacts with the 18 peaceful tribes of the Seqalu, led by the venerable and diplomatic Toketok, and following his death that year, Toketok's adopted son Bunkiet. They were soon handing out Japanese flags, which the local indigenous communities proudly flew as indicators that they were 'good men', not realising that it gave every impression that their villages had become Japanese territory.[29] Their arrival was the perfect chance for Toketok to deal with the difficult Botan people himself, leading to his volunteering of assistance in tracking and fighting their mutual enemy, a thorn in his side since at least the time of the *Rover* incident.

Eventually, a mandarin arrived from Fujian, accompanied by a French agent, to demand that the Japanese go home, the mission having presumably accomplished its original aim, to enact vengeance on the murderers of the Ryukyu fishermen. Saigō gave the Chinese official an audience, disingenuously claiming that he was unable to leave without orders from Japan (the same orders he had ignored while leaving in the first place). Besides, he did not have enough ships to move his men away. In stormy support, the monsoon started up, forcing the remaining Japanese gunboats to steam out of local waters, marooning the soldiers in their increasingly permanent camp, and forcing the Chinese official to return home by a circuitous land route up the west coast to a more favourable port. He did so after distributing a wounded proclamation to the locals that was the precise opposite of previous Chinese diplomatic bluster.

> Now the [Botan] savages who killed the [Ryukyuans] are certainly barbarous murderers; but as the place where they live is under Chinese government, if the treaty is to be observed, they of course should be punished by China ... We therefore issue this notification distinctly ordering the headman of each village concerned, to give our commands to the inhabitants of the savage villages and the like, to go on quietly with their daily occupation, and not to be alarmed. We ... will certainly find means to protect you and keep you from harm if you are unoffending.[30]

Saigō maintained that his mission was not yet over, and that there were multiple incidents of earlier shipwrecks that needed to be avenged. The Chinese, now treating the Japanese expedition as the invasion that it truly was, began to amass a counter-strike fleet at staging posts in Fujian and the Penghu Islands, although the Japanese were facing a far more formidable foe in the form of the Taiwanese summer and outbreaks of disease. Eventually, the Chinese agreed to pay an indemnity for the deaths of the Ryukyu fishermen, and Saigō was ordered to leave when the arrival of the north-east monsoon made such an exodus possible, in December 1874. He did so after having lost a dozen men to indigenous attack, and another 550 to malaria.

The Japanese expedition achieved a cunning underhand aim, not in a punitive attack on Botan tribesmen, or even an abortive settlement in south Taiwan. Its immediate effect was in the establishment of a new premise that had been overlooked in much of the negotiations. The Ryukyu Islands, after all, were supposed to be a *Chinese* vassal. A more forceful China might have been able to argue that the massacred fishermen were Chinese subjects, and hence a matter for local enforcement, not requiring Japanese meddling. Instead, the mere existence of the Japanese expedition established thereafter the idea that the Ryukyu Islands were an inalienable part of Japan.

Despite recognising the underhand methods of the Japanese expeditionary force, the British sea captain Bonham Ward Bax could not help noting that it took a foreign incursion into the south of Taiwan before the Chinese started to take any genuine interest in the island. It was, for example, only after the Japanese incursion that the Chinese started sending gunboats to establish a military presence along the eastern coast, calling ashore at numerous indigenous villages to assure them that the Japanese were unwelcome and illegal visitors (since nowhere nearby was a treaty port), and that the Chinese would do their utmost to protect the locals from further harassment.[31]

It was only after the settlement of the issue of the massacred 'Japanese' fishermen, in 1875, that China lifted its blanket prohibition on migration to the island and dispatched a progressively minded mandarin to reform local affairs.[32] A new governor, Liu Mingchuan, arrived with a mandate to 'open the mountains and pacify the barbarians' (*kaishan fufan*), in which the Qing rulers walked back their previous strategy of leaving the indigenous people to their own devices. Without a change in policy, the Chinese risked further intrusions by Japanese taking them at their word that the eastern coast of Taiwan was not Chinese territory, and hence there for the taking.

With the Japanese planning on a continuation of their 'warlike enterprise', the Taiwanese intendant sent a memo to the Chinese emperor, outlining the benefits of relaxing the restrictions on migration to the island.[33] If anything was going to keep the Japanese out, it would surely be an increased Chinese presence in the Taiwanese hinterland:

> with the exception of the lands occupied by the aboriginal tribes, the whole interior of Formosa is entirely uninhabited. Lands which might be cultivated lie waste, overgrown with forest and sending forth pestilential miasma, a refuge for savage aborigines who lie in wait there for victims of their murderous designs.[34]

The memo seems confused about whether the land was 'uninhabited' or not, since it also complains about just how inhabited it is, with the wrong sort of people, something that the authorities hoped to address by finally assenting to widespread and legal settlement on previously unopened lands.

The 1880s were characterised by a grudging, tardy attention from Beijing — a performance designed to establish that Taiwan really was part of China, and not, as the Chinese themselves had previously claimed, a largely lawless wilderness. It was not until 1881 that the south tip of Taiwan gained a lighthouse in order to prevent further shipwrecks. Its first keeper, George Taylor, wrote of the 'new and peculiar difficulties' facing its construction, including the hazards of getting materials through the mountains and ravines occupied by hostile Formosans. Taylor did not relish the dangers of being the sole beacon of civilisation on the edge of tribal lands, occupied, in his words, by 'the most feared tribe of aborigines in Formosa, the Southern Paiwans, whose head-hunting propensities and general unamenableness were notorious'.[35] The land for the lighthouse was somehow officially purchased from Koalut chiefs after 'the most delicate and tedious negotiations', such that Taylor himself reported friendly encounters with the self-same Koalut tribesmen who had massacred the crew of the *Rover* only a generation earlier.

The lighthouse itself was suspiciously military in its bearing. It comprised a 50-foot wrought-iron tower, built by Armstrong & Co., looming above a fortified compound, with walls and barbed wire atop a 20-foot surrounding ditch. Construction also entailed the dynamiting of a local reef, in order to create a suitable dock to land supplies. When the construction crew departed, the lighthouse keeper was left with a garrison of over a dozen soldiers, and weapons emplacements for two 18-pound cannons, two Gatling guns, and a mortar. The staff resided in bungalows in the compound, but these were connected to the lighthouse itself by corridors thick enough to withstand gunfire. Thus, the lighthouse could still be operated in the event of a siege.

Artillery assaults were beyond the means of the Formosans, but the British on Taiwan had other possible threats to consider, as did the Chinese. The new governor, Liu Mingchuan, had in fact been appointed with a specific aim of defending Taiwan from foreign assault, not only from the Japanese, but from the French, who in 1874 had snatched the Indochinese state of Annam (Vietnam), nominally a Chinese vassal, and declared it a French protectorate. It was Liu Mingchuan, called out of retirement after an illustrious military career on the mainland, who determined that Keelung harbour was the key to the mastery of Taiwan, and that consequently it needed to be heavily fortified against a possible attack.

In 1884, an undeclared war broke out over French advances into the Gulf of Tonkin and onto Chinese territory. The French warship *Villars* dropped anchor in Keelung harbour, immediately risking an international incident, since it had its guns trained on Chinese forts within sight of the German freighter *Welle*, which was bringing in vital military supplies for the Chinese. Rather than risking running guns, sea-mines, and ammunition under the noses of the French, the captain of the *Welle* instead made for Tamsui, where he off-loaded his explosive cargo onto Chinese middlemen.

In August, the ironclads *La Gailissonière* and *Bayard* arrived at Keelung and bombarded the fort, landing marines with the intention of seizing both the town and the vital Keelung coal mines. The French were beaten back with two dead, against substantially higher casualties sustained by the Chinese defenders, but by the following day the French were triumphantly flying their flag from the smouldering rubble of one of Keelung's minor hillside defences.

The French, however, had trouble getting off the beach. Liu ordered the sabotage of their main objective, the Keelung coal mine — the machinery was destroyed, the pits flooded, and an apocalyptic bonfire of 12,000 tons of stockpiled coal was set ablaze with kerosene.

The impasse wore on throughout the month, with the French blockading Keelung, watched over by the British gunboat *Cockchafer*, in place to prevent any shelling of the town itself, with its British trading community at risk. France's leading officer in the field, Admiral Amédée Courbet, wrote angry communiqués back to Paris, demanding to know what idiot had approved such a 'terrible idea' as relying on Keelung coal, when the fleet could have surely found supplies elsewhere.[36]

Liu Mingchuan telegraphed the mainland for assistance, but while Chinese reinforcements trickled in by the hundred, having to land in the south and march north, French troops arrived by the thousand. The French commander signalled the *Cockchafer* with the ominous message that bombardment of the town was about to commence, and that 'European residents should seek their own safety'.

Liu eventually retreated from Keelung in early October, leaving the city to the French, in the hope that a subsequent advance on the northern city of Taipei would be delayed by the poor conditions of the local terrain. Instead, he concentrated his defences on Tamsui, the other port in north Taiwan, in perilously close reach of Taipei. Tamsui was protected by a maze of sea-mines laid across the seabed, and navigable only by the pilots of the ships that had put them there. This kept the French at bay for many weeks, during which time the trading community tried to continue its usual business, bringing in the tea harvest in hope of better times.

The 'French' forces were a strikingly international band, including Foreign Legionnaires, Algerian conscripts, and several African companies alongside native Frenchmen. Courbet was irritated at their lack of leeway on land — despite high Chinese casualties, the marines were unable to advance further.

By April, the French were thinly spread. An occupation of the strategically crucial Penghu Islands was successful, but left so few warships spread across such an expanse of the Taiwan Strait that reinforcements and resupplies were able to sneak onto Taiwan from the mainland. The blockade was finally lifted in the summer of 1885, after the Chinese conceded to Annam becoming a French protectorate, on the condition that the Penghu Islands and Taiwan were left alone.

With the French gone, Taiwan was detached from its previous status as a mere marine dependency of Fujian, and accorded full provincial status, with Liu Mingchuan as governor and Taipei as its new temporary capital (permanent after 1894). It was now, to coin a phrase, officially *part of China*. The Hakka leader Qiu Fengjia wrote in 1887 that, regardless of multiple places of origin on the mainland, the Chinese people who had migrated to Taiwan now very much felt that it was their home:

After two hundred years of growing and expanding
Sojourning grasses were deeply re-rooted.[37]

But it was Taiwan's ongoing liminal status that made it such a tasty prospect for investment. While many progressive developments still faced opposition on the mainland, Taiwan had missionary schools and hospitals, and a thriving community of entrepreneurs raking in foreign currency for exports in camphor, sugar, and tea — all this taking place amid the indigenous peoples, still written off as 'cannibals' by foreign authors, even though the only evident cannibalism on the island came from an unexpected quarter.

Liu Mingchuan launched over 40 campaigns to suppress indigenous unrest, some of which took on ghoulish aspects. The American consul, James Davidson, was horrified at stories of the Chinese soldiers butchering and eating dead Formosans:

> One horrible feature of the campaign against the savages was the sale by the Chinese in open market of savage flesh. Impossible as it may seem that a race with such high pretensions to civilization and religion should be guilty of such barbarity, yet such is the truth. After killing a savage, the head was commonly severed from the body and exhibited to those who were not on hand to witness the prior display of slaughter and mutilation.[38]

Davidson reported that kidneys, livers, hearts, and soles of the feet were the most desirable elements, usually cut very finely and boiled in broth or gumbo, and claimed that this was due to an 'old superstition' that cannibalism would impart strength and courage.

> During the outbreak of 1891, savage flesh was brought in — in baskets — the same as pork, and sold like pork in the open markets of [Daxi] before the eyes of all, foreigners included; some of the flesh was even sent to Amoy to be placed on sale there. It was frequently on sale in the small Chinese villages near the border, and often before the very eyes of peaceful groups of savages who happened to be at the place.[39]

George Mackay, a missionary, reported similar behaviours in the 1890s, noting that the standoff between Chinese colonists and indigenous head-hunters found both sides unrelentingly vicious with each other. He witnessed the public execution of one Formosan, and the veritable feeding frenzy as the Chinese crowd descended upon the headless body 'for food and medicine'. Observing that human bones could be boiled into an anti-malarial jelly, he archly noted that the scene was 'illustrative alike of the character of both races'.[40]

Despite such atrocities, Liu Mingchuan's reign is usually remembered as one of welcome development of infrastructure and the rule of law. But when Liu retired in ill health in 1891, he was replaced by two more carpet-baggers determined to line their own coffers, and the island fell into decline again. Beijing had other things to worry about, specifically the outbreak of war with Japan in 1894. Although the war was fought largely in Korea, Taiwan was dragged into the conflict in its closing days, as the Chinese toyed with the idea of luring in French assistance, and paying for it with the 'loan' of the Penghu Islands.

The Japanese instead proposed that Taiwan be thrown into the negotiations as a bargaining chip — a handy territory on the end of the now-Japanese Ryukyu archipelago, that might be handed to Japan in order to offset some of the cost of the war reparations demanded from China. Whereas it had been annexed by the Manchus in 1683 only with great reluctance, it was now widely regarded on the mainland as Chinese territory, and protestors in Beijing argued that handing it over would be tantamount to 'severing the nation'.[41]

The Japanese response was an underhand military campaign that got underway even as treaty negotiations were ongoing. While Li Hongzhang and the Japanese dickered in Shimonoseki about likely peace terms, the Imperial Japanese Navy sent a taskforce rushing south to seize Taiwan.

In the middle of the negotiations, Li Hongzhang secretly regarded Japanese designs on Taiwan as a welcome distraction, and had trouble concealing his glee.

> It is true that when Marquis Itō made stipulations as one of the chief terms of peace of the cession of Formosa, I immediately declared that I was willing to agree to almost anything, yet, had I been in another apartment all alone, I would have danced with joy in spite of my infirmities.[42]

Eventually, Li agreed to give up Taiwan as a spoil of war. In 1895, the Manchu Qing state signed away its island province to the Japanese 'in perpetuity'.

The people of Taiwan had other ideas.

CHAPTER SIX

PERFECT PANIC

The Republic of Formosa (1895)

The Japanese had little interest in the people of Taiwan. With the announcement that the island would be granted to Japan as a spoil of war came a concession by the Japanese that there would be a two-year grace period, in which inhabitants were free to gather up their possessions and leave — the implication being that only a madman would choose the Chinese mainland over life in a new Japanese colony.[1]

But the Chinese did not have much interest in the people of Taiwan, either. Two days after the decision, Governor Tang Jingsong received notice by telegram that he and his staff should pack up and return home immediately. Lien Heng's *General History of Taiwan* characterises Tang as the polar opposite of a military man, 'a literary man with no long-term strategy'.[2] Nevertheless, Tang commenced a series of intrigues designed to keep the island out of Japanese hands, beginning with secret messages to Britain and France, offering them Taiwan as a protectorate.

It was only when these offers failed to secure any interest that he chose a new path, proclaiming the independent Republic of Formosa, with himself as its first president. In doing so, he managed the unique achievement of disobeying both his old masters in China, and his new masters in Japan, who were already preparing to unload their new administrators at Keelung. Tang pleaded with Beijing that he had been urged to establish this new position by 'the people of Taiwan' (*Tai min*), a delegation of whom showed up at his office at the beginning of May with a ready-made presidential seal. The visitors comprised spokesmen for the well-to-do Chinese in Taipei, led by the Hakka strongman Qiu Fengjia, who telegraphed Beijing with a declaration of their intent:

> We have repeatedly begged governor Tang to represent to the [Chinese] throne the views of Formosa on this matter, and our feelings on finding the matter is beyond recall are as intense and poignant as those of a little child that has lost its father and mother. We would humbly point out that since His Majesty has abandoned Formosa, its people have noone to look to for aid. They can only defend and hold to the death as an Island State.[3]

Tang was a reluctant appointee, convinced that the Japanese would kill him if he resisted, but that the Chinese would kill him if he didn't.[4] He had already managed to evacuate his mother to the mainland in late April, in a chaotic incident that demonstrated only too well the level of his authority. Mother Tang's baggage train was ransacked on the way to the docks, on the grounds that it might contain 'treasure', and her departure with bodyguards also served as a signal for six would-be thieves to raid Tang's offices. Tang was rescued by a party of marines, who fired into the mob that had surrounded his building. Later accounts suggested that the crowd did not comprise concerned citizens, but angry and unpaid soldiers.[5]

The Chinese original of the Republic's declaration of independence has been lost, but has been preserved in English translation. Part of it reads:

> The Japanese have affronted China by annexing our territory of Formosa, and the supplications of we, the People of Formosa, at the portals of the Throne have been made in vain. We now learn that the Japanese slaves are about to arrive.
>
> If we suffer this, the land of our hearths and homes will become the land of savages and barbarians, but if we do not suffer it, our condition of comparative weakness will certainly not endure long. Frequent conferences have been held with the Foreign Powers, who

all aver that the People of Formosa must establish their independence before the Powers will assist them.

Now, therefore, we, the People of Formosa, are irrevocably resolved to die before we will serve the enemy. And we have in Council determined to convert the whole island of Formosa into a Republican state, and that the administration of all our State affairs shall be organized and carried on by the deliberations and decisions of Officers publicly elected by us the People. But as in this new enterprise there is needed, as well for the resistance of Japanese aggression as for the organization of the new administration, a man to have chief control, in whom authority shall centre, and by whom the peace of our homesteads shall be assured — therefore, in view of the respect and admiration in which we have long held the Governor and Commander-in-Chief, Tang Jing-song, we have in Council determined to raise him to the position of President of the Republic.[6]

'If it has been conceived altogether by Celestial [Chinese] minds,' wrote James Davidson from Taipei, 'we are emboldened to believe that there is, after all, a new China in the nursery from whom great things may eventually be expected.'[7] Other observers were less enthusiastic, with William Pickering writing: 'It is to be doubted whether any of these patriots could imagine what form of government is implied by the term "republic".'[8] The *North China Herald* was even more cynical, noting that it was less an 'official declaration of independence' than it was an 'independent declaration of officials':

The people are unconcerned, but the grief of the mandarins and their paid followers at the prospect of being separated from their appropriations has found vent in memorials ... against the cession of their rich and beautiful land of the eternal squeeze.[9]

The historian Niki Alsford offers a more nuanced interpretation, suggesting that while the Republic in the north was a matter of the wealthy trying to hang on to their possessions, the people in the south were 'perhaps housing a more patriotic fervour'.[10] Down in Tainan, the old heartland of Koxinga and the Kingdom of Dongning, there was even a faction of idealists who regarded the proclamation of independence not a matter so much of resisting the Japanese, but of finally throwing off the yoke of the Manchus. Somewhat optimistically, the scholar Xu Nanying wrote a muddled celebratory poem:

> Parliament widely extends the Republic
> The land reverts to the sacred Ming Dynasty![11]

Depending on how one interprets the idea, the Republic of Formosa was either a pointless paper tiger, a doomed ideal that lasted less than two weeks before its founders fled the country, or a notion that inspired a resistance that fought on for several months and took years to truly fade. It was a concept rejected at the time by many Taipei residents, who instead welcomed the Japanese as liberators from the declining Qing regime. But it was also a tiny spark in history — a moment of disruption that would continue to shine. The people who gave their lives for Tang's short-lived Republic would be hailed a century later as vital historical actors — the founders and defenders of a new state that broke with Taiwan's Chinese past and established it as an independent island nation. Belief in the existence of that state, even if only for a few days, even if it was the product of a cynical upper-class clinging to its privileges, would create a thorny legal precedent in the 20th century. In 1945, when Taiwan was 'returned' to its rightful owners after World War II, who were those owners — the political inheritors of Manchus who had given it away, or the Taiwanese who had fought for it?

As the new state stumbled, James Davidson was soon walking back his own enthusiasm, while other commentators referred to the Republic variously as a 'hoax', a 'joke', or according to Li Hongzhang himself, 'strange words'.[12] Tang Jingsong had admitted weeks before the Japanese arrival, in a proclamation to the island shortly after the Chinese New Year, that defence of Taiwan would be all but impossible in the event of the loss of the Penghu Islands, which could be used as a marshalling station for an attacking fleet — the islands were occupied by the Japanese on 24 March, two months before Tang would proclaim independence.[13]

In a post–World War II Nationalist-sponsored education system determined to downplay the Japanese colonial era, the rebels of the

Republic of Formosa were praised as heroes not only of anti-Japanese resistance, but also of pro-Chinese belief. This was also the mindset of many of the rebels of 1895, including Tang himself, who changed the date of 1895 to Year One of 'Forever Qing' (*Yong Qing*), and approved the design of a national flag depicting a tiger, the symbolic counterpart of the imperial dragon in Chinese geomancy.[14]

Despite proclaiming himself the ruler of a republic, with the promise of free and democratic elections of a parliamentary assembly, Tang stressed to his people that their new state remained indelibly Chinese:

> Although [Taiwan] has today declared itself to be a state, it feels gratitude due to its Chinese benefactors, the sages and emperors, and it will continue to honour the reign of China, be its distant vassal state, and maintain close affections, being no different from the territory of China.[15]

The historian Harry Lamley has no qualms about calling Tang's new state 'a sham affair unworthy of its republican label'. The very idea of there being a new republic in Asia, caught between two imperial predators, was a calculated ruse — a last-ditch dog whistle in the hope that a Western power would come to its aid if it could somehow hold out 'for six months or a year'.[16] Tellingly, Tang Jingsong continued to use his titles and protocols as the 'acting governor' of Taiwan province in all his dealings with the Qing officials in Beijing — he only styled himself as 'president' when communicating with the foreigners he hoped would step in.[17]

Tang's hope of a foreign intervention was not without justification. On 23 April, less than a week after the Treaty of Shimonoseki had been agreed in Japan, foreign powers did indeed object to its terms, with the Triple Intervention of Russia, Germany, and France preventing Japan's occupation of the Liaodong Peninsula on the Yellow Sea. Lacking support from any other power, Japan was obliged to concede, although ironically it might have put up more of a fight if the bulk of its navy were not off on a foreign adventure in Taiwan.[18] In such a situation, it was not unreasonable for Tang and his fellow republicans to hope for Taiwan to be added to the conditions of the Intervention. Tang did his level best to pretend that the matter was already under discussion, performatively summoning the local consuls representing Britain, Germany, the United States, Norway, and Sweden to his office, to ask them if they had received assent from their governments to intervene. None of them had, but the meeting still looked good from the outside.[19] He also boasted to Beijing that the commander of the French cruiser *Béautemps-Beaupré* had urged him to proclaim independence in order to attain foreign protection; a bold assertion made by a sea captain who promptly steamed for Nagasaki, vaguely promising that he would mention it to the French government.[20] Two German steamships, the *Arthur* and *Martha*, were commandeered by the Republic government and put to work on a constant loop to and from the mainland, bringing ammunition and other supplies.[21] Tang's officials were offered the preposterous promise that if they held out until 12 June, China would send ten warships to their rescue, led 'by foreigners in Chinese costume'.[22]

James Davidson noted that the new Republic began without much fanfare, lacking pomp and ceremony, and that its first official day of existence was characterised by nothing but drizzling rain. In search of vox pop commentary, Davidson quizzed a local tea merchant, and attempted a phonetic rendering of his reply — that it was all very well, but everybody was really busy right now: '*My talkee that new fashion blong velly good, but just now my too muchee pidgin no have got time.*' I have often wondered if the tea seller meant he had no time for the Republic, or no time for Davidson.[23]

Local representatives for foreign powers acted with remarkable diffidence. Britain's maritime customs officer, responsible for collecting taxes on behalf of the Chinese, refused to fly the new tiger flag above his office. Out in the harbour, a Japanese warship loitered menacingly, while Chinese officers onshore fretted about the sight of 'saucy marines' openly taking soundings in a harbour that the Japanese navy was sure to soon be attacking.

Tang's own government included several factions out to get him, including Qiu Fengjia, who was instrumental in setting up multiple militia outposts across Taiwan, ready for an expected Japanese assault. In 1894, Qiu had sold his possessions in order to fund his military exploits, and claimed to have 100,000 'men' spread across 140 camps, ready to resist the Japanese — I use quote marks because accounts of the Hakka resistance repeatedly mention women also taking up arms, a rare sight among the Hoklo Chinese, but seemingly commonplace among the Hakka. As a Cantonese-speaking Hakka, Qiu had little love for the Qing regime in Beijing, yet on the occasion of the cession of the island, he had sent a petition calling for the Qing Emperor to reconsider the decision:

> Your humble subjects shall either live or perish with the native land. We vow to guard it with our lives. Should failure fall upon us, please await our death prior to considering cession.[24]

When this failed to find sympathy, Qiu was drafted into Tang's new administration as the vice-president. Tang did so in order to prevent Qiu, who had been Tang's protégé in his younger days, being hailed in an altogether more powerful role. Qiu had, after all, struck something of a dash among the literati of 1880s Tainan, and been hailed in some quarters as 'the child prodigy of Dongning' — a spiritual successor to Koxinga, with whom he shared a coincidental birth-year in the Chinese zodiac.[25] As noted in an aside in the *North China Herald*, Qiu was already the de facto ruler of Taiwan's Hakka strongholds:

> during the present weakness and loss of Governmental authority, one of the old Hakka chiefs, Ku Hong-kok [i.e. Qiu Fengjia], *has proclaimed himself 'King' of a portion of the island* ... His strength is growing daily, the natives near his district flocking to join his standard ... *all central Formosa has been declared independent* and neither China nor Japan shall be its rulers.[26] [My emphasis]

The commissioning of Qiu as Tang's vice-president was an under-the-table effort to hold his new state together, lest it immediately prove to have splintered into *two* republics. Such a consideration should be borne in mind during events of the next decade, as the Hakka people proved to be some of the strongest rebels against Japanese occupation.[27]

Qiu was, at least officially, a militia leader, not the general of Formosa's armed forces. That was Liu Yongfu, a fantastically flexible military man, having fought in the course of his life under several different flags. Another Hakka by birth, Liu had begun his military career during the long-running Chinese civil war known today as the Taiping Rebellion. He was a member of a force that proclaimed allegiance to the failing Taiping rebels, before carving out a realm for himself as the leader of the 'Black Flag Army' in what is now northern Vietnam, offering refuge to a multi-ethnic company of Chinese and European mercenaries, deprived of an income source after the fall of the Taipings. It was, in fact, the efforts of the French to contain his predations in Indochina that had escalated into the Sino-French War in the first place, and so there is a certain historical symmetry in placing Liu, in his late fifties, back on the sharp edge of history, facing the oncoming Japanese invaders.

The only reason that Liu was in the south at all was because Tang had sent him there. During a meeting in Taipei the previous year, Liu had suggested that Tang handle all civil matters on the island, while Liu dealt with matters military. Seeing this for the underhand power play it most likely was, Tang ordered Liu out of Taipei, removing him from the shaky centre of power, but giving him ample time in Kaohsiung to prepare for the arrival of the Japanese. Asides in consular reports suggest that Liu's Black Flag Army was unwelcome in Taiwan, and that he had refused to evacuate his 'Cantonese soldiers' without payment of a bribe of $100 a head.[28]

The resistance to Japan was mounted by at least four different factions, with the Imperial Japanese Army first having to fight through the 'bandit troops' hastily ferried over from the mainland in the north, through Qiu's Hakka militia strong points and the troops of the Hsinchu garrison as far as Taichung, and then through Black Flag territory further to the south. North Taiwan did not present much of a problem for the Japanese, with local defenders buckling at their arrival in Keelung. Tang Jingsong had already admitted to the foreign community that he was unable to control the thousands of newly arrived mainland soldiers, who were running amok all over the island.

'The officers were all losing control of their men,' wrote James Davidson, who had hoped to cover the defence of Keelung, 'quarrelling among themselves, killing their officers, robbing and looting at every opportunity.' His interpreter and assistant already having fled the scene, Davidson gave up any attempt at war reporting, and instead fought his way through the 'perfect panic' at Keelung station to get a place on the train to Taipei.

The place was strewn with guns and ammunition boxes, spears, banners, broken furniture ... and hundreds of villagers, women with children in their arms were begging [for] places in the cars, while the men were crowding and pulling them back to make room for themselves. Even among the men it was a fight for places, and the weakest were forced off the cars to add their angry yells to the cries of the women and children.[29]

As the last train out of Keelung 'literally ploughed through the hundreds that surrounded it, a cry of despair arose that was heartrending in the extreme'.

President Tang headed the other way, disguising himself as a woman and sneaking off to a German ship at Tamsui that would evacuate him from the disaster. When confronted by an officer with the news that a prominent fort was just about to fall, Tang flung his attaché case at the man, proclaiming: 'The army's orders are all in there. Do it yourself!'[30]

Tang secured his passage out of Taipei by bribing his own men with $50,000 from the Republic's coffers. Clambering aboard the *Arthur* to escape, he found himself under bombardment from his own former subjects in the Chinese fort above Tamsui. The German warship *Iltis* came to his rescue, opening fire on Republic positions in order to cover the escape of the Republic's erstwhile president.[31]

When other Republic soldiers arrived at Tang's headquarters in search of their own handouts, they found that their leader had already gone. Instead, they started plundering his residence, which was soon in flames. Further fights broke out in the streets outside, over the thousands of silver dollars scattered by fleeing soldiers unable to carry it all.[32] Others began looting anything they could carry, creating a lightning-fast criminal economy of muggers and thieves, looters and entrepreneurs, not only inside buildings, but in the street, as thieves found themselves unable to carry certain items swiped in haste and tried to fence them on to passers-by. Weapons swiftly changed hands, with deserting soldiers offloading their rifles and other equipment — James Davidson turned down the tempting offer of a brand-new Gatling gun for 'a few dollars'.

An overwhelming Japanese force disembarked at Keelung — Davidson reported that 'Cantonese' soldiers (presumably mainland transplants, but he may have meant Hakkas) offered the bravest resistance, though much of their firepower was turned against other Chinese, as hundreds of Republic troops fled past their camp.[33]

Taipei, too, was burning, and overrun with Chinese looters, leading to a division among the local population akin to class war. Those with nothing, including the many thousands of newly arrived mainland soldiers, were grabbing everything they could, while those with something to protect were begging for help from the approaching invaders.

> Now that affairs were every hour growing more serious, the Chinese merchants prepared a petition to the Japanese, requesting them to come on to [Taipei] with all haste, that the dangerous class of Chinese might be driven away and the indiscriminate burning and looting of property might cease ... The capital city had been fired, the arsenal had been stripped, the saw-mill and timber-yard had not a movable object remaining, the powder mill was burnt, the magazine exploded, and, frenzied by their success and encouraged by lack of opposition, the looters were looking about for more plunder. Nothing now remained but the private property of foreigners and Chinese ...[34]

Soon, Taipei was in Japanese hands, the president of the putative first 'republic' slipping across to the mainland for a life of obscurity. The Japanese presided over a prize in flames, the city looted by its own residents, with reports that 'rioters have destroyed many buildings at [Taipei] and plundered Government property to a large amount'.[35]

A town crier ran through the streets of Taipei, proclaiming that salvation was at hand: 'Do not despair, have courage, for the great one-eyed lion will come tomorrow from the south with twenty thousand fierce braves who will drive the cowardly invaders back in the sea whence they came.' Nobody except the reporter from the *North China Herald* paid any attention.[36]

The Japanese were forced to contend not only with sporadic attacks from Qiu's militia, but also with the awful conditions of Taiwanese roads, which forced their leader, Prince Kitashirakawa Yoshihisa, and his cavalry to dismount and walk in heavy rain, and their artillerymen to dismantle and carry their own gun carriages.[37] It did not help that the bulk of the force had arrived from Manchuria in China's far north, and consequently were equipped for winter conditions, not a scorching Taiwan June.

Among the defenders, there was a continued factionalism, often through the resurrection of old enmities between Fujianese and Hakkas — James Davidson reported one incident in which 'Cantonese' soldiers, heading south to join Liu Yongfu, were wined and dined by Taiwanese villagers, and persuaded to discard their weapons so they would not be revealed as combatants if they ran into a Japanese patrol. The villagers then turned the confiscated weapons on their former owners.[38]

Now accompanying the Japanese on their southward advance, Davidson noted the wavering nature of the Chinese resistance. He reported, on occasion, deadly barriers, fortified strong points, and harsh fighting, but also many townships with all the buildings flying white flags, through which the Japanese marched unmolested. At the Hakka stronghold of Hsinchu, the Japanese expected a fierce resistance, only to discover that the thousands of brightly uniformed Chinese defenders had evaporated into thin air.

From furious soldiers in battle array to peaceful smiling merchants and smirking coolies would be quite a feat for European soldiers: but the Chinese accomplished it in the ten minutes' interval between the time when the first Japanese soldier scaled the wall and when the Japanese were in complete possession ... It is difficult for a civilian to realise the sickening disgust of a soldier who, after plodding along in the heat, day after day, to attack the enemy, finds his opponents discarding all warlike equipments, and coming forward smirking and disclaiming all knowledge of the enemy.[39]

The transformations continued. Davidson reported with wry amusement that free gifts of tea and cakes, brought out for the Japanese in Hsinchu, soon turned into business opportunities with ever-rising prices as the Japanese continued to behave themselves and the Chinese locals grew bolder. One Chinese entrepreneur also enjoyed a brief career as an insurance salesman, going from door to door selling flags that purportedly declared each building safe from Japanese looters. He was soon arrested after making the mistake of offering his services to a shopkeeper in the presence of Japanese journalists, who were consulted about the fairness of his prices, after which they reported him to the military police.

The civilians and fair-weather soldiers in Hsinchu did not present a problem to the Japanese, lulling them into a false sense of security in their push south. Their column marched along bad roads through forested ravines, straight past platoons of concealed resistance fighters, who then threatened to cut off their lines of supply and communication back to Taipei.

> The greatest obstacle that the Japanese encountered was the smiling villagers who stood in their doorways, over which they had flown a white flag, watching the troops go by. For these natives the Japanese had at first a kind word and a smile. But scarcely were the troops out of sight before guns were brought out through the same doorways and shots fired at the first unfortunate party whose numbers were sufficiently small to make it appear safe to the treacherous occupants.[40]

Further to the south, a confusing resistance awaited, which was, depending on whom one asked, a movement of locals who refused to give up their status as part of China, or the continuation of the Republic. Niki Alsford notes that James Davidson's own account of the Japanese advance changes its tone after the fall of Hsinchu, referring not to a 'resistance movement', but to 'rebels'.[41]

With the loss of Taipei, the new base for the resistance was Tainan, where Liu Yongfu refused to accept the title of president, but did preside over a hastily convened 'government' on the understanding that someone would find the means to fund it. With the knowledge that he only had enough silver in his coffers to fund two further weeks of military wages, Liu gave free licence to money-making exercises, including the issuing of government bonds named after Guanyin, the Goddess of Mercy. His best wheeze, however, was suggested to him by C.A. McCallum, a British customs officer who had until recently been nothing more than a third-rate cargo inspector, propelled swiftly up in rank by the mass exodus of other consular officials, until he became one of Liu's most trusted confidantes.[42]

McCallum suggested to Liu that the best way to rake in cash from overseas was to issue a number of postage stamps in the name of the newly proclaimed Republic of Formosa, thereby cashing in on 'the stamp mania now universal'.[43] Liu's Republic swiftly issued several thousand stamps bearing the image of the Formosan tiger, without which no mail was permitted to leave the island. The stamp thus issued was spartan in the extreme, based on hastily cut dies, leading *Stanley Gibbons' Monthly Journal* later in the year to proclaim: 'Whether it represents a dragon or a squirrel or a landscape or anything else or even which is the right way up we have not been able to discover.'[44]

Even with the issue of thousands of Republic stamps over the next few weeks, various authorities observed that it was highly unlikely that their face value would have amounted to the revenue Liu accrued. The only possible explanation was that a foreign stamp-collecting consortium was muscling in on the issue and overpaying for entire sheets of the early stamps, in the expectation that even if (and especially if) the Republic of Formosa fell, the stamps it issued in its lifetime would experience exponential increases in subsequent value.[45]

Regardless of the degree of philatelic skulduggery, Liu's stamp business kept the money coming in to pay his soldiers. Meanwhile, Liu doggedly avoided much of the implied politics of an actual republic, announcing that he was merely fulfilling his obligation *to the Chinese Emperor*, who had ordered him to defend Taiwan from the Japanese, and had yet to countermand that order — a somewhat pigheaded reading of the situation, since the Emperor had already agreed to hand Taiwan to the Japanese.[46]

Liu instead made the matter of the Republic a logistical issue — he was getting on with his job of defending Taiwan, and it was up to the people of Taiwan to determine for themselves the form that entity took. In the meantime, he required those same people to support his military efforts, making the Tainan organisation less of a government than a military requisition authority, leaning on local bigwigs and businesses to keep it funded and supplied, and paying them with notional positions in the theoretical state.

News of such activities drifted north, and in a prolonged case of 'Chinese whispers', magnified with the telling, so much so that the Japanese military advance stalled in the expectation that substantial reinforcements would be required before taking on Liu's Black Flags, who, in the words of

James Davidson, 'had been represented by all as blood-spitting monsters who, under command of the fearful Pirate Chief [i.e. Liu], would give the Japanese the greatest trouble'.[47] As June turned to July, with increased risks of typhoons and landslides, the road south became even tougher, while supposedly subjugated areas, including the 'friendly' streets of Hsinchu, were subject to repeated insurgent counter-attacks from guerrillas.

Davidson was particularly taken with the tale of one Captain Sakurai — in command of 35 men dispersed across 18 Chinese riverboats, charged with taking rice provisions upriver to Daxi in what is now Taoyuan county — who was surprised at a rest stop by an unspecified number of resistance fighters. Sakurai and his men fought on for three long hours, until, their numbers already dwindling, they mounted a bayonet charge into what they presumed to be the weakest point of the enemy advance. All but one were killed.

That single soldier, Private Tanaka, survived by wading for eight hours, up to his neck, through riverside rushes. After word of his adventures, which came complete with many an account of wounded Japanese soldiers proclaiming their love for the Emperor as they slit their own throats, got back to his superiors, they responded by sending a cavalry squadron to the nearby town of Banqiao, where, once again, they found nothing but white flags and welcoming smiles, and the idyllic sight of men and women picking tea on a hillside, and rice paddies shining in the sun. Advancing in single file along the limited pathways beside the flooded rice fields, the cavalry was surprised by another insurgent attack. 'The peaceful tea-gatherers of an hour before were now loud, shouting rebels,' writes Davidson, 'even to the women, who joined in the fight.'[48]

The cavalrymen scattered through the rice fields, hobbled by the muddy waters, but presenting a more diffuse target. One man, Sergeant Muramatsu, was able to charge through a group of the insurgents, and fled towards Banqiao, his retreat aided to some extent by the distraction presented by a fellow officer, who was pulled from his horse and went down fighting beneath a pile of rebels. Muramatsu left his own horse dying at the edge of town, riddled with bullets from the pursuing Taiwanese. He eventually made it to the fortified mansion of the local potentate, one of the famously rich Lins of Banqiao, where he and three fellow survivors were treated with kindness, further confusing them about who was friend or foe.

The Japanese followed up with a pincer movement by an even larger force, descending with artillery and infantry on several insurgent villages in the area — Davidson does not supply any explanation of how the baffled Japanese were suddenly able to distinguish between the common people and the rebels, and one suspects that his rose-tinted view of Japanese soldiery blinded him to escalating atrocities against innocents.

June was not kind to the Japanese. Liu's veterans were experienced in jungle warfare, and inured to tropical storms and perishing heat. Their guerrilla campaign tied up the Japanese on the road to the south, while the elements did much of their fighting for them. Disease, in fact, proved to be far more damaging to the Japanese advance than the Chinese resistance, as it had also been during the expedition of 1874. Although it is likely that a hundred or more Japanese casualties in battle were attributed to disease in dispatches in order to save military face, thousands of other Japanese lives were lost to dysentery and malaria. Even as the army advanced south, thousands of the marines and sailors who had occupied the strategically crucial Penghu Islands were suffering from cholera and other afflictions. Many of the 12,000 Japanese soldiers on Taiwan itself also suffered from numerous intestinal or parasitic disorders. By the time they reached Zhanghua in central Taiwan, their fighting capability had been reduced by almost half.[49]

Zhanghua was a walled city, protected by artillery batteries on the nearby Baguashan (Eight Trigrams Mountain) — 'if the mountain falls, so too does the city.'[50] A lucky shot from the Chinese gun battery killed the Japanese second-in-command and wounded Prince Kitashirakawa himself, but the Japanese soon had the upper hand. This was because the Chinese had concentrated much of their tactics around a river ford, expecting that the Japanese would have to cross at that single point. Their enemies found another, substantially less convenient crossing point a mile away, and were able to surround them. As the fleeing Chinese ran for Zhanghua, hoping to defend from behind its walls, the Japanese turned their own cannons on them from the newly occupied mountain fort.

Qiu Fengjia, the apparent 'King' of the Hakkas, held on until sometime in August, before fleeing for the mainland with the promise of returning to fight another day — he was talked out of taking his own life in protest. For the rest of his life, he would be a staunch advocate of

Chinese republicanism, participating in many revolutionary activities on
the mainland, but his swift exit from the defence of Taiwan would haunt
him for years. He would write of repeatedly waking up from dreams
of a Taiwan that was still Chinese, only to be confronted with the real
situation.[51] His son, Niantai, whose name literally means 'Remember
Taiwan', would later publish a poem that Qiu had written as he fled,
claiming that his motives were just, whereas Tang's were merely cowardly:

> The ruler may cede the land
> His underling alone, has no power to restore heaven
> Shipped away ahead of the barbarians
> I grieve, gazing back at the rivers and mountains.[52]

The resistance continued without him as the Japanese made their way
along the road south.

There, Liu Yongfu had many weeks to prepare the defences at
Kaohsiung, his somewhat mercenary troops kept in line by payments from
a shipload of 'treasure' that had arrived in Kaohsiung in February on an
unnamed ship flying a British flag. They had, in fact, been so enthusiastic
about receiving their wages that they had boarded the ship and started
to ransack it, before the arrival of the British cruiser *Mercury* persuaded
them to wait their turn.[53]

In an increasingly tense situation at Kaohsiung, with the foreign
community fretting about the threat to its members from both the
Chinese and Japanese, Liu commenced the fortification of the town and
harbour, laying sea-mines in the approaches, and putting his men to work
on a three-kilometre bamboo bridge that linked the fort on Shoushan, the
hill that overlooked the harbour entrance, to the city on the other side of
the harbour lagoon. This would prevent the garrison on Shoushan from
being cut off in the event of a blockade. The observer from *The Illustrated
London News* was impressed that the bridge was completed in only three
days, but lamented Liu's priorities:

> It seems nothing will teach the Chinese the fallacy of the idea that
> a fort is only to be attacked from the front; They still persist in
> occupying their whole time piling obstacles on their front and leaving

the rear quite open. One thing they never forget, that is to leave a good road for retreat.[54]

Since the British consulate was on Shoushan, the writer presumably didn't object to a similar avenue of escape being open to his countrymen.

The preparations at Kaohsiung were all for nothing. In a crushing blow to Japanese morale, their leader, Prince Kitashirakawa, died of malaria on the outskirts of Tainan. The new leader of the Japanese forces would be Kabayama Sukenori, the former navy minister, now promoted to full admiral, ennobled as a count, and somewhat pre-emptively handed a medal, the Order of the Rising Sun. Kabayama wrote personally to Liu Yongfu, assuring him of clemency if he would spare both sides the tribulations of a full-scale battle.[55]

Tainan itself gave up without a fight, with a delegation of the town's European occupants coming out to meet the Japanese and welcome them — the town had effectively been occupied by British marines since May, and was hence spared the chaos of the fall of Taipei.[56] It was supposedly Liu's stamp adviser, C.A. McCallum, who 'saved thousands of innocent civilians' from a similar fate to that of Taipei, by arranging for the Chinese soldiers in Tainan to be disarmed and assembled in front of the Customs Office, from which they were shipped back to the mainland by the Japanese.[57]

With the Japanese army entering the city, and the Japanese navy dropping anchor in the port of Anping, Tainan was under Japanese control. 'And so,' wrote Lien Heng in his *General History of Taiwan*, 'fell the Republic of Formosa.' In doing so, he attributed substantially greater longevity to it than the ten days it had lasted under Tang Jingsong.[58]

Liu Yongfu, leader of the Black Flags, was nowhere to be found. Off the shores of Amoy, the Japanese cruiser *Yaeyama* halted a steamship, the *Thales*, on a tip-off, boarding her in search of fugitives from Taiwan. The Japanese marines were intensely suspicious about the behaviour of seven Chinese labourers, but after ten hours were shooed off the ship following protests from its captain. Two Japanese officers were left aboard the *Thales*, with the intention of arresting the suspects when they departed from foreign jurisdiction onto the quayside at Amoy. There, however, the seven men were spirited away through a distraction by the British consul, allowing Liu Yongfu, for he was indeed among them, to escape.[59]

The Japanese had already held a celebratory parade at the fall of Taipei, but held another in Tainan. Pointedly, they gave thanks at the Shrine of Koxinga, the Japanese mother of whom had now achieved a new political importance, as a shaky claim for the island's original liberator having been sort-of Japanese himself.

Writing some years later, the anthropologist Janet McGovern found local attitudes towards Koxinga deeply ironic and opportunist:

Previous to 1895, the name of Koksinga [sic] was in Japan held up to universal execration. He had been a 'villainous Chinese pirate; one who had behaved in Taiwan with the usual cruelty of his race' (i.e. the Chinese). Since 1895 when the Japanese came into control of Formosa, and, in turn, dispossessed the Chinese ... he was Japanese — and a hero.[60]

CHAPTER SEVEN

TAKASAGO

Taiwan Under the Japanese (1895–1945)

The newly admiralled, newly ennobled Kabayama Sukenori was now rebranded yet again, as the first Governor-General of the Japanese province of Taiwan. He soon issued a notice that, while a trifle condescending, assured the locals that Taiwan would be better off under its new masters:

> The island of Taiwan is a new territory in our great Japanese empire, a land that does not yet bask in imperial grace. Today, when we enter this land, we will cause the people to gladly return [sic] to the benevolence of our emperor, who adheres to the principles of educating and pacifying, but we must at one and the same time combine grace with force, preventing the people from responding with a contemptuous heart.[1]

The whole matter was regarded by the Chinese as a sorrowful loss of territory, and by the Japanese, thanks to some careful massaging of the historical record and some judicious forgetting of the facts, as some sort of restoration. For many in the younger generation of Japanese, such as the 30-year-old author and journalist Takekoshi Yosaburō, it was an inspiring territorial acquisition, and the chance for Japan to clamber up into the club of imperial powers. Takekoshi wrote:

thus the island, which China had torn from Koxinga's descendants by intrigue bribery and brute force *passed again into the hands of the Japanese*, in whose veins flows the same blood as filled those of Koxinga.[2] [my emphasis]

Now retired and writing up his action-packed memoirs, William Pickering, the veteran of the indigenous squabbles of yesteryear, thought Japanese control could only do good:

There can be little doubt that the change of government will benefit the Japanese, the inhabitants of Formosa, and the civilised world generally ... This, however, cannot surprise anyone who is acquainted with the real state of things. The Chinese governed the portion of the island under their control merely for the benefit of the officials, and in many parts of Formosa ... anarchy prevailed for generations. However much the Chinese inhabitants may have been oppressed by their own mandarins, it is certain that they will not submit quietly

Tainan effigy of Koxinga, deified by both the Manchus and the Japanese for his unwavering support of the defeated Ming dynasty.

even to just and good government, when exercised by a nation whom they have been accustomed to call 'dwarf slaves'.[3]

Pickering incisively identified the issues facing the island as not being so easily divided into a mere matter of local Chinese and a scattering of indigenous Formosans.

Much firmness and great tact will be required, as although the aborigines, both savage and semi-civilised, will cause little or no trouble, yet the Hakkas, who have never submitted quietly even to the government of their own empire, will be amenable only to the sternest measures, and the large population of [Fujianese], whilst gladly accepting the protection of their conquerors in their commerce and agriculture, will in their hearts despise what they deem to be the rule of an inferior race, and will therefore be open to the influence of intrigue from the mainland.[4]

The dream of the republic did not fade immediately. Hakka villagers acquired guns from deserting Chinese soldiers, and staged a rebellion on New Year's Day 1896, raiding several Japanese settlements and killing 128 colonists. The Japanese responded with six weeks of reprisals, massacring many innocent Hakkas simply because of their race, and dragging their neighbours to witness 'post-mortem abuse', designed to play on the Hakkas' belief that the victims would remain maimed in the afterlife. The Taiwanese, wrote one author, came to fear the police 'as if they were ghosts'.[5]

That June, there was a second uprising by Hakkas in the countryside near Tainan, led by a man who believed that Britain, Germany, and Russia were about to send forces to liberate the island. Instead, Japanese colonists hid in the local fort, while a military retaliation force sallied out to burn 30 villages to the ground. As late as 1897, there were upstart proclamations in the hinterland of the Republic's re-establishment by various partisan groups, and multiple uprisings thereafter. As with the various revolts during the administration of the Qing dynasty, it is difficult to determine precisely where loyalist actions were replaced by sedition over more prosaic matters. Back in Tokyo, factions within the cash-strapped Japanese

government wondered aloud if Taiwan was really worth all the trouble,
and seriously suggested offloading it onto the French for a bargain price.[6]

Writing in 1907, Takekoshi Yosaburō seemed dimly aware that the
Japanese were partly the authors of their own fate:

> As fast as one band had been broken up, new bands arose in other
> places, and both soldiers and police were wearied out, without
> having apparently accomplished anything. It is true that in each
> expedition some brigands were killed and thus they were weakened
> to some extent; but the fact that occasionally peaceable inhabitants
> were mistaken for brigands and treated accordingly by the punitive
> expedition, led some of these to turn to brigands.[7]

Takekoshi blamed multiple factors, including the first few governors'
insistence that governing Taiwan was a primarily military matter. He also
cited language as an issue, particularly among untrustworthy interpreters
who both shielded true bandits from retribution and falsely accused
innocent Taiwanese of being criminals. But he also noted that Taiwan
itself was famous for its contrary attitude.

> From the time Formosa passed under Chinese rule, after Koxinga's
> defeat and death, down almost to the present day, there were continual
> disturbances, at least twenty of which were outbreaks of some
> importance; in short, the island was never entirely free from rebellion.
> True, there were brief periods of apparent peace, but the authorities
> secured these by bribing the brigand chiefs and governed with their
> assistance for the time being. The inhabitants, therefore, came to
> regard the brigands as their possible future rulers, and felt that any
> turn of fortune's wheel might make them their actual governors.[8]

Even geography suggested that the Japanese had bitten off more
than they could chew. Seven of the mountains in the new province of
Taiwan were taller than Japan's Mount Fuji, causing consternation for a
propaganda regime that had insisted it was without equal anywhere in
the empire. The highest peak in 'Japan', Jade Mountain (*Yushan*), now
renamed Mount Niitaka, was actually in Taiwan.

For the rest of the 1890s, the encroachment of the Japanese on the hinterland led to a constant litany of almost daily 'incidents' — 303 in 1898 alone, resulting in 557 deaths among railway surveyors, lumberjacks, policemen, and the like. Despite claims to rule the whole island, the Japanese authorities soon resurrected the 'guardline' of the Qing era, now a north–south series of outposts, a 'savage boundary' (*fanjie*) wreathed in barbed wire and staffed by paramilitaries, ostensibly to protect the lucrative camphor forests from encroachment by tribes from the outlaw east. Tribesmen crossing what had once been virgin forest now faced electrified fences and landmines.[9]

Throughout Taiwan's five decades as a Japanese province, its governors would be drawn from the ranks of the military or police. Its civil administrators, flocking to the opportunities afforded by a 'new' territory, were often progressively minded graduates or ambitious technocrats, ready to use Taiwan as an experimental testbed for initiatives to export to the Japanese homeland. By 1901, Taipei had a 'Grand Shrine' in the Japanese style, across the Keelung river from downtown Taipei, set into the slopes of Yuanshan mountain. Reached across an ornate bridge, it was set into the mountain itself as a series of terraces: a grand courtyard, with steps to two further sanctuaries. Ostensibly conceived as a monument to the luckless Prince Kitashirakawa, it also venerated the Three Deities of Pioneering, ancient figures from Japanese folklore who had been instrumental in the breaking open of new lands and contacts. The shrine used a large amount of Japanese lumber in its construction, with hinoki cypress trees imported from several Japanese prefectures. Its inauguration ceremony in October 1901 was attended by a who's who of the Japanese aristocracy, including the widow of Prince Kitashirakawa, another imperial princess, several former governors-general, and multiple marquises, dukes, and barons.

The opening of the shrine was part of a series of grand schemes set in motion by the head of the island's civilian administration, Gotō Shinpei, who was responsible for a huge number of initiatives designed to solidify Taiwan as a productive and peaceful element within the Japanese Empire. Part of his achievements included the establishment of the Provisional Council for the Investigation of Old Habits of Taiwan (*Rinji Taiwan Kyū Kanchō Sakai*), which would continue to sponsor the authorship of massive reports on elements of Taiwanese culture for the next decade.

These included the landmark, eight-volume *Research on Taiwanese Tribal Customs* (*Taiwan Banzoku Kanshū Kenkyū*), which, at almost 4,000 pages, would become the cornerstone of much subsequent anthropology.

One spin-off from Gotō's research programme was an intricate series of measures to deal with Taiwan's opiate addiction crisis. Infamously and illegally supplied to China in industrial quantities by the likes of the British, opium had become popular in Taiwan initially for medical use, offering some respite from the effects of malaria and other tropical diseases. It was, however, also fiercely addictive, regarded by the Japanese authorities as a danger no less threatening to social order than banditry.[10]

Gotō, who had trained as a medical doctor, recognised that Taiwan's 170,000 opium smokers (6.1 per cent of the island's total population) were a drain on resources, on the labour market, and on civil order. He used his new role as a test case in demonstrating how a drug problem widespread in all China could be dealt with through the right measures in a province under benign rule.

Gotō recognised that an immediate ban on all opium would create more problems than it solved, pushing addicts into withdrawal, and incentivising criminals and smugglers. Instead, he instituted a 'gradual ban', forbidding access to opium for new users, but offering existing addicts a licence to buy their supplies from a government monopoly.

Over the next 20 years, the number of opium addicts in Taiwan fell drastically to 60,000. Meanwhile, the state monopoly on opium supply proved so lucrative to government coffers that it was soon expanded to other commodities — salt, camphor, tobacco, petroleum, matches, and liquor. In a quirk of history, one of the Monopoly Bureau's officials saw an artefact on display in the Governor-General's museum that he thought would be nicely appropriate for a trademark. As a result, the logo for government-supplied tiger-bone liquor ironically employed the image of the Republic of Formosa's tiger flag.[11]

Gotō hoped Taiwan would ultimately prove not to be a burden on the Japanese Empire, but a net contributor. To this end, he set up the Bank of Taiwan to channel funding into infrastructure projects, along with a Twenty-Year Fiscal Plan that would annually reduce the subsidies from Tokyo. Gotō did not stay in office long enough to see the plan to fruition: he was whisked away to work similar miracles on the Manchurian

Railway, the Japanese government, and, eventually, as its mayor, Tokyo. But left to run without him, Taiwan would achieve financial autonomy two years ahead of schedule, in 1907.[12] About 85 per cent of Taiwan's 'exports', including its coal, its petroleum, and much of its agricultural produce, actually stayed within the empire and went back to Japan. The acquisition of Taiwan also brought with it a new, sweeter tooth for the Japanese, who now enjoyed a boom in candies, cakes, and desserts, fuelled by the Taiwanese crops of sugar cane, bananas, and pineapple.[13]

Gotō's earnest hope that even the indigenous peoples could be eventually lured and guided into becoming model citizens did not always work on the ground, where frictions continued, and were answered by his counterparts in the military. In 1900, Atayal tribesmen in Dakekan mounted so many attacks on camphor prospectors in the hinterland that a 300-strong punitive force was assembled, including soldiers and boundary paramilitaries accompanied by indigenous bearers and guides. Repelled from Atayal forests by a strong resistance, the soldiers retreated to a nearby mountainside and commenced shelling the Atayal lands with artillery.

The Dakekan campaign also saw the employment of a new tactic, a blockade (*fūsa*). 'There will be a strict enforcement of a complete shutdown,' wrote the Taipei prefect, 'meaning savages are forbidden from moving about, as well as receiving armaments, munitions, food, salt and naturally everything else. This will result in the destruction of their vitality, to the point of life or death.'[14]

Blockades on intractable communities could stretch on for years, squeezing not only the perpetrators of crimes, but their innocent neighbours. Inevitably, some of the tribes turned on each other. In a case in 1903, a subtribe of the Atayal, the Seediq people from Musha, struggling and starving after six years of restricted access to supplies, sought help from their traditional enemies, the Gantaban subtribe of the Bunun. The Gantaban offered a parley and a peace treaty at a nearby site, which turned out to be an ambush that led to the deaths of a hundred Seediq men — a cataclysmic loss of life for two villages, leaving them largely populated by widows and orphans.[15]

Rumours persisted that the Japanese had been complicit in the Gantaban atrocity. They were certainly directly involved in another tribal grievance in 1903, when Saisiyat people in Miaoli rose up in protest at lapsed payment for camphor logging rights on their territory. Surprise attacks on boundary outposts met with initial success for a small party of Saisiyat raiders, only for the Japanese to retaliate, once more, with artillery.

With an 'incident' of some sort roughly every 30 hours, year after year, and periodic escalations requiring a more involved military response, the Japanese military began making pre-emptive plans. Administrator Mochiji Rokusaburō issued a chilling *Report Concerning the Governing of Savages* (1903), advising a more active genocide against the indigenous peoples, on the grounds that they barely counted as human beings:

> the suppression of raw savages from the standpoint of international law cannot be called a war. As a result, although from a sociological point of view the savages are human, from the point of view of international law they are more like animals.[16]

Mochiji's report was a subtle correction of his own Emperor's proclamation about the position of the people of Taiwan as Japanese subjects. The indigenous peoples didn't count — they were better regarded as an unpleasant infestation of Japan's new colonial acquisition. Mochiji knew that Japan could not afford an all-out war on two-thirds of the island, but instead suggested a policy of 'benevolence in the south, suppression in the north' (*nanbu beibatsu*), in which military operations were reserved only for the areas experiencing the most indigenous resistance — which were, conveniently, the camphor forests.

By the end of the decade, the Japanese military had hatched a Five-Year Plan to Pacify the Northern Savages, in which continued embargoes went hand-in-hand with military operations, often exploiting local enmities to set tribes against each other. Not to be left out, the Imperial Japanese Navy shelled indigenous villages from the sea.

In 1910, the circle returned to the Seediq Atayal, an ever-bellicose group that had angered the Japanese authorities by staging attacks on understaffed guard-houses while officers were away fighting a different war with the Gaogan Atayal. After a four-day artillery bombardment in December, the first village surrendered, handing over 1,200 rifles and thereby limiting its ability to resist in future. The artillery squads repositioned their guns to commence bombarding the next, and the next, until the Musha area was declared 'pacified'.

But the indigenous tribes were not the only likely source of trouble. In 1912, over on the mainland, after more than two millennia of imperial rule, representatives of 17 Chinese provinces proclaimed the establishment of the Republic of China. It began as a shaky and fragile regime — its first president, Sun Yat-sen, was an ailing revolutionary who lacked an army to back up his decrees and was soon forced to compromise with the first of many local warlords. For the next 30 years, mainland China would be plunged into a series of local conflicts between imperial loyalists (who would briefly claim the empire restored), local warlords, and foreign opportunists. The Republic would eventually be pushed off the mainland by the victorious faction in all this fighting, the Communist Party under Chairman Mao Zedong, although as later chapters of this book show, this republic's influence on Taiwan would continue long after its mainland defeat.

The existence of the Republic of China, even only in theory, also led to a series of declarations made in pretence, such as the Republic's refusal to admit that Mongolia was an independent state. As part of its geopolitical to-do list, Sun Yat-sen's new state also described the Japanese presence on Taiwan to be an infringement of its people's right to be Chinese. From the very start, Sun's provisional government included a seat for a Taiwan delegate — the first person to hold the post was the 48-year-old Qiu Fengjia, the exiled 'King' of the Hakkas, who died shortly afterwards.[17]

Back in Taiwan, the writer Lien Heng poetically celebrated the founding of the Republic of China as a long-awaited return of the spirit of Koxinga, somehow nurtured through nine generations, even on a Taiwan occupied by the Manchus and then the Japanese:

> Now the leader of the invaders has resigned, and the south and the north have become whole again. Heaven's mandate constantly renews itself. As people rise up with vigour and rigor, may your spirit abide with us.[18]

With the Manchus overthrown, and a republican entity on the mainland openly suggesting that Taiwan deserved to be part of the

Republic of China, seditious activities on the island took on a new, political dimension. In 1915, a crazed revolt escalated in the space of two months from simple, local issues of poverty and resentment, to attacks on government officials, to the proclamation of a coming apocalypse and the restoration of the Ming dynasty, before Japanese retaliation wiped it out. The setting was the hinterland east of Tainan — hilly, forested areas ill-suited to farming, and hence struggling in the newly agricultural environment promoted by the Japanese colonists. Unable to grow rice in any useful quantities, the locals were pushed into assigning more and more land to sugar cane or other plantation crops, although these, too, failed to match returns from other parts of the island. The area, particularly around the town of Jiaxian, was also notable for a strongly diverse intermixture of locals. Before pressure from the Japanese, the Hoklo and Hakka immigrants from Fujian traded and married with both the indigenous plains and mountain dwellers, enjoying thriving local barter in deer hides and similar items.

This fragile status quo was steadily upset, not so much by immediate Japanese incursions, but by the arrival of a handful of police officers, who were expected to impose new imperial policies over thousands of locals, many of whom had been previously managing their own affairs through a network of headmen and temple affiliations.

A significant number of the rebels were affiliated to local martial-arts schools or secret societies. Soldiers were recruited amid apocalyptic prophecies — claims that recent typhoons were the first signs of a looming revolution that would cast out the Japanese and all who sympathised with them, amid seven days and seven nights of poisonous black rain. True believers, it was said, needed to swear undying allegiance to the cause, drink sacred water, and purchase amulets of loyalty and invulnerability from approved local temples.[19]

Their nominal leader was Yu Qingfang, who was proclaimed as the new messiah or at least the messiah's herald. Yu led blood rituals of allegiance, pledging his followers' fealty to a deity described by survivors as either the Goddess of Mercy or the Dark Maiden of the Ninth Heaven. Imposing severe military discipline on his growing horde of Chinese, Hakka, and local tribes, he dispensed 'Beheading Official's Red Banners' allowing certain minions to execute anyone who infringed his unnamed order's regulations. On several cases, the banners became the focus for rituals of human sacrifice, making examples of local resistance, criminals, and in one case, the wife of a local police chief.

Despite such colourful and dramatic evocations, using language and rituals that deliberately suggested the re-establishment of the Ming dynasty, Yu Qingfang's new world order soon crumbled in the face of Japanese counter-attacks. His most fanatic followers, the 30-strong Drawn Sword Squad, died in a suicidal, naked charge against Japanese soldiers. Others, in the self-proclaimed Songjiang Armies, died in their dozens before it became obvious that makeshift weapons and magical amulets were no match for the Imperial Japanese Army.

Japanese clampdowns on head-hunting led to the thinning of tribal traditions. By 1917, the Paiwan were glumly substituting a bundle of bamboo for the freshly removed human head that once formed the 'ball' lanced by the winner in their tribal *Mavayaiya* game. The Puyuma were no longer sending out expeditions for ritual head-hunting. Instead, they would annually capture a monkey from the forest, tie it to a tree outside the bachelors' hut, and let the young men fire arrows at it, before conducting a libation and ceremonial celebration at its corpse. 'The old people of the Puyuma,' wrote Janet McGovern, 'explain that in the "good days of old", when their tribe was a large and powerful one, a prisoner, captured from some other tribe, was always sacrificed on these festal occasions, but now they, like the Paiwan ... have to be satisfied with an inferior substitute.'[20]

Janet McGovern reported seeing the telltale chin tattoo of an accredited head-hunter among the Atayal people, but by that time it had evolved into a more ceremonial function, denoting that 'these boys were the sons of famous head-hunters and that their hands had been laid upon heads decapitated by their fathers; or that they have carried these heads in net-bags upon their backs'.[21]

Posterity has been unkind to the Japanese colonial period, which was, after all, tied inextricably to imperialism, the rise of a militarist nation, and in the eyes of the successor regime on Taiwan, an enemy to be eradicated from historical memory. This is not how it looked on the ground to the Japanese, who saw themselves as plucky saviours, arriving to drag Taiwan out of the stagnant swamp of its former Chinese administration. Liu Mingchuan's infrastructural improvements, left to ruin since 1891, were polished up and renewed — railway, port organisation, and telegraphs all back up and running. Slum clearances and swamp drainage in the west of Taipei created a new, more modern city for the colonists, while officials tried to make sense of the resources and population realities of an island that, while not uncharted, was certainly inadequately surveyed.

Even today in Japan there is a thriving publishing industry of tourist guides to Japanese Taiwan, pointing the curious visitor at repurposed colonial-era banks and government buildings, entire Taipei districts of surviving red-brick houses and shopping streets, stone staircases, water towers, and lighthouses. Other Japanese relics are less obvious — such as parts of the sewage system and many inland roadways. But even today, it is possible to walk in old Taipei, and discern faded logos and worn carvings where there were once Japanese factories and stores. The influence, of course, also went both ways, with many elements of Japanese life also reflecting its colonial era — not merely the Taiwanese influence on 'Chinese' food in Japan, but also the legacy of Taiwanese labour in everything from Japanese road building to coal mines.[22]

Sometimes such enterprises became muddled and misunderstood. Taiwanese folklore retains elements of what must have been Japanese attempts to win over superstitious locals who had concerns about feng shui and local geomancy. A 'stone chain' in the river waters at Jinxing is the surviving remains of a Japanese colonial-era weir, with two four-metre-tall cones of concreted rubble, linked by a smaller line of rocks, designed to prevent flooding. Local legend, however, ascribes the building of the weir to a project initiated by a vision from the sea goddess Mazu, who told the authorities to build it.[23]

Among the achievements of the Japanese era, much of which must be credited to the thousands of Taiwanese labourers who did the actual work, we might include the incredible stretch of railway designed to improve access to the lumber in the Alishan mountains, crossing steep ravines and edging along sheer precipices to climb 3,000 metres in less than a hundred kilometres. Another major project, a ten-kilometre canal from Tainan to the sea, undid the damage caused by the silting up of the Luermen lagoon in the 19th century.[24] In many cases, the long-term dividends for such projects did not manifest until after the Japanese era was over, when talk of Taiwan's dark years as a colony was suppressed, and new rulers took the credit.

One of Japan's interests in Taiwan was its unexploited agricultural lands and other resources. Japan had been facing a series of food shortages since the late 1880s, which continued to manifest as outbreaks of riots and local unrest all through the early 1890s. Above the pre-existing cash-crops of Taiwan — including camphor, which revitalised the Japanese doll-making industry with lacquer and early plastics, and sugar cane, which transformed the market for Japanese candy — the real prize was rice.

Taiwanese native rice was unappealing to the Japanese — it was a long-grain *indica* variety, often called 'red rice' from its colour, itself caused by a lack of nutrients in the soil. By 1915, Japanese scientists were trying to breed a variety of *japonica* rice that would flourish under Taiwanese conditions, eventually reaching a breakthrough with a fast-growing, high-yield strain that would please the home market. It was named for the Penglai islands, the isles of the immortals in Chinese legend, pronounced *Hōrai* in Japanese. From a small experimental plot of 96 hectares near Taichung, Hōrai Rice spread swiftly through the island. Today, it accounts for 93 per cent of all Taiwanese rice production.

The joys of Hōrai Rice were celebrated in a propaganda song issued by the colony's Food Department, 'Hōrai Rice is Delicious':

Taiwan has become a rice-producing island
Both old and young dance over the bountiful year
The people will have a prosperous century
Hōrai Rice, acquainted with the stars
Hōrai Rice, a treasured brand.[25]

The rice itself was only part of the battle. It was dwarfed in the achievements of the colonial government by the infrastructure that supported it, particularly in the part of the island south of Chiayi, where climate conditions had previously made farming difficult. The Japanese hydraulic engineer Hatta Yōichi remains something of a local hero even in modern Taiwan, for his lifelong project to bring water to the plain between Chiayi and Tainan. Sometimes this is mistranslated, using pieces of the two cities' names, as the Chia-nan *Canal*, as if it were a single waterway. But, in fact, Hatta's project was to create a vast irrigation network over hundreds of square kilometres, smoothing out the uneven quantities of water dumped onto the region by the monsoons and mountain run-off, alleviating the dry seasons and containing the periodic floods. Completed in 1930, Hatta's irrigation network increased the arable land on the Chiayi–Tainan plain from 5,000 to 150,000 hectares, and made it possible for the formerly annual rice crop to become thrice-yearly.

This, in turn, was fed by grand hydro-engineering projects, including Hatta's pride and joy, the Wushantou Dam, which created the Wushantou Reservoir. Today it is a much-loved scenic area, dominated by a replica of Beijing's Temple of Heaven, with long, twisting fingers of forested land reaching into the waters — the sight of which from the air has given it its modern nickname, the Coral Lake. Built with an earthquake resistant 'hydraulic-fill' method, the Wushantou Dam was completed in 1930, and would be the largest dam in the world for the next six years, until it was trumped by the Hoover Dam in the United States. It also supplied immense amounts of hydroelectric power, making Japanese Taiwan an icon of renewable resources, and tamed the watercourses of the western Taiwanese farmlands. It was not without its cost — a memorial on the site today commemorates over a hundred labourers who died in its construction, including several dozen blown apart in a gas explosion during the excavations of one of its feed tunnels.[26]

Another of the colonial era's projects had a visible effect on the scenery, and continues to do so today. Completed in 1934, the dam on the Sun-Moon lakes created substantial hydroelectric power, but also raised the water levels so that the twin bodies of water, separated in the hottest weather, turned into a singular lake. The Thao people, who had dwelt for centuries in the nearby wetlands, were forced to move to higher ground. Their sacred island was substantially reduced in size.

•

For the engineers and scientists who laboured over rice strains, outreach programmes, irrigation networks, and hydroelectric schemes, the beginning of the 1930s was the culmination of a generation's work. Some of that work remained unwelcome in the hinterland, particularly among indigenous Formosans who objected to the encroachment of transport links, plantations, and educational initiatives that taught their children to sing the Japanese national anthem.

In 1930, the most notorious of the incidents arising from these rural tensions would shock the Japanese media. It all started so simply in Musha, home of the Tgdaya subtribe of the Seediq, with a wedding, and a Japanese policeman, Yoshimura Katsumi, walking by. A young Tgdaya tribesman, Dadao Mona, his hands bloody from the wedding livestock slaughter, beckoned Yoshimura over for a drink, which the officer refused. Affronted, the drunken tribesman grabbed at the officer's uniform, his bloody hands staining the pristine cloth. The officer slapped the tribesman away with his cane, and was jumped in turn by Dadao and his brother Bassao, who beat Yoshimura up.

The next day, the youths' father, Mona Rudao, visited the police box with bottles of millet wine and offered his apologies. His attempt to smooth things over was to no avail. The local police chief refused to let the matter lie, and announced he would instead be reporting the incident up the chain of command. A simple brawl was liable to be written up as a tribal 'incident', with uncertain consequences. Mona's sons might be arrested, or even made the cause of a punitive expedition launched against the entire village.[27]

That, at least, is the official version of events, which ignores the reason why there might be a Japanese police officer wandering past a tribal wedding in the first place. The Seediq people saw things differently. Their way of life had been disrupted by multiple factors, beginning with a road driven through the forest to make easier access for lumber companies. Then came the lumber companies themselves, transforming the local villages, plundering the menfolk for cheap labour. The previous generation, the formative years of Mona's sons, had seen a succession of directives chipping away at Seediq *gaya* — their own term for the many unspoken traditions and rules that formed the bedrock of their culture. In 1911, the Japanese authorities had made the Seediq hand over their prized human-skull trophies; in 1916, they were prohibited from smoking opium; in 1917, tattooing was outlawed; in 1918, the men were forced to get 'modern' haircuts, and forbidden from selective tooth extraction — once a feature of a tribal manhood ritual. In 1922, the Japanese interfered in funereal customs, forbidding indoor burials. And then in

Mona Rudao (centre), leader of the 1930 Musha rebellion,
pictured with Seediq leaders.

1926, they confiscated many of the Seediq people's guns and most of
the ammunition.[28] In 1927, the Musha area was listed in the Taipei press
as one of 12 'scenic spots' recommended for Japanese tourists — six
hours by pushcart railway and road vehicles from the rail head at Puli,
but nevertheless further increasing the number of visitors to the area, to
whom the tribes were nothing but a bit of local colour.

By 1930, Musha was a picturesque huddle of buildings on a hillside
above the forest, boasting a single main street with two general stores, a
doctor's surgery, a post office, a school, and a police station. It was home
to 36 Japanese families and 23 Chinese families. Down the hill and down
the road was a less organised, less familiar collection of huts, the homes
of the Tgdaya Seediq people — some accounts deliberately use the term
'reservation'.[29]

Head-hunting was now illegal, and even *hunting* was frowned upon
— the men of the Seediq, if not working for the logging company, were

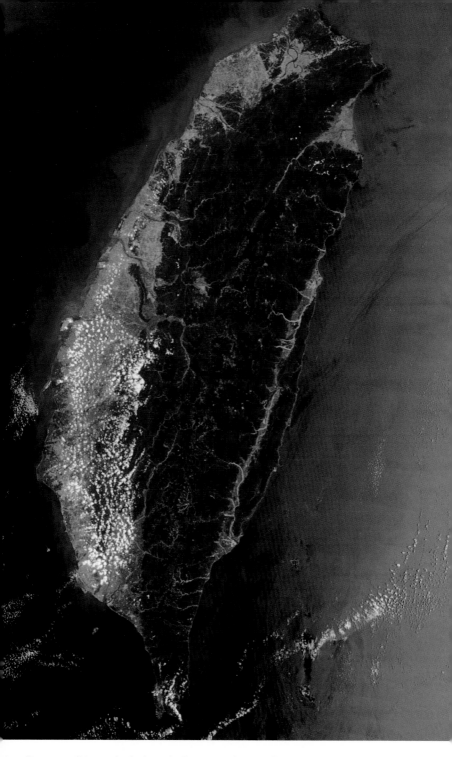

A satellite image of Taiwan clearly shows the demarcation between the mountains and plains.

Left: A Spanish image of an indigenous couple from 'Tamchuy' (Tamsui) in northern Taiwan, found in the Boxer Codex (1590).

Below: Bunun tribespeople photographed around 1900.

Below left: The paSta'ay ceremony in 2006, in which the Saisiyat people atone for the genocide they committed against another tribe.

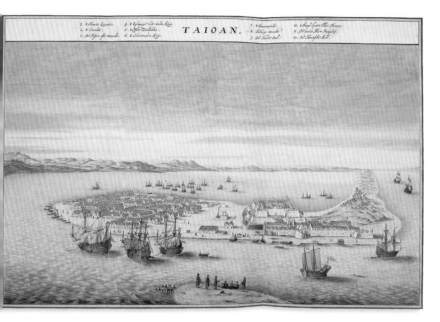

Above: The Dutch base at Fort Zeelandia, built in 1623–34 near what is now Tainan.

Below: A propaganda print from the People's Republic celebrates Koxinga as a national hero for banishing European imperialists. He is shown backed by a rainbow coalition of indigenous peoples.

Above: Manchu artillery makes short work of Lin Shuangwen's rebellious stronghold at the battle of Dali, in an engraving made as a collaboration between Chinese and European artists.

Left: A Chinese representation of Tainan and its Anping harbour, looking eastwards from the sea across a lagoon thick with junks. Remnants of Dutch-era architecture can be seen among the local houses.

Right: Chihkan Tower, formerly the Dutch-era Provintia in Tainan. The steles in front of it commemorate the suppression of the Lin Shuangwen rebellion in 1788.

Top: The tiger flag of the Republic of Formosa (1895).

Above: The lion emblem of the Republic of Formosa, as seen on one of the stamps issued to generate revenue for the short-lived state.

Right: The Grand Shrine in Taipei, painted here in 1930, was the spiritual centre of the Japanese colonial era, built into the mountainside where today's Grand Hotel now stands.

Above: Crowds gather outside Taipei's civic hall in October 1945 to celebrate the departure of the Japanese and the handing of the island to the Kuomintang, whose flag looms large.

Above: US President Dwight D. Eisenhower walks in Taipei with Soong May-ling and Chiang Kai-shek in 1960. Eisenhower had been responsible for the 1955 Formosa Resolution that granted the US president the authority to intervene militarily in the event of Chinese aggression in the Taiwan Strait.

Left: 'We shall certainly recapture Taiwan', claims a propaganda poster from the Communist-led People's Republic of China.

Above: Opened in 1980, Taipei's Chiang Kai-shek Memorial has become a focus of commemoration and of protest.

Right: Displaced statues of Generalissimo Chiang Kai-shek dotted around the memorial park in Cihu.

Right: A jubilant Chen Shui-bian and his running mate, former political prisoner Annette Lu, acknowledge the crowd on 18 March 2000 in Taipei, following the Democratic Progressive Party's victory in Taiwan's second presidential elections.

An iconic symbol of modern Taiwan, the skyscraper Taipei 101 was the tallest building in the world from 2004 to 2010, and is an annual focus for firework displays on New Year's Eve.

expected to farm the land that had been cleared by the destruction of the forest. The Seediq women were encouraged to intermarry with Japanese colonists, a romantic spin on the colonisation of local sexual relations, which often ended badly. Mona's own sister, Tiwas, was herself the abandoned 'wife' of a Japanese visitor, who had returned to his homeland without her.[30]

For many previous years, the Japanese and the Seediq had practised a form of 'wet' diplomacy, hammering out any disagreements or proposals over a boozy night of heavy drinking. However, a directive had recently been sent down from high command, instructing officers that such community relations were no longer standard operating procedure, and that officers would do well to distance themselves from the local headmen, whose time was coming to an end. When Dadao Mona drunkenly offered a drink to Yoshimura Katsumi, he was not only extending tribal hospitality, but engaging in a ritual that had previously been the very foundation of Formosan–Japanese relations in the neighbourhood. Instead, he was slapped away by a jumpy policeman.[31]

Matters came to a head on 27 October 1930, at the annual Musha sports day, held on the grounds of the elementary school, attended by the colonial provincial governor, high-ranking police officers, various other officials, and their families. Festivities began at eight in the morning, as the Japanese flag was raised above proceedings, and the assembled Japanese, Chinese, and Formosans began to sing the Japanese national anthem.

Suddenly, there was a shriek from somewhere in the crowd, and a disembodied head was hurled into the air — it was the first victim, the Taichung police commissioner. Amid the ensuing chaos, only those who spoke Atayal languages understood the yells of men in the crowd: 'Do not spare any Japanese!'

Formosan women fled the scene with their children, as the Chinese and Japanese reeled in confusion. Three hundred Tgdaya Seediq men waded through the crowd with muskets and knives, grabbing rifles and swords from the fallen police. When the bloodshed finally ended, the bodies of 134 Japanese, many with severed heads, were strewn around the blood-soaked playing field.[32]

In the eyes of the Tgdaya, the attack on the sports field was not merely a fight. It was a ritual, a mass sacrifice designed to reclaim their *gaya* and appease restless ancestral spirits.[33] Among the killers were teenage tribesmen executing their former teachers. A detailed report by the colonial authorities recognised all of the above, and noted several other possible contributions to the uprising. Mona Rudao's eldest son, Dadao, was at the forefront of the killing, propelled to action by his fear of reprisals for the assault on the police officer. His brother Bassao, who had come to his aid in the original incident, was reputed to be particularly keen on displays of manly violence, in the hope that acting like a traditional, head-hunting Seediq would impress his new love interest. Nor was it lost on the authorities that the Musha elementary school itself had been a flashpoint of tensions, after local tribesmen had been drafted into the arduous and underpaid task, not only of 'cutting down the trees that saw their ancestors', but of carrying lumber through the forests for the construction of its new dormitory. Moreover, there were manpower issues, lax discipline, and petty crime among the local authorities, and the prospect that two indigenous police officers who committed suicide had done so to conceal their foreknowledge of their relatives' plans.[34]

In response, the authorities mobilised 1,303 Japanese soldiers, alongside tribal auxiliaries deliberately recruited from the Tgdaya people's neighbours and sometime rivals, the Truku Seediq and Toda Seediq. The campaign verged on the genocidal, with planes overhead dropping experimental incendiary bombs and spraying mustard gas into the forests. By the end of the first wave of the campaign, half the people of the six villages were dead, including Mona Rudao himself, who committed suicide along with many of his men. The survivors were corralled into two 'detention centres' where, six months later, the unarmed men, women, and children therein were massacred by Toda tribesmen armed with guns. Japanese officers, who had suspiciously looked the other way during the assault, returned for a photo opportunity when the grisly work was done, posing in front of a mound of 101 severed heads. A mere 293 people survived from the six villages held culpable. They were moved off their land and resettled 40 km away as farmers, far from their ancestral homeland.

There was a suggestion, muddied by later fictionalised accounts of the incident, that Mona Rudao's massacre of the Japanese was intended as the first step in a suicidal guerrilla campaign, reframing his actions as those of a type of apocalyptic cult, bestowing one last chance for emasculated Seediq men to hunt heads and thereby gain the right to cross the 'Rainbow Bridge' when they died, attaining a paradise that would otherwise be denied to them. The Musha Incident has become a touchstone of indigenous Formosan history, celebrated in the 21st century as an early assertion of Formosan resistance and pride. It also remains highly problematic. Among multiple quibbles and queries about the events at hand, it is notable that Mona Rudao, who is celebrated with a statue today, was previously a collaborator with the Japanese, participating in a campaign against *other* Atayal in 1920. He was, in fact, a respected figure among his people precisely because he had the necessary livestock to provide banquets after hunting expeditions, a form of wealth he had acquired by working for the Japanese.[35]

Nor is the incident universally valued among Formosans. Mona Rudao is not regarded as a hero among the Toda and the Truku, because acknowledging him as such would require them to also acknowledge their own communities' complicity in the massacre of the surviving Tgdaya.[36]

Back in Japan, the incident was a colonial embarrassment, with only the most desultory of medals handed out for what was regarded as a regrettable mop-up operation rather than a war. In a cryptic comment appended to his 1931 article on the incident, the Japanese officer Hattori Heijirō wrote that he hoped that the 'next time' the Seediq fought, it would be on the side of the Japanese.[37]

•

With the rise of radio and the phonogram, recorded music began to form a part of the wallpaper of Taiwanese life. One of the first acknowledged hits in Taiwanese popular music was 'Embrace the Spring Breeze' (*Wang Chun Feng*, 1933):

> Wishing he could be my groom
> But hiding my love in my heart
> Waiting for the day he comes to pick
> The flower of youth in full bloom.[38]

Listeners were soon ready to hear a subversive message in a song that was purportedly about a lonely young girl thinking about unrequited love. The promise of spring after the harsh conditions of winter came to be a metaphor for a different Taiwan, a coded message of hope for a Taiwan without the Japanese, and in later generations, a song of gentle protest against Taiwan's new masters.[39]

A more obvious protest song, the first to be banned by the Japanese administration, was 'Unemployed Brothers' (*Shiye Xiongdi*, 1934), which presented everyday life not as a glorious colonial paradise, but as a ramshackle slum, from which the colonial authorities squeezed all the resources, manpower, and money they could:

> The economy gets worse every day and my feelings sink along with it.
> The boss isn't making money, and now we're laid off. *Ai-yo! Ai-yo!*
> We're brothers with no road to follow.
> It's not because our fate is cruel.
> So hating the gods is unfair.[40]

Some of the 'unemployed brothers' of Taiwan were being put to work in the service of Japanese imperialism overseas. The acquisition of Taiwan in 1895 had also presented the Japanese with literally millions of new subjects, fluent in at least one form of Chinese. Some of these were soon put to work on the mainland as Japanese agents, exploiting the extraterritoriality to which Japan was entitled under its treaties with China, to indulge in illegal activities, including the sale of opium, but also sedition and espionage.[41]

On the mainland, the struggles of the Republic of China and its Communist rivals had been suspended to deal with a new threat. Having acquired Taiwan in 1895 and Korea in 1910, the Japanese empire was extending its reach further onto the Asian mainland, setting up puppet states and staking territorial claims in Inner Mongolia and north China. By 1937, the Japanese army was carving out new territory for itself in Shanghai and along the Yangtze River, in an ill-advised campaign that Emperor Hirohito had been promised would only last three months. In fact, this undeclared Sino-Japanese War would drag on for another eight years, eventually segueing into World War II in the Pacific. The Japanese empire, and its Taiwan province with it, grew ever more militaristic and authoritarian, devoted to a total war effort that would ultimately consume the country.[42]

As the war in East Asia came to occupy increasing attention in Japanese industry and media, the Taiwanese were exhorted to support the troops on the home front. One song suggested that even the Taiwanese indigenous peoples were integral to the war effort, valorising them in 'From a Native Warrior' (*Kyōdo no Butai Yūshi kara*, 1939):

On the sentry line of a moonlit camp
Across the sea under a distant night sky
My homeland, luxuriant with coconut leaves
Is recalled in my eyes.

Heroes trained on the island
Are high in spirit and full of vigour.
They are used to landing in the face of the enemy.
With high morale they march long rivers and a thousand miles.

In 1941, Japan escalated the war by mounting a pre-emptive strike on Pearl Harbor in Hawaii. The coded command to commence the surprise attack was 'Climb Mount Niitaka' — a reference to the tallest mountain in Taiwan and the Japanese empire.

Before long, the Japanese military were also retooling the most popular songs with new lyrics to support the war. 'Flowers on a Rainy Night' was converted into a song of praise to workers in military support industries. 'Embrace the Spring Breeze', in the hands of the Japanese propaganda office, became 'Call of the Earth' (*Daichi wa Maneku*, 1941). Instead of a heartsick girl thinking about boys, the singer was transformed into a farmer intent on ploughing everything he could find.

Asia's cold and wintry wind
Has stopped unnoticed.
Looking up, as the five-coloured flag shines in the sun
Fluttering high in the blue sky.

Look at our power burgeoning out
Across the endless earth.
When we take up a hoe in the green field
It carves a happy smile in the soil.

Because I am a young man
Born in this growing country
I shall devote my body to the country; now let's go
The earth is calling and the spirit is high.[43]

By 1942, the military authorities had started rounding up indigenous youths to form the core of the Takasago Volunteers, eight companies of special forces, trained in jungle warfare for use in Japan's war effort across South-East Asia. The total number of indigenous men drafted into the Volunteers would ultimately be around 8,000 of a total indigenous population of 200,000.[44]

Indigenous Taiwanese soldiers in the Takasago Volunteer Corps,
a highly decorated unit of the Imperial Japanese Army.

Few of them would return. Many found themselves at the front line of Japan's efforts to hold off the Allied counter-offensive, and the clandestine nature of their activities, coupled with the post-war stigma of having serviced in the Japanese military, often left their stories redacted. Every now and then, there would be a mention in dispatches, such as one delivered by a major in New Guinea shortly before his base was overrun:

> Yamamoto praised the Takasago's expertise in jungle combat, their great spiritual strength, their fine-tuned sense of hearing and sight, their alertness in detecting enemy movements and airplanes, and their sharpshooting skills ... It is no exaggeration to say that only the Takasago soldiers maintained their fighting strength.[45]

Among the 23,000 Taiwanese who served alongside the Japanese army during the war, Takasago Volunteers were valued much more highly by the Japanese military than those of Chinese origin, who were written off as 'untrustworthy'. Repeatedly in Japanese accounts of Takasago fighters in New Guinea and the Philippines, there is a sense that they are pinnacles of fighting men. One officer wrote:

> When I was first appointed to instruct the Takasago soldiers, I was a little apprehensive. But when I actually saw them, I found out their skin colour was also fair, their features good-looking, and they didn't waste time on idle conversations. Their hearts were ablaze with the ... spirit of patriotism and loyalty to the Emperor. In this, they were much superior to new recruits from Japan itself.[46]

Used to jungle survival, the Takasago Volunteers saved many Japanese lives, partly through their ability not only to find food in troubled times, but to work out which unfamiliar plants were edible. 'When we trapped birds,' wrote the Atayal marine Pawan Taimo, 'we would always examine the food inside their stomachs. Plants edible to birds are equally safe for humans.'[47]

Famously, the last of the Takasago Volunteers did not return home until 1974, when Attun Palalin, an old hermit living in a hut on Morotai Island, was persuaded to give himself up to the authorities. Although the media assigned him names in both Chinese and Japanese, he was an Amis tribesman by birth, who doggedly refused to accept the news of Japan's surrender. He would ultimately return to a Taiwan somewhat embarrassed to receive him, as he was a reminder of a colonial past that Taiwan had spent many decades trying to erase.

Attun Palalin aside, the official last hurrah of the Takasago Volunteers was at Leyte, when a suicide squad was crash-landed onto the American airstrip in an attempt to destroy the facility. But despite assurances to the contrary, the Allied counter-attack was already closing in on the Japanese empire.

In 1944, to rustle up a bit of divine support, the Japanese authorities officially enshrined the Sun Goddess Amaterasu in Taipei's Grand Shrine. Plans were afoot to give the entire complex a substantial makeover, and building materials were brought on site to upgrade the shrine itself, as well as its distinctive gates, stone lanterns, and sundry decorations. It was hence doubly damaging when a plane crashed into the side of the mountain in October 1944, not only wrecking the shrine, but destroying much of the carefully acquired materials. The site would remain in ruins for the rest of the war, as the authorities had other priorities.

Hatta Yōichi, the architect of the grand irrigation schemes that had transformed Taiwan, was killed at sea when the ship he was travelling on, the *Taiyō Maru*, was torpedoed by the submarine USS *Grenadier*. His body drifted for a week in the sea before it was picked up and identified from his clothes and personal effects, the skeleton having been picked clean by fish in the interim.

On 15 August 1945, on hearing the news of the Japanese surrender, Hatta's widow, Toyoki, walked in heavy rains to the spillway of the Wushantou Dam. There, she took off her shoes, placed them neatly on the concrete siding, and threw herself into the flood-waters.[48]

CHAPTER EIGHT

THE LAW OF SQUEEZE

Taiwan within the Republic of China (1945–1950)

On the mainland, the Republic of China was in the hands of Generalissimo Chiang Kai-shek, the former lieutenant of the late president Sun Yat-sen and the architect of a prolonged military campaign that had wrested north China from warlord control and strengthened the notion of a single Chinese republic.

The young Chiang had been a product of China's self-doubt over modernisation, packed off to study in Japan in 1906 as part of the generation that sought to learn from the enemy in order to prevent any further embarrassments like the seizure of Taiwan. He was fast-tracked into the leadership of what was then called the Chinese Revolutionary Party in 1916, after his predecessor was killed by a northern warlord. Thereafter he walked a difficult line between military necessity and dirty politics, remaining a powerful figure in the Nationalist Party (the Kuomintang, or KMT) through his control of the military.

He had been instrumental in the ongoing war against the Japanese invaders, but also a passionate enemy of the rising Communist Party, and was responsible for a 1927 massacre of Communist sympathisers in Shanghai that would return to haunt him. Through the 1930s, he led the Republic of China as it struggled against both Japanese invaders and a lookalike upstart, the 'Reorganised National Government of the Republic of China', which was actually a Japanese collaborationist regime based in Shanghai.

In 1941, when Japan attacked Pearl Harbor, it dragged the United States into the war in Asia that Chiang had been fighting for the previous decade. Even as the fires were still burning in Pearl Harbor, and corpses pulled from capsized American vessels, Chiang danced for joy in his residence, putting on a gramophone record of 'Ave Maria' and thanking the Lord for such a timely intervention.[1]

Pearl Harbor transformed Chiang's China from a beleaguered Asian state into the front line of the Allied world war against Nazism and Fascism. Allied aid bolstered his ongoing war effort against the Japanese, while his new backers enthusiastically hoped that he would also win out against the Communists, turning China into a great new hope for democracy, capitalism, and Christianity.

This, however, was only part of the story. Chiang's Republic of China was losing the war on the ground, while the Communists enjoyed increasing support at a grassroots level. Hobbled by ties to organised crime and smuggling, not to mention decades of struggle and deprivation, the Republic of China was riddled with corruption and graft. Chiang continued to present himself to the international community as a statesman and sympathiser, although not everybody saw him this way.

When Chiang arrived in Cairo in 1943 for a fateful conference between the Allied powers, a British general described him as a 'ferret ... Evidently with no grasp of war in its larger aspect and determined to get the best of the bargain ... a shrewd but small man ... very successful at leading the Americans down the garden path.'[2]

Chiang's greatest ally in this venture was his wife and interpreter Soong May-ling, a wealthy, charismatic heiress whose early education at various American schools allowed her to win over US politicians and the public by addressing them in perfect English. With her flirtatious banter, and cast-iron political will, Soong was the star of the Cairo negotiations, edging her way into photographs of her husband with Winston Churchill and Franklin Roosevelt to effectively double China's apparent weight and presence relative to Britain and the United States. The British general Sir Alan Brooke found her to be 'a queer character in which sex and politics seemed to predominate, both being used indiscriminately, individually or unitedly to achieve her ends'.[3] It was through her that Chiang apparently made his demands — although some claim that more of the ideas came

Chiang Kai-shek, Franklin Roosevelt, and Winston Churchill in Cairo in 1943, along
with Chiang's wife and interpreter, Soong May-ling.

from Soong herself — for the strategy of a counter-assault against Japan
in Asia, and for the policies to be followed after the defeat of Japan.
Notably, Chiang (or Soong) pushed for the Allies to exert a lighter touch
against a defeated Japan, cautioning them that the time had passed for
white men to tell Asians what to do. They also successfully argued for a
policy of post-war restoration of Chinese possessions, sealing the fate of
Taiwan.

At Cairo, the leaders of the Allies agreed among themselves that:

All territories Japan has stolen from the Chinese, such as Manchuria,
Formosa and the Pescadores [Penghu Islands], shall be restored to
China.[4]

This decision might have looked good on paper, but ignored the
context of its handover to Japan in the first place — we might remember
that Japan annexed the island of Taiwan at least in part in reaction to the
admission that only a third of it was under Chinese control, and that in
some cases the Chinese had been glad to be rid of it. George Kerr, who at

the time was a 'Formosa expert' in the American State Department, wrote of a lack of attention to 'the dangers inherent in such unqualified promises to alter boundaries and transfer millions of people from one sovereignty to another without due precaution and reserve'.[5]

With the end of the war in 1945, the Allies chose to ignore any concerns about a 'Formosa Question', preferring to act as if Taiwan had always been a Chinese province, and reattaching it was little more than paperwork.

The news was greeted back in Taiwan with much the same confused reaction as the cession to Japan 1895. Former collaborators with the Japanese regime now frantically asserted their loyalty to the KMT or went into hiding, exuberant nationalists proclaimed their hatred for the departing Japanese, and criminal elements used the regime change as an excuse to settle scores and make powerplays. There was even an abortive movement to proclaim a new Republic of Formosa, in order to keep out the mainlanders.[6]

The general tone of the mass media in the first, heady days, was one of celebration. In Taipei, wrote the author Wu Zhuoliu:

> The whole city seethed with excitement — long-hidden lanterns, garlands and silken banners were brought out, firecrackers exploded endlessly, and Taipei was transformed into a whirl of colour and noise ... Six million islanders fervently hoped to turn their home into an even finer paradise than it had been in Japanese times.[7]

Three decades after the declaration of the Republic of China on the mainland, which had indeed included a delegate for the lost province of Taiwan, the island was finally incorporated within the state. Freed from Japanese restrictions, media figures began to proclaim the best courses of action: an emphasis on learning Mandarin, all the better to interact with the new rulers and fellow citizens, as well as a series of articles and proclamations concerning the Three Principles of the People (*San Min Zhuyi*) — the political philosophy of the Republic of China's first president, Sun Yat-sen. These called for a people's nation, a people's franchise, and a people's life (*Minzu, Minquan, Minsheng*), and even formed the basis of the Republic of China's national anthem:

Three Principles of the People
The foundation of our party
Using this, we establish the Republic
Using this we advance into a state of total peace
Oh you, righteous men
For the people be the vanguard[8]

Sung at mainland public occasions since 1930, 'Three Principles of the People' contained a number of problematic lyrics. Feminists might bristle at the assumption that it only appears to address gentlemen (*shi*), but the bigger political issue was that 'our party' referred to a single political entity, the Kuomintang. The KMT emblem, a ten-pointed star, even formed the top-left field of the flag of the Republic of China. It all seemed to suggest that there could only ever be one party.

Generalissimo Chiang Kai-shek appeared on the surface to be offering new hope to the Taiwanese, announcing in an August 1945 speech:

> If frontier racial groups situated in the regions outside the Provinces have the capacity for self-government and a strong determination to obtain independence — and are politically and economically ready for both — our Government should, in a friendly spirit, voluntarily help them to realise their freedom and forever treat them as brotherly nations and as equals of China.[9]

There were an awful lot of ifs in the statement. It has been cited by Taiwanese secessionists as a demonstration of putative government policy towards the indigenous Formosans, but was more likely to have been intended to put a discreet, positive spin on the looming Mongolian referendum, undertaken at Soviet insistence at the Yalta Conference, and fated to lead to an official declaration of Mongolian independence several weeks later. Chiang's words seemed intended to refer to those parts of China that were annexed during the Qing dynasty's era of 18th-century expansion, not the province of Taiwan, the acquisition of which arguably began that year.

Chiang was busy on the mainland, fighting a Communist insurgence, led among others by a young Mao Zedong, that was soon to break out into open warfare. His delegate to oversee the newly acquired province of Taiwan was a fellow mainlander, Chen Yi, the former governor of Fujian province, whose Japanese schooling and Japanese wife were presumed to be benefits in dealing with the formerly Japanese island. However, he refused to use his fluent Japanese in his dealings with the Taiwan administration, forcing the locals to default to their often-inexpert Mandarin.

Under Chen, a substantial number of the new administrators were 'Half-Mountain People' (*banshanren*), a pejorative term for Taiwanese-born Chinese who had spent the war working on the mainland for the KMT. They were fast-tracked up the promotional ladder for their local knowledge, but dismissed as outsiders by the Taiwanese who had stayed on the island.[10] For the mainlanders' part, the Taiwanese were regarded with suspicion as a bunch of foreigners who had, until only recently, been supporters in some form of the Japanese war effort. The people of Taipei did themselves no favours by rushing out to welcome Chen Yi's triumphant motorcade with enthusiastic shouts of '*Banzai*', the Japanese war cry.[11]

There were frequent expressions of concern that the Taiwanese had been dangerously 'Japanised' (*Ribenhua*) or even 'enslaved' (*nuhua*).[12] The terminology, warned the local newspaper *Minbao*, 'represented the sort of insult that turned the island's people against outsiders'. Other writers went further, actively arguing that China had abandoned Taiwan to its fate in 1895, and that all talk of 'restoring' it to Chinese control was misplaced. After 1895, they argued, the Taiwanese had been left 'with no nation and no family' (*wu guo wu jia*), and they could hardly be 'restored' to an authority that had not existed 50 years earlier.[13]

The activist Peng Ming-min's memoirs give some sense of the surprise and disappointment among many of the Taiwanese as the island was 'saved' from its Japanese masters only for the KMT to be 'pulling us down to the general level of chaotic life in continental Chinese provinces'.[14]

His family's first sense of the new order came in 1945, when his father, a respected local figure in the Chinese community, was approached by the outgoing Japanese administrators and asked to be an interim manager for the handover of power. Inspired by the enthusiastic propaganda leaflets that had been airdropped by Allied planes, he agreed, only to be roped into the logistics of a welcoming committee for the KMT soldiers. The

Kaohsiung townsfolk hung out the bunting and prepared firecrackers and banners, along with a buffet of expensive and perishable foods, only for the ship to be a no-show. It was only on the fourth occasion, with much food wasted amid post-war austerity, that the long-awaited ship finally showed up, to be greeted by a smartly turned-out honour guard of Japanese soldiers, themselves awaiting repatriation.

'The first man to appear,' wrote Peng, 'was a bedraggled fellow, who looked and behaved more like a coolie than a soldier ... Others like him followed, some with shoes, some without. Few had guns.' The battered, careworn mainlanders, many of them 'country conscripts with not the least sign of understanding the welcome arranged for them', seized food at the dockside, ignored the crowd, and stumbled into town, seizing whatever they wanted as if plundering a conquered town. Peng's father was soon called in for a meeting with the officers, who immediately demanded to know how much money was in the local bank vaults. Officers began requisitioning local houses, evicting homeowners to seize the best quarters. Peng's family began to understand that the common soldier was looting on an individual level, while the upper echelons were plundering Taiwan to support the ongoing war effort against the Communists on the mainland, seizing 'foodstocks, scrap metal, machine tools, and consumer goods of every variety, destined for private sales along the China coast'.

'As far as they were concerned,' wrote Peng bitterly about the newly arrived mainlanders, 'the Formosans were a conquered people.'[15]

George Kerr, now a naval attaché, at least had some empathy for the Chinese arrivals:

> We had no reason to be surprised when the ill-disciplined, ill-fed and underpaid men pilfered war-damaged buildings and unguarded private property. They were expected to fend for themselves on Formosa as they did on the mainland, and here they did very well.[16]

Overnight, the Japanese occupiers were reduced to the bottom of the pile, scrabbling for work and scrounging a living. Many became enthusiastic volunteers for the various relief efforts, although others were targeted by vengeful Chinese for reprisals. The status of Taiwan as a former Japanese colony also afforded multiple opportunities for accusations and finger-pointing. 'When a Chinese [mainlander] with some influence wanted a particular property,' wrote Peng, 'he had only to accuse a Formosan of being a collaborationist during the past 50 years of Japanese sovereignty.'[17] In one of the most scandalous enclosures, the Chinese Air Force, annoyed that there was no Japanese Air Force to hand them spoils of war, simply seized control of 'a huge block of urban real estate' near Taipei's Songshan airport, allowing residents 48 hours to flee before all property in the area was forfeit.[18]

Peng's anecdotes of the mainlander arrival, some of which may have been tales that grew taller with the telling, are a catalogue of disasters. He writes of an ignorant bumpkin who thought that water comes magically out of faucets, and that all that is required to make them work is to push them into a wall and turn them on; another who immediately puts his hands up in a barber's shop, mistaking a hair dryer for a pistol. On more than one occasion, Chinese officers were involved in car crashes, having requisitioned a vehicle they were not qualified to drive.

Peng's examples have the ring of comedy sketches, but systemic corruption was no laughing matter. Keen to latch on to local sources of funding, mainlanders flooded the Taiwanese political and business worlds with cronies and family members, pushing unsuitable and often corrupt officials into positions of influence. Peng cites a minister managing a fleet of smuggling junks, a police chief with 40 friends and relatives on his payroll, and a YMCA secretary from Shanghai suddenly rebranded as a suitable man to manage the Taichung Pineapple Company, even though he had never set foot in a pineapple plant before.[19] Similarly, George Kerr reported trash piled high in the streets (the garbage trucks having been commandeered to drive loot to the docks), while the heroic efforts by Taiwanese and Japanese engineers to restore power and communications were thwarted by nightly pilfering by scavengers who stole copper telephone wires and even pipes and plumbing. The squeeze took many forms, including a multi-week programme to extort money from the wealthy of Taipei, whose arms were twisted to donate funds to replace a statue of a prominent Japanese official with a gilded effigy of Generalissimo Chiang Kai-shek.[20]

Time and again in accounts of the post-war Nationalist arrival, there are moments of black humour when the mainlanders are confronted with a Taiwan that is years ahead of their own experience, even in the classroom. Allan Shackleton, a UN industrial-rehabilitation officer sent to oversee the reconstruction of Taiwan, recalled one story about a Chinese schoolteacher, enthusiastically addressing a class with an exercise about counting the number of legs on a chair.

> After suffering this for some time, one bright boy in the class proffered the information that the last lesson they had received was on the subject of quadratic equations. The 'Professor' finding that this was algebra had to admit that he did not know algebra, and retired ...[21]

The new Chinese masters started to wear out their welcome within weeks. Within four months, a more systematic looting began, as the Nationalists proclaimed that anyone who uncovered hoarded supplies would be immune from accusations of criminal damage — a licence to plunder, and an incentive to accuse victims of being black-market entrepreneurs.[22] Within a year, the US State Department was warning its officials that the Taiwanese were angry at a political situation that did not banish the Japanese so much as it restored Taiwan's subaltern, unloved status, attached to a corrupt and inefficient Chinese regime. 'These Formosan appeals,' wrote George Kerr, 'begged the United States to remember that Japan had surrendered Formosa to all the Allies and not to China alone, and that all bore a share of responsibility for what was then taking place.'[23]

There was no choice as there had been in 1895. The 350,000 Japanese on Taiwan, up to half of whom had been born there, were shipped back to a 'homeland' that many of them had never seen. In a particularly cruel touch, biracial married couples were obliged to pick one country for them both. Chinese citizenship was guaranteed to the children of a Chinese mother, but not a Japanese mother.[24] Taiwan also faced a vagrancy problem from those Japanese who could not leave: 800 homeless Ryukyu Islanders camping in ruins or on parkland. They were unable to return to their home on Okinawa, which had been so ruined by the last battles of the war that it was unable to take more refugees. Elsewhere, the deportation of thousands of Japanese smashed huge holes in the island infrastructure, especially where it deprived industries and amenities of engineers. By

1946, the shortage of fertiliser and the decline of agricultural manpower was leading to food shortages. The depletion of the water supply, often through the looting of fixtures that led to continued leaks and drops in pressure across the network, fostered local outbreaks of cholera, malaria, smallpox, and tuberculosis. Meanwhile, four cases of bubonic plague were confirmed on a refugee ship arriving from the mainland.

•

Among the immediate musical hits of the post-war period, several pop songs reflected the melancholy and displacement of the people on Taiwan. 'Come Home Soon' (*Wang Ni Zaogui*, 1946) was widely understood as an allusion to the many Taiwanese still overseas on Japanese military posts, awaiting repatriation, but also, families left behind on the mainland.

> I miss you, alone every day, unable to meet
> Like mandarin ducks and teals in pairs
> From time to time, doubtless they will be parted
> The Cowherd and the Weaver Girl meet but once a year
> What if you are gone, never to return?[25]

In the case of some indigenous people, the lyrics alluded to an even more troublesome issue. When American soldiers reached a mountain police station, abandoned by the Japanese and ignored by the Chinese, they were approached by Atayal women begging them to 'send back the men'. Many of the Takasago Volunteers had been lost in action, in remote locations and desperate situations that left little opportunity for paperwork. However, until an Atayal woman had official confirmation of her husband's death, she was not permitted to remarry.[26]

Those Takasago Volunteers who did make it back alive faced another issue. Some might have been reluctant porters and scouts, but many others had joined the military as genuine patriots, elated at the opportunity to live as 'warriors', in a fashion previously denied them by the colonial administration. Some even expressed their military service as an opportunity to expunge the stain on the indigenous record caused by uprisings such as the Musha Incident. Raised in the colonial education system that had often taught them only Japanese, they returned to their island as defeated collaborators, speaking a language that was itself now forbidden.[27]

Allan Shackleton reported back to the UN on a number of issues that seemed likely to hamper the island's improvement. He found coal mines that had fallen into disrepair, deprived of workers by wartime conscription, damaged by Allied bombing, and then flooded by pumps that had been unmaintained, or lacked electricity. On the Penghu Islands, he witnessed a fishing industry devastated by the wartime requisition of fishing boats, and people driven further into poverty by the removal of crop surpluses to feed hungry mouths on Taiwan itself. He also noted the vicious cycles that made it difficult for reconstruction to get off the ground. It was all very well, he wrote, for the authorities to get a pineapple cannery back online, but its production was still hampered by a number of issues, starting with the fact that farmers under austerity conditions had given up on pineapples in favour of rice.

There were, in addition, not enough cans to go around, owing to a shortage of tin. If 60 per cent of the price of a can of tinned pineapple paid for the tin it came in, then a further 10 per cent of the cost went on the sugar that kept it sweet. However, many sugar-cane growers, who had enjoyed a Japanese government subsidy in the colonial period, gave up on the low returns of sugar-cane plantations when the subsidy disappeared. Like the pineapple farmers, they had switched to the far more lucrative crop of rice, which could be harvested two or three times a year and sold at ever-increasing prices to meet the needs of the vast refugee population. Even if they could be persuaded to go back to sugar cane, wrote Shackleton, the slow-growing crop would take 18 months to reach its first harvest. As a result, one pineapple cannery, reopened with great fanfare in 1946, barely managed to reach two days' worth of its previous output in its first *year* of operation. Nor was there much chance that consumers in war-torn Shanghai, the largest mainland urban export market, could even afford such treats anymore.[28]

Such issues paled in Shackleton's mind before a far greater problem. While the Taiwanese had initially welcomed the Kuomintang as their saviours, many soon came to resent them as corrupt carpet-baggers and robber-barons.

They said that the Japanese regime had been hard and strict, but the law was clearly defined and provided they kept within it, they could go about their business in peace, security and comfort: and the Formosans found the Japanese honest in their dealings. But when the Chinese came from the mainland, a Formosan once remarked, there was no law but the law of 'Squeeze'.[29]

In a bitter joke about the level of corruption in the new administration, Taiwanese talked about needing to pass a 'Five-Part Imperial Exam' to secure government contracts by handing officials particular treasures: gold, cars, positions, houses, and women.[30] Despite the enthusiastic attendance at Mandarin classes by Taiwanese locals, their ability to speak standard Chinese was so rare that even government meetings required interpreters.

Aping their Japanese forerunners, the KMT maintained a strict monopoly on certain commodities in order to generate revenue. This inadvertently led to the most controversial and enduring event in post-war Taiwanese history, when a confrontation over black-market trading escalated into island-wide unrest.

On 27 February 1947, authorities received a tip-off that a boat approaching Tamsui was carrying 50 or more cartons of matches and cigarettes. Six officers from the Monopoly Bureau and four uniformed policemen were dispatched to the scene, but only found five boxes of cigarettes.

Getting a second tip-off, that the missing cigarettes were being off-loaded at the Tianma Tea Store in Taipei, they drove to the new location, took a suspiciously long time over their dinner, and then strolled into the store only to discover no sign of the alleged smugglers. It was then that they noticed Lin Chiang-mai, a 40-year-old widow, selling cigarettes, accompanied by her two young children.[31]

Assuming that she was selling some of the very contraband that they were searching for, they demanded that she hand her stock over. She pleaded with them that she would be unable to eat unless she could keep her legal due — the wording suggests that at least some of her stock was indeed illegal. She grabbed one of the investigators to ask him for mercy, but he struck her on the head with the butt of his pistol. This only angered the gathering crowd, who began shouting at the investigators that they were 'evil pigs' and should give Lin back her cigarettes.

In the struggle that followed, the investigators fled the scene, one of them turning and firing a shot from his pistol, wounding the brother of a known local gangster. The crowd set fire to the investigators' abandoned vehicle, and then went to the police station to demand the execution of the officer who had fired his pistol.

By nine in the evening, the crowd had failed to disperse, and attacked the car of the police chief sent to assess the scene of the original altercation. Demands continued for the immediate and summary execution of the investigators, from a crowd that now began chanting: 'The Taiwanese want revenge now!' and an additional slogan that amounted to a call to arms for any 'real Taiwanese' in the fight against their oppressors.[32]

By the following morning, the altercation had expanded into a riot. The word 'China' was violently erased from several street and shop signs, and a banner was raised in Japanese, proclaiming: 'Down with Military Tyranny'. A mob in front of the Taiping Street police station failed to disperse when the police chief fired his gun into the air, instead rushing the building, beating him up, and smashing the windows.

Reading between the lines of the slogans and news reports, the incident appeared to unite several interest groups — the family and friends of the wounded gangster, a bloc of traders annoyed with the past behaviours of the Monopoly Bureau and its stranglehold on trade, and locals angry at the arrival of the Chinese from the mainland. The Monopoly Bureau's offices were next in the line of fire, attacked at noon on 28 February 1947. A mob beat two officers to death and seriously injured four others, while setting light to the on-site contraband, and dragging office furniture into the street to start bonfires.

By one in the afternoon, the mob had turned into a column of marchers, a group of which seized control of the local radio station. Several were killed by outnumbered police officers, and a new, sinister form of call-and-response arose, in which anyone the crowd encountered was interrogated in Japanese. Anyone who could not respond in kind — which is to say, anyone who failed to pass the shibboleth of being able to speak the island's lingua franca from three years earlier — was assumed to be a Chinese carpet-bagger and beaten up.[33] In a sonic rebellion,

Taiwanese began playing old Japanese songs on record players in the street, the volume turned up as high as it would go.[34]

At Taipei Railway Station, the Shanghai journalist Wang Kang watched from his hotel window:

> Just at that moment, a passenger train had disgorged its passengers. Some of them, Mainlanders, had just emerged from the railway station only to be beaten severely; many were wounded and others killed. They never knew why they were attacked. There were two military men ... quickly surrounded by Taiwanese, who used their fists and rocks to beat them.[35]

The radio broadcasts had the effect of transmitting the unrest further afield, with copycat incidents in Keelung and Banqiao, and before long, in Hsinchu and Taichung. Citing rising rice prices because 'the Mainlanders were eating it all' and demanding 'Let Taiwan rule itself!', the protests spread elsewhere in the island. All along, it was framed by both sides as an assault by Taiwanese locals upon the new arrivals from the mainland who could not speak either Taiwanese or Japanese. In the aftermath, the government was eager to blame Communist agitators, despite evidence that the few genuine Communist participants had been greatly outnumbered by aggrieved Taiwanese.

Amid frenzied meetings and appeals for calm, a group of activists in Taichung began setting up a paramilitary unit, sourcing weapons, and repurposing vehicles for a much more deadly and wide-ranging assault. In Chiayi, protestors threatened to attack the airport unless the police and army surrendered their weapons, leading Governor Chen Yi to telegraph his local officers with the words: 'Fight to the end; troops will arrive soon.'[36]

A Chinese general estimated that around 100 military men had been killed, along with 64 civil servants. Many hundreds more were wounded, but the damage to the local population was substantially higher, with author Wu Zhuoliu noting that the Nationalist police had killed more of the Taiwanese people than wartime Allied bombing raids. Even though most Communists had very likely already fled to the mainland, the frantic search for 'Reds' led to an enduring 'White Terror'. At the height

The Terrifying Inspection, a woodcut by Huang Rong-can depicting the White Terror that followed the February 28 Incident.

of national paranoia, it was even regarded as seditious to publish a book with a red cover.[37]

Reprisals by the Nationalists against alleged insurgents led to multiple killings, as reported by George Kerr:

> One foreigner counted more than thirty bodies — in student uniforms — lying along the roadside east of Taipei; they had their noses and ears slit or hacked off, and many had been castrated. Two students were beheaded near my front gate.[38]

Alluding to the change-over in the Chinese zodiacal year a month earlier, graffiti around Taipei commented: 'Dogs leave; Pigs come' (*gou qu zhu lai*), a pithy summation of local attitudes towards the regime change that has endured in Taiwanese historiography for decades since.[39] Paranoid about Communist infiltration and an anti-KMT fifth column, which were not necessarily the same thing, the Nationalists forcefully put out a message of a single, mandatory, unified purpose for the administration on Taiwan. Paramount in all Taiwanese thought and action, until further notice, was the plan of resisting the Communists and restoring the nation (*fan Gong, fu guo*).[40]

Steven Phillips, in his account of the five years that Taiwan was truly a province within a mainland-based Republic of China, notes that the February 28 (or '228') Incident had a more momentous impact on the Taiwanese than the handover of the island itself two years earlier. The deaths in the uprising, and the subsequent clampdowns and arrests, silenced even the more moderate political opposition, depriving the island of some of its best-educated potential reformers. Thrashing around in search of enemies of the people, Governor Chen Yi not only mounted savage purges of suspected Communists, but banned all Japanese flags, colonial-era memorabilia, and Japanese-language publications, including phonograph records.[41]

In Nanjing in 1948, the newly formed National Assembly passed the *Temporary Provisions Effective During the Period of National Mobilization for Suppression of the Communist Rebellion*, a series of sweeping powers designed to keep China (including Taiwan) under control for as long as it took to arrange a successful counter-attack against the Communists. A garrison command allowed for the institution of martial law on Taiwan, and Chiang Kai-shek and his vice-president were exempted from the usual two-term limit on re-election until the need for the provisions had passed. The plan, at least in the beginning, was that the powers would only be in place for three years. This not only had the effect of placing Taiwan under martial law for the indefinite future, but also locked in the incumbent administrators and policies of Taiwan as a mere province of the Republic. The local administration became top-heavy with superfluous levels of 'national' government, likened by the anti-KMT activist Annette Lu to 'putting a grandmother's old, dilapidated nightgown on a new-born baby — it was just too large, too old, and too worn-out to fit.'[42]

The new governor, the Republic of China's former foreign minister Wei Tao-ming, became so frustrated with the inadequacies of the administration that he even suggested to American diplomats in 1949 that 'Taiwan be severed from the mainland politically, develop its own economy, and welcome American investment and loans'. His proposal, made in secret with General Sun Li-jen, was discreetly put aside by the US Department of State, which remained determined to support

Chiang Kai-shek, and not to encourage factionalism among his underlings.[43]

Among the common people, the mood of the times was summed up in a popular hit that was soon banned by the Nationalists. 'The Broken Net' (*Bu Po Wang*, 1948), as ever, purported to be an innocent song about fishing tackle, but alluded to a state of dilapidation and disaster, and was also a convenient pun on 'lost hope'.

> Looking at the net with reddened eyes
> A great hole is torn through it
> I want to make up for nothing
> Who knows how I have suffered?
> Right now, everything seems hopeless
> Can no-one make this better?

This might have all faded away were it not for the fact that the Nationalists were losing their war on the mainland, overwhelmed by Communist insurgents with ever-growing support in China's vast rural base. Nationalist propaganda continued to define the Communists as 'rebels', but the rebels were soon forming the de facto government in multiple mainland areas.

Many within the KMT could see that the fighting was over. Reassigned after his poor handling of the February 28 Incident, Chen Yi, the former governor of Taiwan, was now in charge of Zhejiang province for the KMT, effectively making him the overlord of the cities of the commercial hubs of Nanjing, Shanghai, and Hangzhou. By November 1948, he appeared to have given up all faith in a KMT victory, and began to make increasingly obvious efforts to placate the Communists, starting with the release of a hundred Communist political prisoners that month. In January 1949, he made plans to defect to the Communist side, but made the mistake of attempting to persuade his garrison commander to come with him. Instead, the commander reported him to the KMT, giving Chiang Kai-shek's son, the ambitious Chiang Ching-kuo, then serving as Shanghai's anti-corruption tsar, the perfect opportunity to make an example of the architect of the February 28 Incident. Chen Yi pleaded in his trial that he had been trying to save Chinese lives from a pointless battle over Zhejiang, but he was indicted as a traitor and executed.[44]

In Taiwan, Chiang Ching-kuo oversaw a ruthless plan to root out moles, spies, and sleeper agents, leading to the purge of over 400 KMT officials. Dozens were executed, the remainder shipped off to the prison on Green Island, off Taiwan's eastern coast, for 're-education'. General Sun Li-jen archly observed to the Americans that while part of the reason was growing paranoia among the KMT, a major contribution to the crackdowns was the presence on Taiwan of huge numbers of evacuated mainland secret police, desperate to look busy.[45]

In April 1949, several members of a KMT delegation, sent to Beijing to negotiate peace terms, including Chiang Kai-shek's personal secretary and one of his most trusted generals, chose to defect to the Communists. So, too, did an entire echelon of 10,000 officer trainees — bolstering the People's Liberation Army, even as it reduced the manpower of the KMT.

Faced with an inevitable Communist victory on the mainland, the Nationalist authorities began to consider a historical precedent. Just as Koxinga and his Ming loyalists had fled to fight another day, they would have to do the same. They eventually did so, along with two million of their followers, cramming the island of Taiwan with a huge influx of hungry refugees.

The evacuation of the Nationalists from the mainland was a remarkable achievement, but came at a heavy cost. Determined to misdirect as many Communist forces as possible, Chiang Kai-shek gave the impression that he was planning to evacuate to Fujian, the south-eastern province that faced Taiwan across the Taiwan Strait, edged with a half-moon of mountains that created a natural fortress. To do so, he sent some of his evacuees in the wrong direction, in the vague hope that they could be rescued later. There were also some strange priorities among the materials that made their way to Taiwan. Even though thousands of soldiers and their families, as well as countless warehouses of military hardware failed to make it to Taipei, there was somehow space in the evacuation ships for the treasures of the National Palace Museum, along with much of the gold from the national bank and a chest full of jewellery confiscated from supposed Shanghai fifth columnists.

Chiang Ching-kuo personally oversaw the transport of the first hundred crates of treasures from the Palace Museum. Ships took the artefacts onboard at Chongqing, and then steamed straight down the Yangtze, without stopping at Shanghai — a measure to limit the chances of any third parties discovering what was on the vessels and where they were going, as the two answers to those questions would give away the Generalissimo's plans.

The younger Chiang did stop in Shanghai himself, where he oversaw the removal of the Central Bank's remaining holdings of foreign currency, gold bullion, and silver coins. The nature of this cargo could not be hidden, but Chiang still tried to confuse the enemy by sending the material to a number of staging posts before heading for its final destination, all the better to keep the Communists guessing about the site of the next planned KMT stronghold.

Before he quit Nanjing for good, he burned his papers and documents, throwing a stack of unused invitation cards onto the bonfire. A Communist informer reported that he had asked Chiang why he was destroying something that had not been written on.

'We will not be inviting people to dinner,' he replied.[46]

On 1 October 1949, far away in Beijing, Chairman Mao Zedong stood on the balcony of Tiananmen, the Gate of Heavenly Peace, and proclaimed to a cheering crowd that China was now a People's Republic. The banished Republic of China, he argued, had served its Marxist purpose as an intermediate, bourgeois stage in the evolution of the state, but the Communist utopia was now fated to arrive. A band played the new national anthem, and soldiers unfurled the new flag, an all-red field, dotted with five yellow stars. As they did so, the last of the Nationalist refugees who had the means were piling onto boats and planes in the south and running for Taiwan. Chiang Kai-shek himself took the old Japanese Governor-General's residence as his new office. 'Like a beached hermit crab,' observed Peng Ming-min, 'he had appropriated someone else's shell for his own.'[47]

Chiang Kai-shek's wife, Soong May-ling, reacted to the news with pious anger. 'How can God allow anything so wicked to happen?' she wrote in a stirring article for *The New York Times*, deliberately intended to whip up the American readership into anti-Communist fervour. 'How can He allow the Communists to overrun the mainland. Doesn't He know they are His enemies?' Soong had spent the previous year in the United States, but announced on US radio that she was choosing to fly to Taiwan to be with her husband and 'my people on the island of Formosa, the fortress of our hopes, the citadel of our battle against an alien power which is ravaging our country'.[48]

The 'Temporary Provisions' on Taiwan, suspending the constitution, freezing most government appointments, and imposing martial law, would remain in place until 1991.

CHAPTER NINE

COLD PEACE

The Kuomintang in Exile (1950–1979)

If divine intervention were possible, Chiang Kai-shek received it in 1950, when the outbreak of the Korean War transformed both American and Chinese priorities in East Asia. With the global superpowers focused on a proxy war in north-east Asia, any confrontation over Taiwan was gradually edged out of priorities — most obviously in the removal of many divisions of Chinese soldiers from Fujian (where they were arguably amassing to attack Taiwan), sent north to Korea to deal with more pressing matters. For the United States, Taiwan achieved a new, tantalising prospect of becoming an 'unsinkable aircraft carrier' on the eastern edge of Asia. However, this would require the United States and its allies to bolster the claims of Chiang Kai-shek's regime to represent *all* of China, not merely an island off its coast. For the next three decades, Taipei would occupy the China seat on the UN Security Council, even though the mainland was clearly run out of Beijing. For the rest of his life, Chiang Kai-shek needed to maintain the image, real or imagined, of being the man who was just about to take China back. For as long as that seemed to be the case, the United States could argue that a free and democratic regime was on the verge of reasserting itself in China as a whole ... by invading it.

'This flawed policy,' writes George Kerr of the US approach, 'asked the world to recognize Formosa as "Free China" when, throughout the decades, the island remained a police state.'[1] The KMT remained the only legal political party on Taiwan — it remained possible for non-KMT officials to run for office, as indeed some did, but they were not permitted to do so as part of a rival organisation. There was only the KMT, and the *not*-KMT, termed *Dangwai* ('outside the Party') in Chinese. Over the years, *Dangwai* came to be a catch-all term for the political forces that would eventually coalesce into a true opposition.

Chiang would be the Generalissimo in charge of Taiwan, in some form or another, until his death in 1975. Despite this, I find it telling that Jonathan Fenby's magisterial biography of Chiang does not dedicate a chapter to those 25 final years of his life, relegating them to an epilogue. With understandable marshalling of resources, Fenby devotes his first five chapters to Chiang's youth, five more to Chiang's political heyday in the late 1920s, five more to his decade in Nanjing, six more to the war, and three to the loss of the mainland and his flight to Taiwan. A straightforward page-count suggests that a historian's assessment of Chiang finds him of relevance between 1926 and 1944, and that all the rest, including his 25 years as the ruler of Taiwan, is little more than a footnote.[2]

Chiang's Republic of China (ROC) continued to dwindle. His soldiers in the south-west retreated across the border into Burma and Thailand, where they subsisted in remote jungles. His supporters on Hainan Island fled ahead of a Chinese amphibious landing in late April 1950. Before long, the 'Republic of China' constituted Taiwan itself and its outlying islands, as well as a scattering of islands just off the shore of Fujian, of which the largest were Matsu (Nangan) and the Kinmen islands (Quemoy), within artillery range of the mainland. Across the Taiwan Strait, the mainland was now the People's Republic of China (PRC). Thereafter, the KMT refused to recognise it, characterising the regime as little more than Communist bandits in temporary control. The first set of foreign states to recognise the PRC were all Communist allies — the Soviet Union and its satellites in 1949. However, in 1950, other states started to shift their definition of China's legitimate government to Beijing, including the United Kingdom, India, Pakistan, Switzerland, and Finland. When Israel jumped on the bandwagon, the KMT vengefully expunged it from locally printed maps.

•

In 1954, with the distraction of the Korean War finally over, the several dozen islands and islets in the Taiwan Strait became a flashpoint of the First Taiwan Strait Crisis, when the People's Liberation Army captured two of them, and prepared to land troops on the over-garrisoned Matsu and the Kinmen islands. Backed, it has been suggested, by threats of nuclear intervention from both the United States and the Soviet Union, the crisis lessened in 1955, only to flare up a second time in 1958. On both occasions, it might be productively envisaged in relation to issues *within* the People's Republic, as its government first lost its support from the Soviet Union, and then turned on itself in a series of purges. For both sides, the presence of ongoing 'hostilities' over Matsu and Quemoy would often make for a handy distraction from domestic issues. Thereafter, the ongoing and never-quite-finished war over Matsu and the Kinmen islands took on a performative component, with each side carefully warning the other of the next coming salvo, and only shelling each other on alternate days, often with little more than propaganda leaflets.[3]

If the stalemate on Matsu and the Kinmen islands seemed oddly theatrical, that could have been because it was a mere placeholder for the resumption of real hostilities. In 1957, the political dissident Lei Chen penned an article for *Free China* revealing that retaking the mainland was a physical impossibility without American logistical help, something which would only arrive with literal Armageddon.

> Call it as you may a civil war quite outside foreign intervention, how can the Kuomintang transport their soldiers to the mainland to begin with, without the United States helping them? In short, they are contemplating such an operation at the outbreak of World War III.[4]

Matsu and the Kinmen islands were useful for other reasons. For as long as the PRC and ROC were firing shells at each other, even if only on alternate weekdays by prior agreement, there was still technically a war on, which helped justify Chiang Kai-shek's ongoing State of Emergency and martial law.[5] Moreover, for as long as the ROC had even a toehold on the Fujian coast, the Nationalists could assert that the territory still held by the Republic of China did not merely extend to the island of Taiwan, but also 'parts of Fujian'. The phrasing would occur on multiple documents of the National Assembly over the ensuing decades, as a suggestion that the campaign to retake the mainland was still ongoing, and that elections of the national government involved the participation of more than one province.

In later years, the surviving KMT participants would claim that the long, long period of martial law, and the 'White Terror' that it generated, had been a necessary evil, not only to shield Taiwan from Communist fifth columnists, but to prevent a backlash from the KMT's *far* right. They argued that were it not for the brutal shutdown of all possible dissent, sometimes before it could even happen, paranoia about the challenge to the KMT would have led to far more oppression and deaths.[6]

Despite its wide-ranging impact on island society, the immediate aftermath of the arrival of two million refugees has a fragile historical footprint. In later years, nobody was all that interested in preserving their rows of emergency housing (the 800 *juan cun*, or 'military dependents' villages'), although some of their influence is most obvious in local food traditions. A penchant for 'military food' (*juan cai*) is often manifest in those restaurants and cafés that serve foods from parts of mainland China, including beef noodles and Shandong dumplings, while a substantial Burmese population in Taipei derives from the families of soldiers, many of them of Chinese descent, who fought alongside the KMT in the civil war.[7]

The national mythology favours an image of brave soldiers reluctantly and temporarily conceding their positions, engaging in an orderly tactical withdrawal in order to regroup and prepare for a counter-attack. The reality of the KMT evacuation was understandably far more chaotic, and led to the arrival of a refugee community in Taiwan that was top-heavy with the officer class. Officers were often able to get out with their families and at least some of their fortunes. The lower ranks were less likely to, and Taiwan was flooded with embittered, war-ravaged soldiers, many of whom had been forced to abandon their families on the mainland.

Taiwan already had a reputation for lawlessness and 'informal' business activities, and the turmoil of the end of the war and the evacuation of the KMT to the island led to a new series of tensions. Thousands of families were shoved into 'temporary' accommodation, placing huge strains upon the island infrastructure. Amid such deprivations and a fierce contest over resources, the children of the newcomers often grew up in antagonistic relationships, with many a mainlander street gang claiming to have formed into reaction from bullying by Taiwanese. Between 1961 and 1997, the years in which the children of the 1949 generation reached adulthood, the crime rate in Taiwan tripled.[8]

In a commonly recurring factor in Chinese social history, the nature of the supposed 'black path' (*heidao*) to criminality is fiercely contested, even among those who are purportedly part of it. There is a fine line, particularly for the people involved, between a simple credit union or a martial-arts school, and more sinister elements. As with the various 'secret' societies of the Qing era, many Chinese gangs romanticise themselves as contemporary heroes, cutting through red tape and getting around the strictures of an already-corrupt society, creating an invisible and informal community that serves as a shadow-line of policing, protection, mediation, banking, and (often illegal) services and goods. Defenders have also pointed to an unexpected corollary of strict KMT laws, which is that someone convicted of certain minor offences early in life is forever disqualified from many educational, political, or commercial enterprises, pushing them into the arms of 'brotherhoods' that offer some form of gainful employment. Such a temptation was particularly amplified in a society crammed with exiled mainland menfolk, slowly waking up to the realisation that their cherished desire to return home and see their families was never going to happen.

The integration of the KMT refugees into Taiwanese society was encouraged by some innovative government policies. One of them, the brainchild of Chiang Ching-kuo himself, mandated the compulsory hiring of retired police or military officers into positions on the boards of all major businesses, which in turn helped to head off the ties between certain corporations and organised crime — an association that would grow once more a generation later, covered in the next chapter.

Chiang's appointees could also be found worming their way into the indigenous population, such as the monitors embedded among the Puyuma in the south. They were sent in order to keep an eye on Matreli, a tribal leader whose life was a microcosm of modern Taiwanese history.

Born in Fujian to Han Chinese parents, Matreli had come to Taiwan at the age of four, when his father fled clan violence in their homeland. Adopted by his father's new Puyuma wife, Matreli became a leading figure in the Chulu, the branch of the Puyuma entrusted with an ongoing century-long feud with the neighbouring Bunun people over mastery of the Luye Gaotai hunting grounds.

In his twenties, Matreli was assigned to the Taitung police as an interpreter, and married Salinay, the daughter of the chief of the Chulu Puyuma. Already living a double life — at one point leading an illegal head-hunting expedition against the Bunun and then reporting back at the police station for duty — he resigned from the police force in 1915 at the death of his father-in-law, becoming the chief of the Chulu.

In the first documented case of a full-blooded Han Chinese leading an indigenous Taiwanese tribe, Matreli enjoyed a powerful position between indigenous and Japanese societies. The disputed hunting ground was an important interior access route between the Taitung Plain and the Huadong Rift Valley, and in collaboration with the Japanese, Matreli secured the right to unlimited ammunition, transforming his tribal territorial dispute into an officially sanctioned policing action.

By the 1920s, Matreli was pursuing a peace deal with the Bunun, much to the horror of many of his own tribal elders, suggesting resettlement policies for several clans in contention, and pushing both sides to accept Japanese rule. Eventually, he relinquished the Chulu Puyuma's claim on the hunting grounds, resolving the feud.

With the fall of the Japanese empire in 1945, Matreli briefly became the de facto administrator of Puyuma and Bunun lands, appointing a militia to enforce the rule of law, even to the extent of shooting a disgruntled Japanese officer who attempted to burn down the local arsenal. He similarly took control in 1947 during the February 28 Incident, when Chinese officials fled a local mob, plunging the Puyuma into a small-scale civil conflict under the guise of political unrest. For keeping the peace, he was defamed by Chiang Ching-kuo as a 'bandit leader' and accused of being an agitator and local threat: 'Fifteen peoples, eight races but one leader.' Despite such claims, Matreli was instrumental in pacifying the south on behalf of the KMT, appearing on the local radio to appeal for calm among the indigenous peoples. In the aftermath of the February 28

Incident, he was listed in reports to Chiang Kai-shek's Military Council as one of the 'Eight Great Bandits' of the uprising, and forced to accept KMT political officers at his village for the rest of his life. Instead of bristling at such treatment, Matreli welcomed the government stooges, adopting them into the tribe and finding them local wives.

Reading between the lines, however, Matreli was ever disappointed with KMT rule and policies. Despite touring the island as a figure of reconciliation, he refused the KMT's request to run as mayor of Taitung, pleading old age. He regarded the Japanese era as the heyday of state/tribal relations, and pointedly applied for permission to send his grandson to study in Japan, although this request was refused.[9]

●

The war with the Communists, according to Chiang Kai-shek, was '30 per cent military and 70 per cent political', an attitude which manifested in the foundation of the Political Warfare Cadre School in 1951. Offering degree-level courses in military science and foreign languages, the school's philosophy formed the core of the next generation's political officers. The historian Jay Taylor points out that the media would often behave as if these officers 'mostly organized sports days and handed out doughnuts', but their involvement was far more invasive. In a comparison that would no doubt leave them aghast with horror, Chiang's political cadres operated on very similar lines to their opposite numbers in the Communist Party, assigned to military units as auditors to sniff out dissent, arrange propaganda campaigns (including the airdropping of leaflets over Communist territory), and ensure the maintenance of morale. This last requirement included the administration of war pensions and counselling, but also the management of the KMT's 37 'tea-houses' — military brothels.[10]

For the government-run media thrashing around in search of good news, even corruption and questionable ethics could be turned into human-interest stories. General Sun Li-jun could not evacuate all the men of the KMT army, but did have space on a ship for his three 'military elephants', the last in his possession of the 12 he had acquired from the Japanese in Burma, and which had been used in various construction and engineering efforts. One elephant having died on the crossing, the surviving two were put to work near Kaohsiung, transporting logs at the Fongshan army base.

By 1952, the last surviving elephant was donated to Taipei Zoo, where he enjoyed a long retirement with his newfound mate — not a luxury afforded KMT soldiers who had to leave their families behind on the mainland. Such stories made for better press than the constant paranoia and purges overseen by Chiang Ching-kuo and his secret police. There were, undoubtedly, Communist agents to be rooted out in the fragile post-war territory of Taiwan, but as one CIA agent ruefully observed: 'Ching-kuo got all the Communists but also a lot of others.'[11]

One of the economic casualties of the evacuation had been Civil Air Transport (CAT), the airline formed by Claire Chennault, formerly of the Flying Tigers American Volunteer Group, to supply and transport KMT operations on the mainland. CAT had provided a vital service in the latter days of the civil war, and had been instrumental in many of the most crucial evacuations, but now faced bankruptcy — a fleet of transport aircraft with perilously little to transport. Chennault was persuaded to sell his ailing airline for $950,000 to the organisation that would ultimately be known as the Central Intelligence Agency, thereby leaving the American secret services an entire Taiwan-based air arm, run through various thinly disguised shell companies for the next 20 years.[12] CAT would fly a number of scheduled passenger flights to keep up appearances as an everyday airline, but much of its activities involved surveillance and espionage. In the 1950s, some of its known operations included a famously botched spy extraction from Chinese territory, as well as multiple airdrops to KMT hold-outs in Burma's 'Golden Triangle'. By 1953, CAT planes with fake French insignia would be involved in airdrops to Foreign Legion soldiers hemmed in at Dien Bien Phu in Vietnam. By 1959, the airline had been renamed Air America.

Conveniently offshore, but in range of China, Indochina, and Korea, Taiwan became the CIA's Asian base, and the location of multiple covert operations, including some intriguing special-forces groups: the legendarily undisciplined China Youth Anti-Communist National Salvation Corps, and the 'orphans unit' of 600 children of dead KMT officers, corralled together for guerrilla-warfare training, on the grounds that they would be liable to volunteer for extremely dangerous revenge missions.[13]

The end of the Korean War left the KMT with a new conundrum — 21,000 captured Chinese prisoners of war, held in a camp on the Korean island of Jeju. As Chinese 'Communists', they should technically have been returned to the PRC, although the matter soon became a political hot potato after it became clear that many of them were former KMT soldiers, marooned in China after the evacuation, co-opted into the People's Liberation Army, and then pushed into the front line against the enemy. Still others were Communists with no previous KMT association who asked to be repatriated to the Republic of China instead of the People's Republic. Of these, reasoned the KMT authorities, some were genuine while others were sure to be Communist spies, hoping to reach Taiwan as sleeper agents.

The Jeju camp soon became the site of numerous prisoner conflicts, as the Communist and Nationalist factions among the POWs began revisiting their battlefield enmities on-site. In one incident, Communist POWs even managed to take the American camp commander hostage.[14]

Glad to be rid of them, Chairman Mao agreed that any of the POWs meeting with the approval of an international tribunal were free to leave for Taiwan. KMT cadres coached many of the soldiers on the best ways to answer the questions of the tribunals, leading to many thousands of them being freed from captivity and welcomed 'back' to the Republic of China in a media circus. The more capable and fanatical soldiers among them were soon recruited into the KMT's guerrilla units — indeed, some were soon sent on suicide missions back into Communist territory. Others joined the swelling ranks of KMT veterans on Taiwan, although they remained united by their shared hardships and journeys, leading many to form a new society, the far-right 'Anti-Communist Heroes', who would act as a pro-KMT pressure group and monkey-wrenchers in decades to come.[15]

Another set of tardy refugees in Taiwan arrived in 1953, after the United Nations issued stern complaints about the activities of KMT irregulars in Burma. Not all the KMT had fled China to Taiwan — several thousand soldiers had headed south-west across the border into Burma, where they maintained a guerrilla base, sneaking back to raid the People's

Republic. The presence of this 'Lost Army' (*Gujun*) in the Burmese jungle was a source of some annoyance to the Burmese authorities, not least because they were mixing with the fractious hill tribes of the region, and were funding their operations through the local opium trade.

Eventually, a multinational deal allowed for the evacuation of the rogue troopers, with CAT airlines flying out 5,583 KMT soldiers and their families. This created a whole new set of problems, since some of the 'KMT' soldiers and all their dependents turned out to be people from the Burmese hill tribes. Suspiciously, the evacuees also comprised only 'the very old and the very young', suggesting that despite claims to the contrary, many of the menfolk of the Lost Army had stayed behind to maintain the trade in opium for arms. For many years, the people of the Lost Army, and their dilapidated accommodation in what came to be known as Loyal Village in the Taipei suburbs, were presented as something of an eyesore — a community of drug-addled, unemployed refugee fishes-out-of-water, far from home. This was an image at least partly fostered by their representatives in search of welfare handouts and concessions. In more recent times, Loyal Village has embraced its status as a weird sidebar in the history of the Republic of China, and has rebranded itself as a Thai-Myanmar tourist experience.[16]

Determined to better the experience of diplomats and potential business investors, the KMT improved some of its hospitality, at least for non-Chinese. The Grand Shrine, in a sorry state ever since the 1944 cargo-plane crash, had been further plundered by scavengers in search of building materials. In 1952, the site was repurposed to create the Grand Hotel, a venue designed to host visiting diplomats in ostentatious and conspicuously oriental surroundings. Conceived by the architect Yang Cho-cheng, the hotel was completed in stages, eventually reaching its final, iconic status as one of the world's largest Chinese-style buildings in 1973. It was intended, in part, to impress foreign dignitaries with the Chinese-ness of Taiwan, as was the nearby 'Taipei branch' of the National Palace Museum, a vast edifice in the imperial Chinese style, built to showcase the artefacts shipped away from war-torn China during the Nationalist evacuation. The timing of the opening of the National Palace Museum could not have been better, since it opened its doors in 1965, shortly before the People's Republic was torn apart with the upheavals of the

Cultural Revolution, a nationwide purge that specifically targeted icons of history and culture. Taipei's National Palace Museum was a propaganda coup, proclaiming that Chinese culture was safer in KMT hands. Noting that sometimes the Nationalists seemed to be trying a little too hard, Peng Ming-min wrote that many 'extravagant traditional Chinese folk-customs, so long condemned by the missionaries and discouraged by the Japanese', were being forcefully reinstituted as part of Taiwan's Sinification.[17]

Culture included language. Early policies that allowed for a bit of Taiwanese in public discourse had been walked back after the evacuation. Taiwan, after all, was a province of the Republic of China, and the current site of the ROC government — it was hence a political necessity that the official language should be Mandarin Chinese. By 1956, Mandarin was enforced not only in administration, but in schools. For Taiwan's future vice-president Annette Lu, who spoke Taiwanese Hokkien at home as a child, it was a severe imposition. 'If children were caught speaking Taiwanese in school,' she writes, 'they had to pay a fine, a harsh penalty when most of Taiwan was poor. Even worse, as class leader, I had to enforce this rule when I felt awkward speaking Chinese myself.'[18]

From 1957, Christian missionaries were obliged to use Mandarin, severely restricting their ability to relate to indigenous or rural populations. In 1976, the language directives were applied to radio and TV, heavily favouring a Mandarin media. 'Only two Taiwanese songs could air on TV and radio each day,' writes Annette Lu, 'and there could be no more than two hours of programming in Taiwanese. The rest had to be in standard Chinese.'[19]

Facing intractable restrictions, some of the most enduring forms of dissent slipped into allegory and poetics. Sometimes this was a false rumour, as in the case of 'Green Island Serenade' (*Ludao Xiao Yequ*, 1954),[20] misinterpreted in some circles as a coded reference to lost dissidents locked away in the Green Island prison:

This green island is like a boat swaying in the moonlit night
My love, you are also floating in my heart
Let my song blow open your curtains with the breeze
Let my sincere love flow to you with the flowing water

The long shadow of the coconut tree can't hide my affection
The bright moonlight illuminates my heart even more
The night on this green island is so quiet
My love, why are you still silent?

It has taken decades to unravel the meaning of 'Green Island Serenade'. Long after the death of its author, his daughter pleaded with the media to understand that the lyrics referred simply to the 'green island' on which mainland refugees found themselves living, not the location of Taiwan's toughest prison.

'From a Native Warrior', the old wartime classic, was dusted off and reimagined as a Taiwanese anthem, now evoking the feelings of a military conscript missing his hometown, and retitled 'Mother, I am Still Tough' (*Mama Gua'ia Tsin Iong-kiann*, c. 1960). Although it was eventually banned when its Japanese military origins were exposed, it became part of an entire subgenre of music designed to appeal not only to conscripts far from home, but to the many thousands of migrants who had flocked to the cities to work in Taiwan's vibrant textiles, plastics, and other industries, as the Nationalists pursued ever more ambitious economic Five-Year Plans.[21]

'Hometown in Twilight' (*Hong-hun e Ko-hiong*, 1959) was originally recorded as a Japanese song in 1958, but migrated into a Taiwanese-language version a couple of years later. With a refrain of 'Calling me, Calling me / the hometown at dusk calls me now and then', it might first appear to have been likely to appeal to many a Nationalist in exile. In the wake of the clampdown on the independence movement, it took on new meanings, both for the friends and relations of imprisoned dissidents and for the many activists forced into involuntary exile overseas.

It calls my beaten body, vagabond migratory bird
If loneliness comes to a foreign land
It would miss home every now and then
Today it's calling again, like it's calling me.[22]

Media optics were of vital importance. It was in the authorities' interests to continue to promote the idea that Taiwan was the legendary

'Free China', a beacon of hope for refugees and defectors from a People's Republic that was falling apart at the seams. As part of the narrative, Taiwanese media showcased the arrival of various defectors, after Chiang Kai-shek promised substantial prize money to PRC pilots who would desert to Taiwan along with their planes.

In January 1960, the first high-profile PRC defector arrived in Taiwan in a stolen MiG-15, but having never seen the terrain of Taiwan before, he crashed into a mountainside. This was not quite the propaganda coup that the KMT had hoped for, but was nevertheless spun into proud boasts of a brave martyr and, at the very least, one Communist fighter removed from the roster.

The CIA maintained a covert-operations squadron in Taiwan, established to make airdrops and electronic-surveillance operations over the People's Republic. After various name changes and switches in personnel, it was eventually known as the Black Bats (34th Squadron), its signature insignia featuring the titular animal, overflying the Big Dipper to signify night navigation, its wingtip piercing the red circle of the Iron Curtain. The United States provided aircraft and equipment, while the majority of personnel were sourced from the ROC air force — 148 of whom would be lost in action in the course of the squadron's career. Celebrated today in a memorial hall near its former headquarters in Hsinchu, the squadron's finest hour was the daring Lao Ying (Eagle) #79 reconnaissance mission in 1957, in which a reconnaissance aircraft from the Black Bats left Taiwan to fly a lazy Σ-shape across nine Chinese provinces, before exiting Communist airspace in Shandong in the northeast. Despite 18 defensive sorties by PRC MiG-17 fighter jets, the plane made it home unharmed, with valuable intelligence on the scope of the PRC's radar defence systems. The last mission of the Black Bats before their disbandment was Operation Heavy Tea in 1969, which attempted to drop monitoring devices over the Lop Nur site in Xinjiang, used by China for atomic weapons testing.

The presence of the American guests was not always welcome. There were multiple flashpoints and tensions between Taiwan's Cold War allies and the locals, manifesting in all sorts of small ways, from bar-room brawls to the 'jeep-girl business', in which toughs would throw rocks at any US soldiers seen driving in a vehicle in the company of a local woman.

A visiting US general once famously asked his hosts why they were not celebrating the birthday of George Washington, only to be sternly reminded that: 'We are not a colony yet.'[23]

The worst standoff came in 1957, escalating from an incident in which a US master sergeant, Robert Reynolds, confronted an alleged peeping tom in his yard. Alerted by his wife, Clara, that a man was staring through the bathroom window as she took a shower, Reynolds seized a pistol, and pursued a man as far as the local park. By the time the authorities arrived, the Taiwanese military officer Liu Ziran was dead, and Reynolds was claiming to have shot him in self-defence.

Under American law, in which a man's home was his castle, this could have been a reasonable argument, but in the Republic of China, all violence was criminalised, even if reactive or inadvertent. Reynolds became the subject of a high-profile court-martial, and upon the dismissal of the charges, the focus of a protest outside the US embassy by Liu's aggrieved widow. She justifiably argued that Reynold's acquittal was tantamount to the restoration of extraterritorial rights, which the US had supposedly renounced in 1943. On Friday 24 May, she was joined by a growing crowd of supporters, expanding to a mob of 6,000, that stormed the embassy, tore down the Stars and Stripes, and defiantly raised the flag of the Republic of China.[24]

A group of embassy personnel fled in a slow-motion car chase — frantically pushing their jeep along the road to jump-start it while their driver tried to hotwire it with a pair of pliers and the tinfoil from a cigarette packet. They eventually reached safety, with the mob shouting, 'You kill Chinese, we kill you.'

The 'Black Friday' incident was a low-point in US-ROC relations, leading to the sight of armed guards watching over American children on their school buses, and a plea for calm from Chiang Kai-shek himself. In the years since, it has also become something of a cause célèbre, not only for its illustration of Cold War geopolitics, but also for the accusations, never quite proven, that the embassy attack had been part-orchestrated by Chiang Ching-kuo's secret police, who had paid off some of the agitators, and even helped Liu's widow with her suspiciously bilingual sign.[25]

All the while, Taiwan flourished as a powerhouse of manufacturing, particularly in the sectors that had been noted by US economic consultants as areas in which Taiwan stood a chance of securing an international competitive advantage: plastics, synthetic fibres, and electronic components.[26] Not every American tie-up proceeded to plan. In 1968, Mark Shepherd, the boss of Texas Instruments, visited Taiwan in the hope of setting up a computer chip assembly plant. He was accompanied by Morris Chang, a senior manager of Chinese extraction, who should have helped ease international understanding. Instead, Shepherd was left to bristle when his steak was served with soy sauce, and he veritably exploded when, in his first meeting with Taiwan's economy minister, he was told that intellectual property was something 'imperialists used to bully less-advanced countries'.[27]

Ruffled feathers were soon smoothed, and by 1969 Texas Instruments had built its first chip-assembly plant in Taiwan — one of many foreign companies that turned 'Made in Taiwan' into a common phrase during the economic boom-time of the 1970s. But the arrival of American investments was a veil drawn over the withdrawal of American economic aid, which faded in the mid-1960s. Meanwhile, US university campuses, once training grounds for the civil servants of the KMT government, were fast becoming crucibles of dissidence. The appointment in 1969, for example, of one academic as an economic adviser to Chiang Kai-shek led to an eloquent letter of protest, signed by the 'Concerned Formosans at Cornell'. Playing to the US audience with true flair, it likened the native Taiwanese to the revolutionaries of the American colonies in the 1770s, striving to throw off the yoke of taxation without representation. The KMT, it claimed, were an unelected occupying force without a valid mandate, using the bulk of Taiwan's tax revenue to support an impossible project:

> More than 80 per cent of the national budget is used to maintain the 600,000 troops and at least 300,000 secret police to suppress and intimidate a population of 13 million, 8,000 of whom are political prisoners in 10 concentration camps on the island ... Formosans do not dream of a 'Return to the Mainland'; they are already in their homeland. Why, then, should they be forced to pay for Chiang Kai-shek's fantasy of the 'return'?[28]

The KMT remained paranoid about seditious behaviour, and not always without justification. First published in 1962 during its activist author's exile in Japan, Su Beng's *Taiwan's 400 Year History* now includes a timeline of the nearly four decades of martial law that stretches for 22 eventful pages, including his own plot to murder Chiang Kai-shek, an attempted coup, several armed uprisings, and terrorist attacks on railways and public amenities.[29] In one of the shortest uprisings on record, the commander of an armoured division assembled his men and announced that they and their tanks were about to drive to Taipei to stage a coup, because Chiang Kai-shek was not pursuing the war against Communism aggressively enough. His political adjutant announced his support, marched up to the podium, and then pinned the commander to the ground, ending the 'uprising' in less than two minutes.[30] Peng Ming-min relates another story, possibly apocryphal, of a nervous, sweating graduate about to receive a diploma from Chiang Kai-shek. Reaching into his pocket for his handkerchief, he was shot by jumpy bodyguards who assumed he had a gun.[31]

The Nationalists were just as, if not more, nervous about more-targeted forms of dissidence, arising from the movement that was not yet a movement, defined only by what it was not. If the Nationalist Party was the only game in town, then those who remained outside it could only be described as not-Party: *Dangwai*. A non-Party politician, Henry Gao, ran for election as mayor of Taipei in 1964, a source of considerable embarrassment for the KMT, as he was associated with many independence activists. In order to avoid such an issue in future, the post of mayor was from then on filled by KMT appointment, rather than another inconveniently democratic election.[32]

A group of such activists congregated around Peng Ming-min, who as a legal expert began to draft a 'Declaration of Formosan Self-Salvation' in 1964. This manifesto laid out the many systemic problems tied to the Nationalists' continued assertion of an ongoing war with the People's Republic, particularly in the light of two and a half decades without any sign of the much-promised reconquest of the mainland. But unlike the far-right wing of the KMT, the *Dangwai* activists had no interest in the reconquest actually happening. Instead, they hoped for political reform that would see the minority evacuee population of mainlanders stepping back, shutting down their sham government of faraway provinces, and opening the widely boasted 'Free China' to truly democratic elections.[33]

Aware that any printer would be obliged to report them for subversion, their draft version cunningly substituted a number of keywords, to make it look as if it were an attack on Chairman Mao and the Communists, rather than Generalissimo Chiang Kai-shek and the Nationalists. Peng makes no comment on the Orwellian irony that the two bitter enemies could be so easily switched for one another. After some wrangles with finding a cooperative printer, Peng and his associates eventually hit upon the right ruse: dressing up in military uniforms, speaking only standard Mandarin, and insisting on secrecy because the pamphlets were 'copies of an examination paper that must not be allowed to fall into students' hands'.[34]

Finally, the conspirators were able to substitute their preferred text, with their preferred bugbears, and run off 10,000 copies of their manifesto — only to be arrested by secret policemen who had been tipped off over their suspicious behaviour.

Writers, too, were not spared the attention of the secret police. Reading the works of the author and journalist Bo Yang in the 21st century, his polemics remain ahead of their time — some, in fact, still are. In a rant about Chinese pride, he asked how it was that such a superior civilisation, with 5,000 years of glorious history, could be so roundly battered by Western incursions in the 19th and 20th centuries. How was it that Chinese people did so well abroad, but failed so miserably at home? Maybe, he suggested, it was Chinese culture that was at fault all along? In doing so, he coined the term 'soy-sauce vat culture' (*jianggang wenhua*), in which he likened modern society to a ferment of all that was worst about China, drowning out any intellect or grace.

Unsurprisingly, Bo Yang's policy of trying to annoy absolutely everybody also annoyed the ROC authorities, ending when he was dragged into custody for his inadvisable translation of a *Popeye* cartoon in a local newspaper. Stuck on a desert island with his son Junior, Popeye declares himself president, only for Junior to announce that he will be running against him in the next election, and for Popeye then to issue a veiled threat that he will not tolerate dissent in his 'democracy'. The inadvertent parallels with contemporary Taiwan were obvious enough, but Bo Yang took matters further by swapping Popeye's opening address 'Fellows ...' with the words 'Soldiers and compatriots of our country ...' — a common phrase from the speeches of Chiang Kai-shek.

Bo Yang was arrested in March 1968, and told that he was only being taken away for a brief interrogation. Instead, he was imprisoned for 18 years on the grounds that he was a Communist spy. Even after his sentence was commuted as part of a mass amnesty, the system found a way to keep him locked up, assigning him a new job as a prison officer on Green Island, and thereby not only keeping him in a state of de facto house arrest, but removing him from the official lists of prisoners. It would be another year before he was finally released in 1977, after intervention from Amnesty International and the US government.

Popeye had merely been a pretext; Bo Yang's newspaper editorials had incited government ire for years beforehand. He had, for example, excoriated politicians for applying for a pay rise of up to US$4,000 a month, when the majority of the Chinese they claimed to represent were still trapped on the other side of the Taiwan Strait, looking to the island 'with tears in their eyes'.[35] Bo Yang was similarly fearless in his attitude towards the ROC police force, which he regarded as hypocritically soft on white-collar crime. To tell the truth, Bo Yang could get angry about almost anything. In a righteous appeal to blue-collar readers, he even ridiculed middle-class intellectuals' use of English words as a mark of 'western stooges' (*xi zai*).

The Nationalist authorities, particularly the secret policemen, made life difficult for many a *Dangwai* activist or believer. After pressure was brought to bear by Amnesty International, Peng Ming-min only served 14 months in jail for his pamphleteering, but he was released into a life of constant secret-police surveillance. Peng's escape from Taiwan in 1970 was an elaborate spy game, calling on numerous favours from Amnesty International and politically motivated missionaries, and requiring a careful disguise, as the tall, distinctively featured Peng was also missing an arm — the result of a wartime Japanese bombing raid. He was made up as a hippy guitarist with wild facial hair, his missing arm replaced by a prosthetic in a sling, along with an official story that he had spilled hot soup on it in a Taipei restaurant. His bearded photo was carefully patched into a borrowed Japanese passport, and he checked in at the airport with a shaggy wig and a bulky guitar case. Although there was a tense moment when an official ran out to return papers Peng had left behind in his nervousness, his flight took off for Hong Kong with him on it, and he was able to seek political asylum in Sweden, shortly followed by a long career as a lecturer in the United States.[36]

In an embarrassing epilogue to Peng's escape, it took the Taiwanese authorities three weeks to realise that he had left the country. Peng and his associates had conducted a textbook covert extraction, but they had been helped to a remarkable degree by the incompetence and corruption of the police and Investigation Bureau officers who had been shadowing him. As heads began to roll in a high-level inquiry, it transpired that the police tails had often neglected their duties for weeks or even months at a time. For three weeks after Peng's escape, they continued to submit fraudulent expense invoices, claiming to have still been following him all over Taiwan, in various expensive restaurants and swish hotels, along with several trips to the cinema. The scandal was hushed up to spare the KMT's blushes, but resulted in multiple dismissals and arrests, including of the officers who had most conspicuously threatened Peng, who were now disciplined for pushing him too far. Refusing to believe that a one-armed lawyer could evade the sharpest minds in the Taiwanese security services by dressing up as a hipster, the authorities speculated that he had been spirited out of Taiwan by the CIA.[37]

It was not long before Peng was at the University of Michigan, holding forth on precisely the sort of political issues that the KMT had so desperately tried to silence. He took great pleasure in pointing out that the KMT's hold on power was based on 'government by fiction and government by myth'. It was, he argued, a government that 'represented no one', obviously and violently rejected by everybody on the Chinese mainland, and returned to power by a rigged election in 1947, the results of which had been frozen in time for the decades since, thereby making it highly unlikely that it even represented the will of the people of Taiwan.

It was, he said, clinging to the offshore islands of Matsu and the Kinmen islands in order to maintain a pretence of ongoing war, a 'politics of national emergency' in order to justify the draconian Temporary Provisions. Far from being 'Free China', Peng argued that Taiwan was an authoritarian regime falsely claiming to represent the Republic of China on the world stage, and using this deception to justify an entire echelon of refugee carpet-baggers, including political delegates claiming to have been elected as representatives for Tibet, Outer Mongolia, and Xinjiang, leeching off the people of the sole province they remained in control of, 'to the great detriment of international order'.[38]

Peng's brilliant legal mind, trammelled for so long by the confines of his Taiwanese environment, identified a number of ongoing and convenient myths that the KMT pursued on the world stage in order to shore up its regime. One of these was that Taiwan has been 'and therefore always will be an integral part of China'. His objection to this was based less on his own experience of growing up in a Taiwan that had been part of Japan, than on his understanding of nationhood and ethnicity elsewhere in the world. It was not, he pointed out, compulsory for all English-speaking peoples to be subjects of the British monarch, or for all Anglo-Saxon nations to be part of a single political entity.[39]

Instead, Peng argued that the KMT was swindling the Western powers into cooperating, hoping to guilt-trip them into aiding a Republic of China built on the ruins of foreign imperial aggressions of the preceding century, and offering Chiang Kai-shek's questionable religious affiliations and economic policies as the only reasonable alternative to Communism. It was possible, he argued, to be Chinese in more than one place and of more than one type, and identifying as Chinese did not demand a compulsory acceptance of whatever values were claimed by others. Taiwan was, and had been for centuries, a rebel island.

> Throughout Formosan history, the descendants of Chinese immigrants who settled on this frontier island have struggled constantly to reduce continental Chinese influence in this island's affairs, and even to remove themselves from continental control altogether. This is illustrated in a saying known to all historians in this field: 'Formosa experiences every three years an uprising, every five years a rebellion.'[40]

The United States, which had been instrumental in bolstering Taiwan for 30 years, caved at the beginning of the 1970s. Chiang Kai-shek's son, Chiang Ching-kuo, had an intimation that America was literally no longer a safe haven in 1970, when he escaped an assassination attempt by *Dangwai* activists on a trip to New York.[41]

President Richard Nixon, having swept to power on a ticket that had been partly bankrolled by the strongly pro-ROC overseas Chinese, sold out his supporters by recognising the harsh reality: the Communists were, and had been for some time, the de facto rulers of China, and it would be folly to continue to play along with the fiction that the 'Republic of China' had any realistic claim on the mainland.

In 1971, United Nations General Assembly Resolution 2758 proposed that the People's Republic of China was 'the only legitimate representative of China'. The motion was opposed by a number of countries, including Australia, Brazil, and a scattering of those African republics that had been enjoying the fruits of ROC-funded agricultural programmes, centred around the provision of Hōrai Rice, which continued to work for Taiwan long after it had been created by the Japanese. The United States, which had wanted recognition for the PRC *and* the ROC, voted against the motion, but it passed with significant support. China's permanent seat on the United Nations Security Council was subsequently handed to the People's Republic.

On 27 February 1972, Nixon and his opposite number in the PRC, Premier Zhou Enlai, released the carefully worded Shanghai Communiqué, declaring that the United States 'acknowledges that all Chinese on either side of the Taiwan Strait maintain that there is but one China and that Taiwan is part of China'. For the rest of the decade, the decision would unravel Taiwan's status in the international community, particularly after both Taipei and Beijing began to assert that if there could only be one China, their allies would have to choose. As a matter that would continue to poison international relations for years to come, Nixon also promised to return the Ryukyu Islands to Japanese sovereignty, choosing to throw in a scattering of small rocks at their southernmost extreme, the Diaoyu/Senkaku Islands. Japanese rights to the latter were disputed by both Chinese governments. It was a rare point on which Taipei and Beijing could agree.

If there was only one China, then only one position was available for China on international bodies — not just the United Nations, but any other organisation that wanted the People's Republic to participate.

Taiwan was shut out of everything from the Olympics to the Universal Copyright Convention, the World Health Assembly, Interpol, and the International Civil Aviation Organization.

The news was a great embarrassment to the KMT, but also a critical turning point in what would ultimately be known as both 'Blue' and 'Green' politics — so called because of the blue field behind the Kuomintang's white star emblem, still found in the top-left corner of the flag of the Republic of *China*, versus the predominantly green emblem of the independence-oriented World Taiwanese Congress (formed in 2000), which would depict the island of *Taiwan*, conspicuously all on its own, within a white bar on a green field.

For the KMT, it was a wake-up call to relax its own martial-law provisions and create conditions more suitable to justify its continued claims to be the elected regime in 'Free China'. Some of the quiet reforms would include supplementary elections for the parliamentary bodies that had, until 1972, been stacked with the ageing politicians who took power in the 1940s. It would take more than a decade before all the 'old thieves' (*lao zei*) were removed, but the newer representatives would serve fixed terms and would need to stand for re-election.[42]

For the *Dangwai* opposition, it was a clear indicator that since the rest of the world accepted the PRC as the legitimate government of the rest of China, the long-awaited reclamation of the mainland was not going to happen, and with that in mind, there was little point in maintaining the various legal fictions that kept Taiwan as a one-party state under emergency conditions. There were early murmurs of political dissent, with several activists running for office on the ticket of being simply 'not-KMT'. Failing to be elected in Yilan county in 1975, one further tested the political system by contesting his defeat in the courts.[43]

One of the spin-offs from this gradual, decade-long repositioning was a new empathy in the media for the indigenous peoples of Taiwan, whose voices had been ignored for years in much the same way that Taiwan itself was now being ignored on the international stage. Gao Ziyang, a singer of Puyuma ancestry, wrote lyrics that alluded to the experience of being a second-class citizen, referring to his formative years as one of the 'gypsies of Taiwan' — 'The old days are a dream / A dream that lives in memory / A dream that's still painful.' Born shortly before the implementation of the

Nationalists' Mandarin-education initiative, Gao had grown up in a media environment that denied many aspects of his personal experience — not merely his indigenous background, but references to his 'hometown', and the fact that he would have to leave it if he wanted work, all of which contravened government policy on negative 'blue moods' and 'vulgarity'. He hence appears to have stumbled into political activism simply by writing songs about how he felt.

While assigned to Hsinchu on his compulsory military service, he became involved with a benevolent association that aimed to pool resources in order to help lift indigenous families out of poverty. Several of his songs alluded to the poverty trap in which indigenous people found themselves, and he made the mistake of performing some of them in 1973 at a charity drive.

Gao was implicated in a jackpot of minor crimes in the eyes of the authorities — public assembly and the formation of any private club were both illegal acts under martial law. He was briefly incarcerated, and after his military discharge, he was summoned to the police station under the cruel pretext that his mother had suffered a stroke. Arrested on trumped-up charges of being a gangster, he served three years in prison on Orchid Island. His songs took on a life of their own, despite flirting with further censure by being written in a patois of Puyuma, Taiwanese, Japanese, and Mandarin. Misremembered, perhaps deliberately so, as a 'traditional' song with no known author, his 'We Are Family' (*Women dou shi Yijiaren*, 1973) became a frequent singalong feature of student parties, even in cosmopolitan Taipei:

> Your hometown's in Naruwan / My hometown's in Naruwan
> Once we were one family / We're still all one family
> Hand in hand, arm in arm / Singing from the heart
> Coming together, loving each other
> Because we are one family[44]

Today, the term *Naruwan* is benign and common currency in the Taiwan tourist trade, a local analogue of the Hawaiian *aloha*, deriving from a term in multiple cognate indigenous languages encompassing *welcome*, *community*, and *harmony*. But for Gao to use it in 1973 as some kind of unifying concept, beyond and separate from the nation's compulsory Chinese identity, placed his lyrics on a slippery slope towards indigenous self-determination, and led to his incarceration.

In the mid-1970s, the Nationalists would have preferred that the Republic of China's most popular song was the 'Chiang Kai-shek Memorial Song' (*Jiang Gong Jinian Ge*), a pious anthem celebrating the life of the Generalissimo, who died of a heart attack in 1975 with his dream of retaking the mainland still conspicuously unfulfilled. His nemesis, Chairman Mao, outlived him by 17 months.

Chiang's publicly declared intent to retake China would even affect the treatment of his corpse, the burial of which in Taiwanese soil would have been regarded in some quarters as an admission of defeat. Consequently, the late Generalissimo remained above ground in a black marble sarcophagus, awaiting a day when he might expect to return across the Taiwan Strait to reclaim a modest six feet of earth on the mainland.[45]

Soon after, his government attempted to celebrate him with the memorial anthem, a compulsory component of the school curriculum, its wonderfully tin-eared and overblown lyrics attesting to a Nationalist Party clinging desperately to long-gone glory days:

> President General Chiang, you are the saviour of mankind
> You are the saviour of the whole world
> President General Chiang, you are the lighthouse of freedom
> You are the Great Wall of Democracy
> You eliminated the warlords, fought foreign aggression
> Opposed Communism for righteousness, to seek the renaissance of
>   our race
> General Chiang, General Chiang, your everlasting spirit will forever
>   guide us.
> We shall win against Communism, we shall build the nation
> We shall win against Communism, we shall build the nation

But even Chiang Kai-shek's death was the cause of some political thaws, with his son and heir, Chiang Ching-kuo, announcing a commemorative amnesty and commutation of prison sentences for many dissidents.[46]

Chiang Ching-kuo refused to entertain any overtures from the People's Republic that might have smoothed diplomatic relations. Instead, he threw himself into arms buying, both to bolster the defence of Taiwan and to keep foreign suppliers sweet. Chiang's interest in buying uranium from South Africa kept Taipei's diplomatic relations with Pretoria safe until the fall of apartheid, although his nuclear programme was thwarted by the fact that its leading scientist was a CIA mole. In one embarrassing incident in 1975, his representatives were caught buying 20 forbidden torpedoes from a criminal source in the United States that turned out to be an FBI sting operation. The disgrace was merely the most visible element of a recasting of America not as a staunch ally in the fight against Communism, but as a new battleground for Taiwan's very existence. In the 1970s, clandestine operations by the Republic of China *in* the United States were stepped up, with a huge influx of new agents placed in consulates. Communism was not the only target: as well as espionage conducted against the People's Republic, Chiang's agents kept tabs on *Dangwai* exiles.[47]

Many exiles, however, were returning home to challenge Chiang Ching-kuo directly. In the 1977 local council elections, the KMT crumbled beneath dozens of successful 'non-KMT' candidates, suggesting that grass-roots support was already waning for the Nationalists.[48]

The US president Jimmy Carter delivered Chiang's greatest disappointment late in 1978, announcing that America itself would be switching its diplomatic recognition of the Chinese government from Taipei to Beijing on 1 January 1979. This carried with it an unsettling corollary: if the United States were cutting ties with Taipei, Taipei was also fated to lose its guarantee of US military support by the end of the year, which risked emboldening Beijing even more.

Refusing to buckle under overtures from the People's Republic, Chiang proclaimed the 'Three Noes' that would define the rest of his reign. There would be, he stated, no contact, no compromise, and no negotiation with the Communists.[49]

On Matsu and the Kinmen islands, the relentless alternate-day Chinese bombardment finally ceased. The war between the Republic and the People's Republic was still not officially over, but the People's Republic clearly believed it had already won.

CHAPTER TEN

BLACK GOLD AND WILD LILIES

The Advent of Democracy (1979–2000)

Unable to cause trouble without reprisals in the territory of the Republic of China itself, *Dangwai* activists found some cunning means of doing so overseas. In February 1979, a delegation of ageing indigenous Formosans arrived at the Yasukuni Shrine in Tokyo. A priestly staff member welcomed them effusively, and reminisced about the days when the Takasago Volunteers were some of the fiercest and most loyal troops of the Japanese Emperor. He rattled on for a while, handing out shrine souvenirs, until an old lady interrupted him, and asked if she could have her late husband's spirit back. She was Chiwas-tari, a widow who had lived for 30 years without acknowledgement or reparation for her husband's service in the Japanese Imperial Army. She did not want his spirit to be held prisoner in a foreign city anymore, she said, a thousand miles away from his true home. Surely, she asked, he had given enough to Japan, and she should be allowed to take home his soul?[1]

Whether she knew it or not, Chiwas-tari was demanding a divine impossibility. The Yasukuni Shrine has long claimed that once a soul is enshrined in its precincts, it mixes up with all the other souls and cannot be extracted, which is, incidentally, the official reason why the venue is unable to remove any of the Class-A war criminals who also reside there in spirit.[2]

The Yasukuni stunt might have been heartfelt, but also played into the kind of dog-whistle politics that was on the rise back on Taiwan. It formed a tacit invitation to politicians in Taipei to come out in support of the indigenous people's grievances, marking the beginning of a long, slow rise in attention to indigenous issues in the Taiwanese government. Many Taiwanese dissidents had come to realise that the one-party monolith of the KMT cloaked a number of internal factional disputes, including the presence of KMT members who were quietly supportive of reform.[3] Yu Deng-fa, a former magistrate in Kaohsiung, was arrested alongside his son on vague charges of associating with suspected troublemakers. Yu was no independence advocate — he was a staunch opponent of Taiwanese independence — but he had a habit of slapping down KMT actions where they appeared to contravene its own laws. Believing that Yu was being targeted for making life difficult for the KMT, *Dangwai* sympathisers organised a protest against his arrest in Kaohsiung, thereby breaking the KMT's martial-law proscriptions on public assembly. One of the participants, a Taoyuan country magistrate, was himself suspended from his post as a result.

Such protests ran concurrently with the KMT's supposed relaxation of rules against free speech, which *Dangwai* activists tested with the publication of *Formosa Magazine*, dedicated to 'promotion of a new generation's political movements'. Pointedly, the magazine's title ignored the word *Taiwan*, itself a Chinese imposition, and the KMT concept of the 'Republic of China', utilising instead a word from the days before the arrival of mass mainland emigration.[4]

Its first issue boldly pointed to the elephant in the room — the withdrawal of American diplomatic recognition, which 'announced the bankruptcy of the KMT government's policy for the last thirty years'. Its third issue flirted with controversy by simply pointing out the obvious: that the '*waisheng*' mainland refugees and their families constituted a mere 12 per cent of the Taiwanese people, but constantly dragged the island's politics towards mainland issues.[5]

Before long, the magazine had established several 'service centres' around the island, officially for administrating distribution and sales, but also functioning as political salons and meeting places. It had become, in the words of one of its founders, Shih Ming-te, 'a political party in all but name'. Shih had only been out of prison for a few years, a previous life sentence having been commuted after 15 years as part of Chiang Ching-kuo's attempts to foster a more cordial rule. Among the magazine staff, Shih cultivated the nickname Nori. Based on the Japanese pronunciation of the last syllable of his Chinese name, it became a watchword among activists, and a provocation to *waisheng* supporters since it reminded them of Taiwan's non-KMT past.

The magazine's launch party at Taipei's Mandarin Hotel was a clear indicator of the shape of things to come, attended as it was by a jeering mob of KMT stooges, throwing fruit peel and rocks, and chanting obscenities about prominent activists. This failed to put off the readership — the 25,000-copy print run of the first issue sold out, and the second issue would sell out a print run four times the size.

The KMT attempted to shut down *Formosa Magazine* after the publication of its second issue, on the spurious grounds that one of its articles had offended the South Korean ambassador. Armed wreckers attacked the publisher's office and the Kaohsiung service centre. At the Pingtung service centre, the site of a planned 'Formosa Night', six men with swords and axes smashed up the furniture, destroyed the phones, and briefly held the staff hostage at gunpoint. Undeterred, *Formosa Magazine* staff held their event at a new venue, where it was packed out by curious members of the public.

Twice refused permission to hold an event on UN Human Rights Day, the Kaohsiung service centre went ahead anyway, sending loudspeaker trucks through the street to advertise a meeting. It was a calculated provocation, designed to establish that the KMT's 'Free China' was a lie, and led to confrontations with the police. The trucks were stopped, the tapes confiscated, and one of the drivers broke two of his teeth when he 'hit his head against the stairs' while being taken into custody.

The stand escalated into the 'Kaohsiung Incident' of 10 December 1979, when riot police attempted to blockade 200 activists determined to mark Human Rights Day outside the magazine's local office. They kettled the activists outside the local railway station, and fighting broke out — reports remain varied as to who started it, although it is worth remarking that even those who claim the protestors started it were surprised at how many of the brawling 'activists' seemed to have military crew cuts, as if planted among the crowd to cause trouble.

Fourteen activists were imprisoned, and *Formosa Magazine* had its publishing licence revoked. Shih Ming-te was eventually apprehended in January 1980, having evaded the police for a month, partly thanks to amateur plastic surgery performed on him by a sympathetic dentist. He was sentenced to life imprisonment for a second time. Among the suspects rounded up and held without charge for two months was one Lin Yi-hsiung, whose wounds acquired while in custody led his wife to contact Amnesty International. In apparent retaliation for this contact with outsiders, alleged gangsters raided his family property while his wife was attending the Amnesty International hearing — they killed his mother-in-law and the couple's six-year-old twin daughters, leaving a third daughter seriously injured. The attackers somehow got away with it, even though the Lin home was supposed to be under 24-hour police surveillance.

Support for the movement was readily apparent from the high sales of the magazine, and from the various ways that the activists were attracting new members. Chen Shui-bian, a 29-year-old lawyer, defended the dissidents in court, and would subsequently run for public office, becoming a *Dangwai* member of Taipei city council the following year.

The incident was also associated with a number of popular songs — Chiu Chue-chen, appointed by Annette Lu as 'the official *Dangwai* bard', had serenaded the protestors with the golden oldie 'Embracing the Spring Breeze', and 'The Broken Net', the latter now blended with another song to form 'Love Taiwan Our Homeland' (*Ai Taiwan Zan de Xiangtu*), which spoke of the island 'cultivated by our hard-working grandfathers'.[6]

He also used the event as an underhand album launch for his *Songs of Taiwan*, which framed a number of traditional songs in a manner that the Nationalist authorities regarded as criminally provocative. His fate, and those of others like him, led to a new and pointed nuance in the 1940s song 'Come Home Soon', now frequently sung at public events by relatives and family members of *Dangwai* dissidents serving time.[7]

The Kaohsiung Incident and the trial arising from it became an incubator of dissent and activism — two of its most prominent participants would ultimately become the president and vice-president of Taiwan a generation later. Annette Lu observed that the activists' plight attracted the attention of the world's media, and their suffering under interrogation in custody, while initially suppressed by the Taiwanese media, became a matter of public record when brought up in court.

While the trial of the participants in the Kaohsiung Incident became the centre of a media and cultural storm, the KMT continued to fight back with some of its old-time bravado. This included a military doctrine of Strategic Sustainability, concocted by Hau Pei-tsun, who was chief of staff for the army throughout the 1980s, and premier of the Republic of China (head of the executive branch and chief adviser to the president) for the first three years of the 1990s. Hau had no time for the posturing of either the KMT or its opponents regarding a *possible* conflict with the mainland. With the pragmatism of a military man, he simply did the best he could to prepare. In the event of a 'premature decisive campaign' — which is to say a sudden attack by the PRC — Hau predicted that Taiwan risked losing almost all of its navy and air force, and counselled an initial withdrawal to the east coast to preserve a 'sustainable' fighting force.

'The most important thing for the operation,' he cautioned Chiang Ching-kuo, 'is to withstand the first strike. The situation will change if we are able to withstand the first strike successfully.'[8] The most famous result of his doctrine was the Jiashan 'bunker' outside Hualien — actually dozens of bunkers in a hollowed-out mountain. Long kept out of the glare of the world's media, Jiashan and its related east-coast installations, stretching as far as Taitung, used the shadow of Taiwan's central mountain range to shield them from any ballistic-missile attack from the mainland. They offered underground storage for hundreds of planes, like something out of *Thunderbirds*.

Hau planned for a determined resistance 'at the water's edge' to hamper amphibious landings, but also offered lip service to the long game — the vague possibility that Taiwan would, at some future date, mount an attack of its own on the mainland, that would, by definition, have to be *not*-premature. He hence conceived much of his military policy as a means to 'preserve combat capability, to avoid a premature campaign with the enemy, to wear down the enemy's combat capability piecemeal ... in order to buy time and direct the strategic situation favourable to us.'[9]

The perfect strategic situation for Taiwan, of course, would be a regime change in Beijing. During the initial economic reforms of the early 1980s, such an event briefly seemed within the bounds of possibility, particularly

after Taiwanese business interests (*Taishang*) became one of the primary
investors in China's new export manufacturing boom. Taiwan, however,
also offered individual economic incentives of its own. There was more
than one way, after all, to 'wear down the enemy's combat capability'.

'Fly Towards Freedom' (*Xiang Ziyou Feixiang*, 1979) by Teresa Teng
is the most blatant of the era's propaganda songs. Whereas other tracks
usually kept to hands-across-the-water declarations of internationalism
and brotherhood, Teng's ballad was much more on-the-nose:

> Pluck up your courage / Set your course
> Make your choice / To fly towards freedom
> Fear not the fog / Fear not the turbulent currents
> Let's fly, let's fly / To fight for freedom

The song clearly alluded to the ongoing KMT policy to reward
Communist fighter pilots who defected along with their planes. Nestled
among the more innocent pop songs drifting onto Chinese airwaves
on newly available transistor radios, 'Fly Towards Freedom' also sang of
'drawing back the Iron Curtain', but stopped short of mentioning the
ever-rising value of the money on offer, which would climb as high as $4.5
million before the programme was abandoned in 1988.

The programme might have been a valuable propaganda coup in
decades past, where it handily distracted the population from Chiang
Kai-shek's continued abuse of wartime emergency regulations and
helped accentuate the sense of Taiwan as a 'Free China' alternative to
the Communist mainland, but some of the 'patriots' it attracted were of
questionable provenance. One gang of shifty figures, the 'Righteous Six',
hijacked a Shanghai airliner and flew it to Taiwan, where they were soon
clamouring for a bigger reward, and barging their way into civil-service
positions for which they were plainly unqualified. Two were eventually
arrested and executed for their involvement in a high-profile kidnapping
and murder.[10]

The KMT's charm offensive in-country continued with a gargantuan
monument to the late Generalissimo, intended to stamp the Nationalists'
authority on the heart of Taipei itself. Riding on the media splash created
by the final completion of his Grand Hotel (see last chapter), the architect

Yang Cho-cheng won the contract to create a monument and public space sufficient to keep Chiang at the forefront of the national consciousness. The result was a breathtaking accomplishment reminiscent of an imperial temple. The Chiang Kai-shek Memorial Hall was a massive edifice of white stone with an auspiciously octagonal roof in Kuomintang blue, atop twin staircases with 89 steps, one for each year of the Generalissimo's life. Built into its base were a museum and a library. Visitors who climbed the towering staircase to the central chamber were greeted by a looming statue of Chiang himself in traditional Chinese costume, as if they were entering an audience with an ancient Emperor, attended by a platoon of flesh-and-blood soldiers, whose elaborate and recurring changing-of-the-guard routine also formed part of the ritual theatre. At the beginning and end of each day, visitors were also subjected to a singalong recording of the 'Chiang Kai-shek Memorial Song'.

Officially opened in 1980, the Chiang Kai-shek Memorial Hall recalled elements of Beijing's Temple of Heaven and Washington's Lincoln Memorial, and faced a broad plaza that itself echoed Beijing's Tiananmen Square. In another subtle echo of Beijing, the plaza was flanked on either side by imposing state buildings — the National Concert Hall and the National Theater. It soon became a much-loved public space, attended by crowds of idlers and kite-flyers, not to mention an ever-expanding number of couples using the venue and its gardens as a backdrop for their wedding photographs. It would also become the focus of large public gatherings, and not necessarily in support of the status quo.

The KMT continued to push itself as the rightful ruler of 'Free China', and quietly suppressed the news that there were far more defectors heading west to the mainland than east to Taiwan. Usually, it was cases of disaffected refugees finally giving up and returning to long-neglected hometowns and families. In order to bolster the image of the Republic of China as a beacon to the Chinese who wanted to be free, the KMT-run media continued to brag about its high-profile defectors from Communism, including Beijing Opera star Zhang Ziyun, and the author Zhou Lingfei, who was the grandson of the much-loved mainland author Lu Xun. They were topped in the headlines of 1983 by the arrival of Wu Ronggen, a young pilot who had taken his MiG-19 on an unauthorised trip to South Korea, where he informed the local

The architectural design of the National Theater, opened in 1987,
in Taipei deliberately asserts a strong 'Chinese' identity.

authorities that he was claiming political asylum on Taiwan.

Wu first appeared to be a media darling — an enthusiastic patriot who claimed that he had given no thought to the US$2.21 million awaiting him in Taipei, itself something of a lesser reward, since his actual plane had been impounded and returned to China by the nervous Koreans. Adopted by a KMT official and commissioned as an officer in Taiwan's air force, he was trotted around the publicity circuit on multiple photocalls, from the pious (leaving a wreath at the grave of Chiang Kai-shek) to the populist (fondling a dolphin at the aquarium). His personal highlight was singing a duet with pop star Teresa Teng, cassettes of whose ballads were regularly dropped over Communist territory in hot-air balloons to tell the People's Republic what they were missing.

A photo of their performance at a Taiwanese airbase was subsequently included in the next set of propaganda leaflets to be hurled at the mainland — in a wonderful high-tech 1980s touch, a chip inside would begin to play one of her songs when the booklet was opened.[11]

Several years later, Wu would find himself embroiled in an altogether different media circus, fraught with oh-so-capitalist accusations of gold-digging and extortion. By now a high-profile figure in Air Force Command, he reacted with shifty equivocation when his girlfriend announced that she was pregnant — first claiming that military regulations forbade him from marrying, and then changing the locks on their apartment. Her affronted family fought back by demanding that he pay her off from his defector's reward, bolstering their claim with the aid of a forged marriage certificate. High-level intercessions hushed the scandal up for a while, until it was taken up by a young, hungry lawyer with an axe to grind.

Chen Shui-bian was officially a specialist in marine insurance, but was more than ready to put his legal knowledge to use in humiliating the KMT and its poster boys. He had already proved to be a thorn in the KMT's side when he had agreed to represent the defendants in the Kaohsiung Incident of 1979; now he took up the case of the spurned Miss Liu. For Chen, the air force officer was not a patriot, but merely one more mainlander plundering Taiwan for his own ends. Unfortunately for him, reasonable though it might have been to argue that Miss Liu was the originally injured party, Wu had committed no crime, whereas the Liu family had shaken him down for US$310,000. Chen lost the case, and six members of the Liu family went to prison, but Wu was shunted sideways into a lecturing position and never got his money back. In the process, Chen had made a further name for himself by publicly standing up not only to the KMT and its love-rat pilot, but also to Wu's lawyer, a KMT politician who was sure to have regretted ever taking on the case.[12]

The continued use of America as a battleground for the KMT-*Dangwai* conflicts reached its high point in October 1984, when the journalist Henry Liu was killed in his garage in a San Francisco suburb. Liu had been a prominent critic of the KMT regime, penning articles that called Chiang Ching-kuo the 'last emperor'. His murder was revealed to have been committed by members of the Bamboo Gang, a crime group acting under orders from Chiang's own intelligence bureau. Although never proved, it was strongly implied that they had been sent to kill Liu by Chiang's son Alex, as the FBI soon pointed out. Before long, there were threats that the committing of murder by agents of Taiwan on United States soil constituted an 'act of terrorism' and might even lead to the suspension of arms sales to Taiwan. Keen to establish that the Liu murder happened without his knowledge, Chiang launched a purge of his own organisation, and a nationwide war on organised crime, called Operation

Cleansweep. Behind the scenes, his minions were commanded to cut their ties to organised criminals like the Bamboo Gang, and after many years of lucrative opium-for-arms dealing, the much-denied stragglers of the Lost Army in the Golden Triangle of South-East Asia were finally cut off.

Unfortunately, Operation Cleansweep had an unforeseen outcome. By assembling all the powerbrokers of disparate crime families in a single prison, it pushed them into confrontation with each other. After initial squabbles between young Bamboo United toughs and the other gangs, the prison session effectively turned into an underworld crime summit, resulting in the formation of the Celestial Alliance, a federation of crime families with a unified purpose.[13]

Operation Cleansweep, and its later corrective, Operation Thunderbolt, successfully cleared away many old-fashioned forms of crime, but prompted the criminal fraternities to seek new means of protection. Exploiting loopholes in legislation designed to protect officials from malicious lawsuits, an entire generation of gangsters with mainland affiliations went into politics in the 1990s, a situation that would only add further scandals and corruption to the political scene, even as it liberalised.

In order to maintain its authority within Taiwan, the KMT needed to establish a new claim, *to represent all the people of Taiwan*, which would ultimately mean going to those people to seek legitimation in a general election.[14] As a result, it is in the early 1980s that we see a shift in KMT policies, as it came to reluctantly deal with the possibility of a political opposition, and recognition not just of Taiwanese born before 1949, but of Taiwanese whose families had been on the island since before the 1600s, and of the indigenous peoples, who had been there even longer. The most productive element of this new direction was Chiang Ching-kuo's selection of a controversial figure as his vice-president and ultimate successor.

Lee Teng-hui is a fascinating figure in Taiwanese history: a brilliant academic mind whose 12 years as president transformed the political landscape of his native island. He was also, arguably, the last throwback to Taiwan's Japanese past, being as useful and productive a remnant of the colonial era as the much-loved Hōrai Rice. Born in 1923 and self-identifying as Japanese until he was 22 years old, he was a graduate of the

Kyoto Imperial University, and served in the Imperial Japanese Army as an anti-aircraft gunner, before returning to Taiwan at the end of the war. Such experiences gave Lee a wonderfully liminal position in Taiwanese history. A native speaker of Hokkien, fluent in Japanese, he did not even fully learn to speak standard Chinese until the 1950s, and made a point in later life of claiming confusion at both the Generalissimo's and Madame Chiang's Mandarin accents.

Lee Teng-hui enjoyed a remarkable fast-track into power. Three years after receiving his PhD from Cornell for an acclaimed dissertation on Taiwanese agriculture, he was persuaded to join the KMT by Chiang Ching-kuo himself. His Party credentials no longer in question, he was awarded a cabinet position as an agricultural minister in 1972. It was widely believed that it was Lee, at the president's ear for much of the 1970s, who was responsible for many of Chiang's late-career concessions to the opposition, including public access to the trial of the *Formosa Magazine* dissidents, and the amnesties after the death of the Generalissimo. By 1978, Chiang had appointed Lee as the mayor of Taipei (another cabinet position), and in 1981 as governor of Taiwan province (i.e. with authority over the non-urban areas of the whole island).[15]

Lee was a wolf in sheep's clothing, a man who had spent much of his adult life in quiet disapproval of the KMT and who had been warned by his own colleagues that he risked arrest and censure if he returned to Taiwan after gaining his doctorate. Instead, he became one of Chiang's prominent Taiwanese minions, a visible example to wavering Taiwanese voters and taxpayers that the KMT was open to some kind of mild, slow reform. His Japanese biographer referred to him by alluding to a traditional proverb, that he was a man 'in the tiger's mouth', reforming a system from the inside.[16]

His tenure was not without its controversies. His enemies in both Beijing and Taipei tried to play up his younger days as a soldier in the Japanese empire, and the possibility, never quite refuted, that he had been detained for Communist sympathies in 1947 but had evaded punishment by betraying his Marxist study group to the authorities.[17]

It is very likely that Lee had something to do with the granting of a visa to the US-based Liao Shu-tsung, a prominent independence activist who somehow gained an audience with Chiang Ching-kuo. The president asked Liao in a hurt tone why he insisted on calling his organisation the North America *Taiwanese* Professors' Association. Why not Chinese?

When Liao replied that he was not Chinese, Chiang asked him to explain, then, what being 'Taiwanese' meant.

'Whoever considers Taiwan as a home country,' replied Liao, 'and whoever helps develop Taiwan as a country.'

Liao then suddenly turned on Chiang, asking if he considered himself to be Taiwanese. When Chiang denied it, Liao had his 'gotcha' moment.

'Those who do not identify with Taiwan are ruling the country,' he said. 'This is wrong!'[18]

As mayor of Taipei, Lee had presided over a huge renaissance in the creative arts, although his KMT masters do not appear to have noticed that he championed international, global works rather than the China-focus that the KMT's own policies encouraged. As governor of Taiwan province, Lee brokered a peace deal between the Vat'an and Tavalong, two Amis subgroups who had been in conflict for generations over an old tribal enmity. Lee persuaded their chiefs to put aside their differences and to hold a joint *ilisin* harvest festival.[19]

By 1987, the sense of the KMT's thinning authority led to a number of gentle pokes at its powers. The use of Mandarin in parliamentary debates had never been officially enshrined in law, as the executive had, until very recently, always been in the hands of the Nationalist Party faithful. In March 1987, the legislator Zhu Gaozheng invited controversy by starting to speak in Taiwanese. Despite the horror this initially engendered among his peers, it was part of a groundswell of assertions of Taiwanese culture. Before the end of the year, three government-owned TV stations were adding Taiwanese-language news broadcasts.[20]

In one of the KMT's wisest moves to maintain Taiwan's relevance in a post-Nixon world, it reached out to Morris Chang, a computer engineer whose family had originally come from Ningbo, China, but who had spent much of his life in Hong Kong and the United States, where he had worked for 25 years for Texas Instruments. Chang, in fact, had lived outside China ever since 1949, but had formed a vital link in the negotiations that had put Texas Instruments' first Taiwanese chip factory in place in 1969. He had been lured back to Taiwan in 1983 from his job at General Instrument Corporation to run Taiwan's Industrial

Technology Research Institute. In 1987, the year that Chiang Ching-kuo lifted martial law, Chang founded the Taiwan Semiconductor Manufacturing Company (TSMC), the world's first factory dedicated to the production of integrated computer chips. He did so with substantial investment from the Dutch electrical firm Philips (27.5 per cent), and the rest of the money harvested from wealthy Taiwanese businessmen, some of whom were subjected to significant arm-twisting from the KMT to come up with the cash.[21]

Over the decades that followed, TSMC's constant reinvestment of profits in research and development ensured that it remained at the forefront of the chip market. This, in turn, made Taiwan a vital link in the supply chain for many modern high-tech goods — everything from phones to fridges, many of which are made by 'fabless' manufacturers, companies that lack fabrication facilities to make their own chips, and hence buy them from outside suppliers.

With his declining health necessitating the use of a wheelchair, Chiang Ching-kuo sent strong signals of the way he intended his legacy to be remembered. He did so in an international political context beyond the scope of this book, but worth noting here in passing: *glasnost* in the Soviet Union, a democratic transfer of power in South Korea, and the liberalising of the economy of the People's Republic of China. Referring to his earlier confrontation with Liao Shu-tsung, in which he had refused to call Taiwan his home, Chiang meaningfully announced, 'I am Taiwanese.' Four long decades after martial law had been declared, he ended the State of Emergency, and allowed ageing veterans to return to the mainland to visit their surviving families and relatives.

As part of the fallout from Chiang's reforms, opposition political parties were now legal. The most prominent and influential, the Democratic Progressive Party (DPP), was already in existence, having been illegally founded the previous year by a conclave of *Dangwai* activists at the Grand Hotel. The DPP would win increasing numbers of seats in national elections at every level, but like the KMT its monolithic existence cloaked the jostling for influence within it of several factions and interest groups. Over the years, the DPP's growing influence would pressure the KMT into further reforms and clarifications, yet within the DPP itself there was often a fervid struggle over policy issues. The DPP, naturally, was initially formed by an agglomeration of people who were simply *outside* the KMT, leading to ongoing struggles over whether it should be explicitly and openly in favour of Taiwanese independence or go to the voters with the offer of maintaining the status quo. Moderates within the new party were soon swamped by more-extreme independence activists, ironically as a result of the same suspension of martial law, as hard-line dissidents were finally allowed to return to their home island, where they were less aware of the delicate nuances required to prevent a backlash from either Taipei or Beijing.

Many of the DPP movers and shakers were the victims or relatives of the numerous White Terror purges, including the Kaohsiung Incident. This gave them a certain dynastic authority, not unlike that which continued to rule within their rivals at the KMT. Chiang Ching-kuo, meanwhile, was determined for the presidential family business to end with him. 'If someone asks me whether anyone in my family would run for the next presidential term,' he stated, 'my reply is, "It can't be and it won't be."'[22]

Kinder commentators might suggest that Chiang and his advisers had realised the implications of an enduring stranglehold on power by a single family. His comment on the succession included a second pronouncement against the installation of a military junta, thereby making it clear that he wanted his legacy to be a democratic Republic of China, not a political dynasty or rule by the armed forces. But even at the time, *The New York Times* observed that Chiang's decision had been made for him, since his three (legitimate) sons lacked 'the authority or support to protect the family's dynasty'. The eldest had suffered brain damage while being treated for diabetes in 1970, the second had been suspected of involvement in the murder of Henry Liu in California in 1984, and the third was an extremely reluctant political appointee who strongly disapproved of Lee Teng-hui and the direction in which his father's regime was going. Moreover, on account of their Belorussian mother, all three were only half-Chinese, liable to be a vote-loser in Taiwan's increasingly identity-focused politics.

Chiang hence avoided any discussion of appointing any of his own children as his successor, ending the sense of a political dynasty. When he died in 1988, his vice-president Lee Teng-hui should have been a shoo-in, but faced a brief scuffle at the top as the KMT old guard tried to walk back their leader's deathbed reforms. Among them was Chiang Ching-kuo's youngest son, who would go on to write a waspish article for the press on the subject of 'distinguishing wolves from sheep', before taking a leave of absence that stretched on for so long that he became a Canadian citizen.[23]

As the time approached for Lee Teng-hui to be officially appointed as president in his own right, rather than as a mid-term replacement, student protestors flooded onto the plaza outside the Chiang Kai-shek Memorial Hall, demanding an end to the era of KMT appointees, and a new era of direct and free elections. Acknowledging a symbol of homegrown Taiwanese purity and fortitude, they carried wild lilies, soon adopted as the name for their movement. The tone of the Wild Lilies mirrored that of the students who had packed Tiananmen Square in Beijing several months earlier, prompting Lee to deliberately treat them in as different a manner as possible. Whereas Tiananmen Square had been cleared with tanks and soldiers, Lee sent in food and water for the protestors, and agreed to meet with their leaders. In 1990, appointed to the presidency by the old system, he gave an inaugural address in which he agreed to the students' demands. Six years later, when his term lapsed, he would seek not reappointment by the government, but re-election by the people.

Lee pushed through further reforms, including the long-delayed declaration that the Temporary Provisions Effective During the Period of National Mobilization for Suppression of the Communist Rebellion were now over, 43 years after they had been instituted — the longest period of martial law in history at the time.[24] They had notched up other records, too. Courts martial had processed over 140,000 people accused of dissent and related crimes against the state, leading to up to 4,000 official executions, and an untold number of off-the-books killings, beatings, and intimidations.[25]

The repeal of the Temporary Provisions created a new legal problem, in that they had been instituted in response to the 'Communist Rebellion'. If there was no longer a need for the Provisions, then either the Communist Rebellion had been defeated, or it had been successful, in which case did this mean that the Republic of China was officially recognising the existence of the People's Republic of China? Even if this were the case, and there were plenty on Taiwan who would have accepted the idea, to recognise the authority of Beijing while still claiming authority as the ROC was tantamount to proclaiming the existence of 'two Chinas', and thereby contradicting the Shanghai Communiqué.

Lee Teng-hui made his feelings clear, announcing that the 'One China' dictum was an 'imagined community — it is not something we should recognise, but something we should renounce'.[26] There was, he said, no need to sign any papers or make any official declarations about ending a war that had already ended, or defining a status quo that was already in existence. 'Taiwan is independent. It owns its sovereignty.'[27] With comments such as that, he created rifts within the Kuomintang itself, which started to shed members into splinter groups of its own. The New Party (*Xindang*), founded in 1993, even managed to lure away the premier of the Republic of China, General Hau Pei-tsun, a former stalwart of the KMT, disappointed at the direction in which his old party was going.

Much of the rhetoric of political campaigning, particularly in the Taiwanese-speaking south, involved allusions and callbacks to cultural artefacts unknown to the Mandarin monoglot. There were, for example, recurring references to 'A Poor Man, Down on His Luck' (*Kelian de Luoporen*, 1979), a song written by Gao Ziyang, that same composer who had served time in the 1970s for his earlier use of indigenous subjects. Released from prison and struggling to make ends meet by running a restaurant, Gao had returned to songwriting, with lyrics that lent themselves well to appropriation in many a hustings debate:

You can string me along, / You can use me, too
Even though you don't love me anymore
You should greet me when we meet
I can string you along too, / Or turn my back on you,
Even if I don't call you anymore
You should still greet me when we meet.[28]

It was not long before Taiwanese parliamentarians began to push the boundaries of their newly found freedoms. At Chiang Ching-kuo's last appearance in the parliament, the frail leader had sat, untroubled, while his assistants read out his last proclamation. It called, ironically, for a reform of the National Assembly, taking the wind out of the sails of the DPP protestors present, who had unfurled a banner proclaiming 'OLD THIEVES OUT' even as the president announced that that was what he was just about to order.[29]

In April 1988, two rival politicians fought to occupy the speaker's table in the parliament during a vote-count on a budget proposal. The 'legislative violence' was started by the DPP's Chu Kao-cheng, who was eventually dragged away by ten fellow politicians, but not before throwing a drink at the KMT official who tried to reprimand him for his misbehaviour. Chu would later claim that 'extreme measures were the only way to combat the KMT', which would otherwise continue its decades of authoritarian power under the guise of democracy. He aimed the fieriest of his arguments against the ageing politicians in the government who had been in place since 1947, clinging to outmoded notions of the Republic of China as a one-party KMT enclave that was permanently poised on the verge of resuming the civil war.

'If you vote for me,' he declared, 'I guarantee that I will explode a bomb in the legislature. I will ... smash the mountains, crack the earth and overturn the heavens. Until the KMT agrees to hold full elections, I will not let up.' Confronted by policymakers, he proclaimed that his mission was to send them home to enjoy their retirement — with the implication that their time was over, and Taiwan should reconsider its priorities.[30]

The pattern was set for a performative type of political debate that would be decried in the press as 'Taiwan's shame' — a likelihood of literal brawls in parliament as a means for politicians to demonstrate their passion for their causes to their constituents. Over the next three decades, there would be a newsworthy punch-up in Taiwanese politics roughly once every seven weeks, often attributed to the intractability of the KMT and DPP in compromising on strongly held issues.

Not even statues were safe from grandstanding media assault. The Chinese hero Wu Feng (see Chapter Four), who had supposedly martyred himself as part of a mission to civilise the Tsou, came under increasing fire from indigenous people with greater freedom to protest. A newspaper article in 1980 had outed Wu's story as a 'fabricated legend', and by 1985 indigenous protestors were showing up at the annual Wu Feng ceremony, wearing T-shirts that proclaimed he was no hero. Such gentle dissent became more active after the suspension of martial law, when a Tsou pastor led a delegation to the statue of Wu Feng outside Chiayi train station and vandalised it with a chainsaw in 1988. A year later, in the face of continued protests that the presence of Wu Feng's story in school textbooks was misleading, patronising, and insulting, the Minister of Education withdrew it.

Wu's ninth-generation descendant Wu Liao-shan came out of the woodwork to offer his approval: 'The aborigines say that the story causes people to look down on them, to bully them in school,' he said, 'so I guess it's for the best not to include the story.' A generation later, the former staple of schoolbooks under both the Japanese and the Nationalists is all but unknown to young Taiwanese.[31]

At least part of the media showboating stemmed from the connections of some politicians to the criminal underworld. The crackdowns on crime — Operation Cleansweep in 1984 and Operation Thunderbolt in 1990 — had purged many sectors of visible gangs, but propelled the better organised criminals into businesses with legitimate fronts, even if some of their deals were shady. The blanket protections for elected politicans turned many gangsters into bullet-proof bosses. Among many such cases, we might take as an example Yen Ching-piao, aka Piao the Stone Pumpkin, convicted under Operation Cleansweep for operating illegal gambling dens, in the course of which he had once ventilated a rival's business establishment with gunfire. After serving three years in jail, and several more at the edges of the political realm, Yen successfully ran for office as a Taichung councillor in 1994. His plan to run for council speaker was put on hold after the incumbent's brother was shot, shortly before a gunman also managed to wound Yen himself. Despite such setbacks, Yen ran for the provincial assembly, becoming its youngest-ever member at 35 years old. In the same year, he also became a grandfather.

The following year, Yen was somehow involved in a car chase and gunfight with the local police. Local reporters sat on the story for some reason, but when the news got out, the journalists who filed it were coincidentally attacked by men with baseball bats. In 1996, he was back in the news when he arrived with a gang of strongmen at a local company's shareholder meeting, and was filmed starting a fight.[32]

Nor did the end of the Temporary Provisions deal with the vast expansion of truly criminal elements into the political sphere, which was by then crammed with councillors and officials with strong ties to organised crime. Taiwanese politics, it was said, was a system loaded with 'black gold' (*hei jin*), financed by and often in hock to criminal interests.

Well aware of the problem, the government instituted a third crackdown in 1996, Operation Chih-ping ('Politics Pacified'), which specifically targeted figures in local government with criminal connections. A series of high-profile arrests played out in full view of the media with movie-level drama, as various mayors and councillors were bundled into squad cars and hauled off by helicopters to offshore detention. Yen Ching-piao complained to the media about suggestions he was somehow involved in illegal gambling and stock-market manipulation, and lamented the fact that his brother's recently reported threat to murder one of his political rivals was somehow being linked to him. 'People are blaming me for all the bad things,' he said, shortly before his re-election to Taichung city council, and his appointment as its chairman.

In 1996, Lee Teng-hui broke with KMT tradition by running for his own reappointment in a democratic election, scraping into a second term with 54 per cent of the votes. To get there, he had to walk through a storm of political in-fighting, as well as the unrest caused by the decision by the People's Republic of China to start testing its new ballistic missiles by firing them into the Taiwan Strait during the election campaign — just to make clear what might happen if Taiwan elected a pro-independence candidate. This, along with the presence of two independents, one of whom cultivated the Buddhist religious vote, the other enjoying the backing of the New Party, is likely to have diluted support for the DPP's presidential candidate, the one-armed dissident Peng Ming-min, who lost his chance at the post. To add a little spice to the electoral campaigns, one of his rivals spread the false rumour that his arm had been amputated in a gangland reprisal, and not as the result of Japanese wartime bombing.

In Lee Teng-hui's re-inauguration speech, he flipped the mainland's rhetoric on its head, arguing that China itself was a grand idea that had grown from a tiny region, and Taiwan could be, too:

All the major cultures originated in a very restricted area. The 5,000-year Chinese culture also arose from a small region called *zhong yuan* [The Central Plain] ... Equipped with a much higher level of education and development than other areas of China, Taiwan is set to gradually exercise its leadership role in cultural development and take upon itself the responsibility for nurturing a new Chinese culture.[33]

Just as the majestic nation of China had grown from a tiny polity on the banks of the Yellow River — so small that it could once be crossed on horseback in a single day — puny Taiwan also had the potential to incubate an entire culture, and to profoundly influence the economic and cultural direction of the mainland. Nor were these idle words. The economic miracle that had created a strong People's Republic in the 1980s was founded partly on Taiwanese investment in the Special Economic Zones of Fujian across the Taiwan Strait and Shenzhen next to Hong Kong. Just as mainlanders in the Qing dynasty had illegally flocked to Taiwan to seek their fortune, Fujian investment incentives in 1984 were designed specifically to lure Taiwanese capital, six years before the Taiwanese government made it an official policy. Moreover, after the violent events in Tiananmen Square in 1989 scared away many foreign investors, it was Taiwanese businesses that rushed in to fill the gap. Even as the Taiwanese government decried the human-rights violations of Beijing, its own businessmen were cashing in.[34] Posterity, particularly since the Handover of Hong Kong in 1997, has often obscured the role played by Taiwan in creating the PRC's 'China dream' wealth and attitudes, but so many elements of modern PRC culture — everything from coffee shops, to wedding photography, to pop stars — derive from Taiwan.[35]

Throughout the period, indigenous issues continued to bubble away at the margins. Two years into Lee Teng-hui's presidency, protestors in tribal dress harangued him for not using their preferred terminology — they did not wish to be referred to as 'mountain compatriots' or even 'aborigines', but as 'indigenous people'. In 1993, there were protests concerning the appropriation of indigenous land as national parks, eroding the tribes' own authority on what had previously been their territory. These continued for several years, particularly since the rezoning of tribal lands as parkland had criminalised Atayal hunters under the cloak of ecological protections. In 1997, an amendment to the Aboriginal Labor Law defanged it in the eyes of indigenous peoples, since it allowed foreigners, allegedly taking jobs from indigenous people, to stay longer in the country.[36]

In a case that suddenly dragged indigenous issues onto the world stage in 1998, indigenous performers sued a record company over appropriation of their song. Four years earlier, the German music collective Enigma had used a sample from the Amis 'Elders' Drinking Song' (see Chapter One) as part of their music track 'Return to Innocence'. Shorn of its original context, without translation, it formed a simple, seemingly 'nonsense' chant:

He i yai ha i w way ha i,
he i yai ha i w way hai ye i ya an ho ay yan ho ay ya o hi yan

It was subsequently heard all around the world as the theme music to the 1996 Atlanta Olympics, leading two singers to take Enigma to court. They had been recorded during a tour of France a decade earlier, and their work had been released as 'anonymous' by a French educational foundation. In a spat over intellectual property, the director of Taiwan's Association of Recording Copyright Owners came to Enigma's defence, pointing out that, by definition, *nobody* owned the copyrights in 'traditional' songs. Lawyers for the plaintiffs countered that they were not claiming ownership of the song, merely of the performance, which Enigma had been misled to assume was in the public domain. After a substantial, undisclosed out-of-court settlement, the song now credits Difang and Igay Duana for their contribution.[37]

After serving his two terms, Lee Teng-hui's retirement in 2000 would divide the KMT over the way to deal with his legacy. The official candidate for the KMT was Lee's vice-president, Lien Chan, but he had to deal with James Soong, a former KMT leader who had been expelled from the party for advocating a European-style economic union with the mainland. Although a clear majority of Taiwanese chose a candidate who was KMT or former-KMT, the split between these two 'Blue' candidates proved fatal. It probably didn't help James Soong that, in search of public support in Taichung district, he had sought the endorsement of local powerbroker Yen Ching-piao, the Stone Pumpkin. Three days before the election, the Democratic Progressive Party paid for a media blitz in all the major newspapers, outlining Yen's criminal links, and asking if this was the sort of support a president should be cultivating. The campaign was a powerful argument in favour of the leader of the DPP, the former lawyer and mayor of Taipei Chen Shui-bian, elected to office with a shaky mandate of a mere 39.3 per cent.[38]

'The outcome of Taiwan's year 2000 presidential election,' he said in his inaugural speech, 'is not the victory of an individual or a political party. It is a victory of the people; a victory of democracy.'[39] Even so, he assuaged Beijing fears by promising that he would not declare Taiwanese independence, he would not change the state's name to the Republic of Taiwan, he would not impose state-to-state relations on Taiwanese diplomatic protocols, and he would not invite trouble by putting the matter of Taiwanese sovereignty to the people in a referendum. These 'Four No's' would, at least for a while, keep Beijing happy.

CHAPTER ELEVEN

WILD STRAWBERRIES

An Asian Tiger (2000–2016)

Chen Shui-bian's 2000 inauguration speech offered a warning to the People's Republic that its frequent threats, bluster, and war-games might serve some sort of political purpose on the mainland, but did not do it any favours on Taiwan.

> We can understand why the government on the other side of the Strait, in light of historical complexities and ethnic sentiments, cannot relinquish the insistence on the 'One China Principle' ... If it continues to threaten Taiwan with military force, if it persists in isolating Taiwan diplomatically, if it keeps up irrational efforts to blockade Taiwan's rightful participation in the international arena, this will only serve to drive the hearts of the Taiwanese people further away, and widen the divide in the Strait.[1]

Oblivious to the irony, the mainland immediately made his point for him. A highlight of Chen's swearing-in ceremony was the pop star A-Mei, a Puyuma woman regarded as 'Taiwan's Madonna', singing 'Three Principles of the People', the national anthem of the Republic of China. For doing so, she was cancelled overnight in the People's Republic, losing her fans, her right to enter the country, concert bookings, and a nationwide sponsorship deal that had previously plastered her face on billboards to advertise the Coca-Cola Company's Sprite soft drink.[2]

Behind the scenes, economics could still exert a powerful political influence. Many eyes in the business sector were not on the election but on the degree to which any tension in the Taiwan Strait might affect the global computing industry — Taiwan being the world leader in semiconductor chips, LCD panels, and DRAM memory. An earthquake shortly before the election threatened to shut down the all-important semiconductor manufacturers, which, in an era not only of computers, but of smart phones, smart fridges, and smart everything, were crucial to many other manufacturing sectors, both in China and on the mainland. Despite the disaster unfolding in other parts of the country, four of the five fabrication plants belonging to the Taiwan Semiconductor Manufacturing Company (TSMC) were back up and running within the week, thanks in part to Morris Chang phoning the authorities and demanding preferential treatment to re-establish their electricity supply.[3]

In 2000, even with the continued sabre-rattling over a DPP victory, the People's Republic welcomed the construction of a computer chip factory in Shanghai by TSMC. The PRC was so keen to get those all-important chips made within its territory that it even consented to the construction of an on-site Christian church. The Shanghai plant, along with several others set up around the same time, was intended as an exercise in technology transfer, teaching the Chinese how to make them, although all foreign companies in the sector did their best to keep the Chinese at arm's length from intellectual property or manufacturing secrets.[4]

Defeated in the election, the KMT's spoiler James Soong founded his own organisation, the People First Party. His policies called for Taiwan to have a stronger engagement in international organisations, and the party was broadly in favour of some sort of unification with China, but was still enough of a KMT-lite to qualify as 'Blue'. Over the years, the People First Party and splinter groups like it would shuffle into a 'Pan-Blue Coalition', most notably on the hustings, where delicate deals were put in place to prevent two competing 'Blue' candidates ruining each other's chances in a particular district. Paramount among the promises of the 'Blue' faction was a refusal to consider Taiwanese independence, and hence the surety that they would do nothing to provoke Beijing.

A similar divergence soon manifested within the Democratic Progressive Party, which, like its KMT rival, was an impossibly broad church. Arguably, the DPP had also been taken somewhat by surprise by its victory, and was unprepared for truly wading into government. It faced not only the sudden need to fill posts for an entire administration, often with inexperienced appointees, but also the fact that the Taiwanese civil service had no memory of working for a government that was not KMT — the common concept overseas, of a neutral civil service pivoting to meet the demands of a new government, was wholly unknown.[5]

While some DPP members might easily be described as 'KMT but (hopefully) without the corruption', others were blatantly in favour of Taiwanese independence — a policy that Beijing repeatedly warned would lead to military intervention. Some were even more extreme, regarding the independence of Taiwan as merely the first step in a sundering of all China into separate sectors. In an argument as toxic to the PRC as Kryptonite, they argued that if Taiwan could go its own way, then why couldn't Tibet? Why not an independent Shanghai, Canton, Sichuan, or Manchuria?[6]

In the 21st century, Taiwanese politics broadly split into 'pan-Blue' re-enaction of KMT issues, and 'pan-Green' coalitions of parties prepared to compromise with the aims of the DPP. In a political turnabout that only sealed his renegade status in 2001, the retired Nationalist president Lee Teng-hui showed up on the hustings for the Taiwan Solidarity Union, a splinter group actively in support of an independent Taiwan. Freed of any protocol restrictions, he expressed his belief that Taiwan was indeed a state separate from China, and that the DPP was the party to lead it. For such a performance, he was roundly criticised as a traitor and expelled from the KMT. After reforming the Republic of China from within the Party, he was now created not-Party after the fact. He had been *Dangwai* all along. Chen Shui-bian's vice-president, Annette Lu, would pay tribute to the defeated Lee for nurturing a loyal opposition from within the KMT. 'President Lee did not plant these flowers,' she wrote. 'He watched them bloom and arranged them in a beautiful bouquet.'[7]

The veterans were dying off, and not merely the humans. Lin Wang was the last of several names for the KMT's only surviving war elephant, which had been a fixture at Taipei Zoo since the 1950s. Lin Wang's eventual death in 2003, at the ripe old age of 86, was cause for weeks of national mourning, and even led to President Chen Shui-bian laying a wreath at the zoo, and offering a eulogy to 'our forever friend'. But much of the rhetoric about the death of Lin Wang had something more to it — the mournful recognition that he was merely the most visible, and presumably heaviest, member of the generation of veterans that had been in their youth at the time of the evacuation and were now dying off, the promise of recovering the mainland still unfulfilled. Press coverage focused on Lin Wang's many years of happy retirement at Taipei Zoo, and not on several episodes of animal rage, particularly during the 1990s, when he had turned on his mate, Malan, and his zookeepers over unknown issues, or his prolonged depression after the death of Malan.

Lin Wang in his glory days, with General Sun Li-jen in 1947.

There were plenty of clues as to how Chen Shui-bian would behave when he took office. As mayor of Taipei in the 1990s, he had presided over numerous changes in street names and the removal of portraits of Chiang Kai-shek. Now with a marginal mandate to effect further change, he started to apply DPP policies to other sectors of the government, particularly indigenous issues.

There were, it was true, not a huge number of votes to be won from the indigenous peoples. But the DPP, and increasingly the KMT in opposition, were obliged to show that they were not parties representing the issues of a single ethnic group, and taking up indigenous issues was a good way to do so. For the DPP, it also repeatedly asserted the Austronesian nature of Taiwan's prehistory, challenging at every stage the claims that Taiwan was indelibly 'part of China'. Many of the sources used in this book date from post-2000, when consideration of Taiwan's indigenous past suddenly switched from being a fringe interest to a central issue within national politics. One only needs to look at the dates on a report from the International Work Group for Indigenous Affairs to see the large number of DPP initiatives rammed through during Chen's years in office:

A number of national laws protect their rights, including the Constitutional Amendments (2000) on indigenous representation in the Legislative Assembly, protection of language and culture and political participation; the Indigenous Peoples' Basic Act (2005), the Education Act for Indigenous Peoples (2004), the Status Act for Indigenous Peoples (2001), the Regulations regarding Recognition of Indigenous Peoples (2002) and the Name Act (2003), which allows indigenous peoples to register their original names in Chinese characters and to annotate them in Romanized script. Unfortunately, serious discrepancies and contradictions in the legislation, coupled with only partial implementation of laws guaranteeing the rights of indigenous peoples, have stymied progress towards self-governance.[8]

The Thao people returned to their ancestral homeland, or what was left of it, on the shores of Sun-Moon Lake. The tribe had been devastated by years of incursions — their territory flooded by the damming of the lake by the Japanese, moved to new accommodation both then and after the arrival of Kuomintang developers, and then rendered homeless by the 1999 earthquake. Thinned down by years of attrition and intermarriage, fewer than 300 Thao stepped ashore at Puzi, the spit of land where their ancestors had once been led to the water's edge by a sacred deer. Only the elders spoke the Thao language with any fluency, and although there was celebration at the recognition of the Thao as a separate ethnic minority in 2001, it was tinged with bitterness — they had spent the last century being misfiled as 'Tsou' people, owing to a translation error by Japanese anthropologists.[9]

The past returned to haunt Taiwan in a more direct way after the DPP victory, when the government of the People's Republic of China reacted with strident warnings. For 20 years, the PRC had maintained a military division, the Blue Force (*Lanjun*), specifically training and preparing for the conquest of Taiwan.[10] It regularly greeted Taiwanese elections not only with missile tests in the Strait, but with photogenic war-games in which news cameras were invited to watch staged amphibious landings. As campaigning began for the 2004 presidential election, the PRC leader Hu Jintao restated that it was his country's duty to 'place national sovereignty and security in first place, resolutely defend national interests, and resolutely defend national sovereignty and territorial integrity'.[11]

The braggadocio from the mainland was interpreted in different ways. Among the 'Green' incumbents, it was a clear sign that Taiwan needed to be more forcefully independent. For the 'Blue' factions, it demonstrated that the DPP had failed to competently manage the issue of mainland relations. Lien Chan and James Soong, the two candidates who had previously split the KMT vote in 2000, now ran on a joint ticket, and there was every indication that the KMT would scrape back into power on a thin majority. The Taiwanese electorate were not united in their support for the DPP, particularly in the wake of a commemoration of the February 28 Incident of 1947 (see Chapter Six) some three weeks before the election. Framed as a memorial to an anti-KMT uprising that had been savagely suppressed, it had been intended as a gesture of reconciliation, but for many it displayed what Jonathan Manthorpe calls an 'unattractive element of triumphalism' in the DPP, regarded by many of Chinese descent as an intimidating harbinger of further backlashes against the *waisheng* Taiwanese who had once been the island's masters.[12]

Vice-President Annette Lu fought back by questioning the commitment of Lien and Soong to Taiwan, returning to a common issue of what she called 'toothbrushism' (*yashua-zhuyi*) — the willingness of

KMT grandees to have an overnight bag packed and ready in case they had to make another quick getaway. In doing so, she made a frankly ungracious appeal to local identity politics by dragging in their families' passports.

Neither Lien Chan nor James Soong was born in Taiwan. Their children are US citizens. If their children don't want ROC nationality, what does this say about the loyalty of the Lien and Soong families to Taiwan? What does it say about their confidence in the future of this beautiful and treasured island? A vote for Lien and Soong is a vote to make 'the father of Americans' your president.[13]

Nevertheless, 2004 looked like it was going to be a narrow victory for the KMT, right up until the eve of the election, when someone shot President Chen.

On 19 March 2004, Chen Shui-bian and Annette Lu were riding in an open-top jeep in a motorcade through Tainan, the heartland of DPP support. A 'disgruntled fisherman' with a homemade gun fired two rounds, hitting Lu in the knee and Chen in the abdomen. Neither wound was life-threatening, but the media circus around the sight of the president being rushed to hospital, after being attacked by a mysterious gunman on the eve of a democratic election, was enough to sway a number of undecided voters.

When the votes were counted, Chen and the DPP had scraped back into power for another four-year term, with a majority of just 29,518 votes, barely 1 per cent of the electorate. Their opponents were livid, blustering not only that they demanded a recount, but that as far as they could see, the most likely mastermind of the assassination was Chen himself, who had, they claimed, paid for a hitman to shoot at him in order to grab last-minute sympathy votes. Others pointed fingers at Beijing agents, or organised criminal elements, although the suspect proved hard to question, as by the time he was identified he had already killed himself, and his family had burned his suicide note.

Chen Shui-bian returned to office on the strength of iconic and statesmanlike imagery, of him speaking into his cell phone, still running his campaign, even as doctors tended to a gunshot wound. But his second term would see him losing public favour as he became mired in bribery and corruption scandals. In the meantime, the divisions within Taiwan's party politics continued to fragment and diversify. It was not lost on any of the actors on the Taiwanese political stage that a single percentile had swayed the result.

Political parties in Taiwan came to see the value of so-called 'iron votes' — niche constituencies that could be guaranteed to turn out to vote on single- or minority-issue platforms, particularly if they were told that their interests were being ignored by the major parties. Some exploited a general sense among the Taiwanese that the KMT was chiefly concerned with representing the issues of the descendants of *waisheng* mainland refugees, while the DPP, despite its claims to speak for all Taiwanese, concentrated on the concerns of the Hoklos — nativist Chinese migrants whose families had arrived from Fujian before 1949. Several sops were thrown to prominent interest groups, including the inauguration of a Hakka Affairs Council in 2001, intended to cater to the needs, cultural concerns, and social wellbeing of the more than four million Hakka people in Taiwan.

Surely, it was soon argued, there was a case for a political party that solely catered to the interests of the Hakka, and the Hakka Party was born in 2006. But the Hakka are themselves a diverse community, up to 20 per cent of the population of Taiwan, and so it should come as no surprise on this famously fractious island that within a year, there was also the Taiwan New Hakka Party, then the Chinese Hakka Party in 2010, and the Global Hakka Party in 2011.

The China Iron Guard Party, the emblem of which is the old five-striped flag of Sun Yat-sen's Chinese Republic (1912–29), calls for the reunification of China under the Three Principles of the People — it represents the interests of die-hard former KMT members dismayed at modern compromises, and a dwindling population of veterans. That's nothing compared to the Peasant Party, which draws its rhetoric from the notion that the short-lived Republic of Formosa was sufficient to establish a de jure sovereignty over Taiwan and the Penghu Islands (which, in fact, were already occupied by the Japanese at the time the Republic was proclaimed), and that the territory thus defined should never have been 'returned' to the Republic of China in 1945. Despite this, the Peasant

Party supports reunification in principle, regarding it as a foregone conclusion once the economic conditions on both sides of the Taiwan Strait are so similar that it makes no odds. In 2008, in a move variously seen as dangerously foolhardy or impressively egalitarian, even the Taiwan Communist Party was able to bring an end to 14 years of illegal operation below the radar, joining the ranks of official political parties. Inevitably, it soon had rivals of its own, including the Communist Party of the Republic of China, and the Taiwan Democratic Communist Party, both founded in 2009.

Taiwanese politicians were unafraid to drag other countries into their showboating if it helped land political points back home. In April 2005, Shu Chin-chiang of the Taiwan Solidarity Union paid his respects in a calculatedly provocative visit to Japan's Yasukuni Shrine, final resting place of, among others, military leaders found guilty of war crimes in Manchuria. Shu's actions riled leaders in Beijing, then in the middle of complex negotiations with the Taiwanese government over new commercial connections.

Two months later, a delegation of Taiwanese in full indigenous regalia was detained by the Japanese police as they got off a bus outside the Yasukuni Shrine. The delegation's behaviour recalled that of the 1979 visitors to the shrine (see Chapter Ten), but the Japanese authorities had fair warning of their intent, because they had spent several days previously arranging peaceful protests and media events to put their case — a demand for the removal of their ancestors' names from the Yasukuni roll of honour.

The protestors were led by Kao Chin Su-mei, a former actress and singer of mixed Manchu-Atayal heritage, who has enjoyed a long second career as one of the three elected representatives for Taiwan's Highland Aborigine constituency. Adding to an accomplished record of publicity stunts, her trip to the shrine was a masterstroke of media manipulation — even 'failing' to gain entry provided her with a platform and a message to waiting journalists:

> We just want to liberate the souls of our ancestors. We expect people
> in Japan to support our peaceful demand. Although we couldn't enter
> the shrine today, we will come again with ten times more supporters

until the shrine returns our ancestors' spirit tablets and removes their names from the list.[14]

Except Kao Chin did not 'just' want to liberate the souls of her ancestors at all. Her fellow protestors carried placards calling for the Japanese to apologise for wartime atrocities, and displayed photographs of crimes committed by the Japanese colonial-era government against Taiwan's indigenous peoples. It was a treasure trove of publicity gold, sure to win Kao Chin attention far and wide — the quote above is not from the Taiwanese media, but from Xinhua, the news agency of the People's Republic, which appreciated clickbait when it saw it.

Such tactics also came home to the Taiwanese parliament, where politicians in search of clicks and eyeballs would stage dramatic interventions on the debating floor. Some of the highlights of Taiwanese political fight club over the years have included the brawl that erupted over vote recounts, when Chen Shui-bian was accused of rigging the election in March 2004; a food fight over military procurements in October 2004; a DPP deputy being forcibly restrained from literally eating a white paper proposing direct transport links with the mainland in May 2006; and a contested budget that led to salvos of water balloons thrown in parliament in July 2017. In the most infamous of political protests, in November 2020, KMT legislators arrived for a debate on easing pork imports from the US, armed with buckets of offal. The world's media was treated to the sight of Taiwan's elected officials throwing pig guts at each other.[15]

In the most conspicuous move of the period, the members of the National Assembly of the Republic of China voted to dissolve their rump government in 2005. The 'ten-thousand-year congress' had been something of a laughing stock, with its multiple-decade terms for politicians claiming to represent provinces that had in fact been part of the People's Republic for 50 years. By 2000, most of the powers previously vested in the National Assembly had been reassigned to Taiwanese administration; its function was further chipped away by the removal of its role in conferring the presidency and vice-presidency. It was time, a large majority agreed, to shut down the fiction, and postpone the convening of a National Assembly until 'unification' was achieved. This last clause was inserted in order to make it clear that the Republic of China was not declaring itself over, since that would be tantamount to a declaration of Taiwanese independence.

Amid the fervent rivalries of this diverse political scene, people would try anything. The former Vice Premier John Chang Hsiao-yen, long rumoured to be an illegitimate son of the late Chiang Ching-kuo, announced in 2005 that he was reclaiming his true surname — Chiang — out of 'respect for history, a return to the facts, and a realization of my parents' wishes'. To add fuel to publicity fires, he also announced that the mysterious stomach cramps that had led to his birth mother Chang Ya-juo's death in 1942 had been poison, administered to her by one of his father's aides.[16]

For John Chiang, to give Hsiao-yen his English name, as well as his twin brother, Winston, the president of Soochow University, it was a welcome leap out of the shadows, and handy publicity for his soon published memoirs, *The Chiang Family's Outside Children*. For the KMT old guard, it was an admission that the Chiang dynasty had never really gone away, and that even at the time Chiang Ching-kuo had announced in 1985 that 'none of his sons' would run for the presidency after his death, one of his secret children was just about to be promoted to Administrative Vice-Minister.

John Chiang reclaimed his famous surname just as the DPP were trying to scrub it from public monuments. It irked 'pan-Green' supporters that the capital of their vibrant and increasingly diverse democracy had, at its heart, a massive, imposing square dedicated to a military dictator. They accepted, they said, the legal documentation that demanded Chiang Kai-shek should have a permanent memorial, but contested whether it shouldn't be somewhere a little more discreet, such as at his actual tomb. They proposed renaming the Chiang Kai-shek Memorial Hall as the National Taiwan Democracy Memorial Hall, and its nearby public space as the Liberty Plaza. In order to gain approval for such a proposal, they cunningly rezoned the Memorial Hall and its plaza as a 'temporary historical site', thereby allowing them to run the whole scheme through the legislative wing of government without having to get assent from the executive.

Sure of a hefty turnout from the KMT's supporters, John Chiang held a rally at the site, flipping the DPP's tactics back at it by turning the event into a struggle for recognition and respect for the historical past, instead of a celebration of a politically diverse future. After all, was not his newly claimed grandfather Chiang Kai-shek also part of history? Who were the DPP to erase him from the record? His display was in vain, and on 19 May 2007, not uncoincidentally the anniversary of the declaration of martial law in 1949, Chen Shui-bian hosted a ceremony unveiling the site's new name, on a sign decorated with white Formosa lilies, in recognition of the student sit-in of 1990. Before long, the pious on-site exhibition of the life and achievements of Chiang Kai-shek had been replaced with a display marking landmark events on the road to democracy, and including names of the many dissidents martyred in the White Terror.

The scuffles continued on multiple fronts, including city ordinances hassling the name-changers on technicalities regarding 'vandalism' to a historic monument, and legal challenges in the legislature over who had the right to change the name at all. Just five days after Chen's triumphant stunt, his sign was taken down again by the Ministry of Education, citing the unacceptable costs of the round-the-clock police guard, itself installed after a KMT veteran had spat on the sign. To add to the fun, nitpickers pointed out that the term 'Memorial Hall' usually implied the commemoration of something that was dead, so what did that say about Taiwanese democracy?

The jurisdictional fighting went on for months, while even the instigators of the name change sometimes forgot about it — in an apology for the Ministry of Education's ham-fisted handling of the incident, the DPP's Annette Lu accidentally referred to it as the Chiang Kai-shek Memorial Hall. The entire matter became a cause célèbre in the presidential election, and the reversal of the DPP's decision was one of the political promises of the KMT's campaign. It took barely a week after the election of the KMT's Ma Ying-jeou to the presidency in March 2008 for the White Terror exhibition to be removed. It took until the summer for the name to be officially revoked, and another year before the new signage of the Chiang Kai-shek Memorial Hall was installed, along with the honour guard at the Generalissimo's statue. Having learned their lessons, the authorities did not make a political event of the installation, preferring instead to sneak in and complete the work while the media's eyes were fixed on the World Games in Kaohsiung.

The KMT rode back into power on the wave of electoral dissatisfaction with Chen's administration. With most of the island map except for the Hoklo heartland around Tainan now coloured 'Blue', President Ma Ying-jeou could take a conciliatory attitude towards Beijing, leading to an eight-year thaw in cross-Strait relations, but he soon ruffled feathers at home. He oversaw the adoption of the PRC-approved Pinyin as the official romanisation system for transliterating Mandarin Chinese (see Notes on Names for a sense of this author's palpable relief), and presided over the Three Links — of post, transport, and trade — that normalised communications between mainland China and Taiwan.

Ma fell foul of the Taiwanese people when he hosted a high-profile Beijing dignitary for a controversial visit. Inevitably, the visit of Chen Yunlin, chairman of Beijing's Association for Relations Across the Taiwan Straits, attracted protestors, and the actions of the Taiwanese police to shield him from insult included the confiscation of flags for the Republic of China, and a ten-officer raid on a record shop that was playing the politically coded folksongs from 1979's *Songs of Taiwan* with the doors open.[17]

The younger generation of activists were animated about the fact that Taiwanese law made their actions as illegal as if they had been living in Beijing — a law on parade and assembly forbade them from protesting without government permission.

Four hundred students staged a silent sit-in at the Taiwanese parliament, calling themselves the Wild Strawberries (*Ye Caomei*). The name derived in part from the Wild Lilies of the previous generation, but also from the use of the term 'strawberry' as an insult by the older generation. The youth today, it was said, were insubordinate slackers who 'bruised easily' like soft fruits — the epithet is equivalent to 'snowflake' in English.

Other forms of protest were beautifully subtle. In an indicator of the relentless march of progress, the 5,000 inhabitants of distant Orchid Island gained their first 7-Eleven convenience store in 2014, although they were still awaiting an answer about what was to be done about all the nuclear waste that had been dumped on their land by the Taipower company in the previous 30 years. When Taipower began to provide free electricity, island-wide, as an attempt to buy their silence, residents of

Orchid Island somehow managed to clock up twice the kilowatt hours in power usage when compared to people in other parts of Taiwan. By 2012, the free energy supply to Orchid Island was costing Taipower US$3.33 million a year, including power for one unnamed family that ran up a monthly bill of almost US$4,000, presumably by leaving everything on, all the time.[18]

But the actions of the Orchid Islanders were a sideshow compared to the youth movement in mid-2010s Taiwan. That movement defined itself as 'pro-Democracy', thereby implying that all the claims for Taiwan as a democracy already were worth nothing to the island's younger voters. Again appropriating floral imagery in imitation of the Wild Lilies, the 'Sunflowers' occupied the Taiwanese parliament to protest at the Cross-Strait Service Trade Agreement, a treaty that many believed would expose Taiwanese infrastructure to mainland interference and control. They were evicted by riot police, but were supported by a large crowd marching on the government offices outside.

Initially, the Sunflowers had adopted 'Rise Up' by the band Mayday as their protest song, but the pop group soon gave in to online pressure from their large following on the mainland and disavowed their connection to the movement. Instead, the Sunflowers seized upon a song by the Kaohsiung band Fire EX. 'Island's Sunrise' (*Daoyu Tiangguang*, 2014) exhorted the listener in Hokkien to 'fight the unforgiven ones'.

An angry Ma Ying-jeou, nearing the end of his second term as president, addressed the student demonstrators: 'Is this the sort of democracy we want? Must the rule of law be sacrificed in such a manner? Do we not take pride in our democracy and our respect for rule of law?'[19]

Over in Beijing, the sight of the beleaguered Ma was a cause of some concern to Xi Jinping, the recently appointed president of the People's Republic. Through the Xinhua news agency, he issued a stern warning. If whoever won the Taiwanese election dared to make any public statements regarding Taiwanese independence, 'the earth will move and the mountains will shake'.[20] The cordial relationship Ma had enjoyed with Beijing, and the freeze on PRC troublemaking during his tenure, seemed at risk of coming apart if the voters of Taiwan swung their support to the DPP.

As the 2016 election loomed, Taiwanese politics suddenly turned on an unexpected fulcrum, when the Tainan-born teenager Chou Tzuyu, a singer in the Korean girl-group Twice, waved a Taiwanese flag on-stage on a Seoul TV show. Accused of being an independence activist, she was pressured to issue a public apology, and her group's mainland tour dates were cancelled. Pushed before the cameras in an appearance one step removed from a hostage video, the remorseful, black-clad Tzuyu read out from a piece of paper: 'There is only one China. The two sides of the [Taiwan] Strait are one entity. I feel proud being a Chinese. I, as a Chinese, have hurt the company and netizens' feelings due to my words and actions during overseas promotions. I feel very, very sorry and also very guilty.'

The sight of her apology, and the implication that mainland politics still called the shots even in something so effervescent as teen pop promotion, was claimed to have influenced up to 1.34 million young Taiwanese voters the following day. In the final tally, the independent James Soong won 12.84 per cent of the votes, splitting voters away from the official KMT candidate, Wang Ju-hsuan, with 31.04.[21] The DPP candidate Tsai Ing-wen stormed to victory with a 56.12 per cent share.

Tzuyu was not the only pop star to get into trouble. Shortly after the election, Madonna (yes, *the* Madonna) appeared at a Taipei concert wrapped in the Taiwanese flag. This managed to annoy almost everybody, with complaints not only from the People's Republic, but also from the Taiwanese themselves, who identified the blue-and-red flag with the star of the Kuomintang as a Nationalist emblem, unrepresentative of the DPP-focused electorate that had voted against them.[22]

CHAPTER TWELVE

THE TIDES OF HISTORY

Taiwan Under Tsai Ing-wen (2016–2024)

There were plenty of other reasons why the Nationalists lost the 2016 election. The KMT had been hobbled by the Sunflower protests, which shut down its plans for further cross-Strait ties. It had stumbled once more into a candidate selection that failed to reconcile the factionalism behind its unified party façade. Blaming a Strawberry youth backlash, as some pundits tried to do, because mainland trolls were mean to a teenage singer, was the easy way out. More-informed analysts saw the election as a foregone conclusion. 'The [Nationalist] party expected to lose the presidential election,' writes Shelley Rigger, 'and it did.' However, it possibly lost to a greater degree than it had expected.

> The legislative losses even extended to districts once considered safe; the old political map showing a 'Blue' (KMT-leaning) north and a 'Green' (DPP-leaning) south turned into a fat Green doughnut encircling a much-reduced Blue center.[1]

Among the new politicians voted into office, a stand-out was Freddy Lim Tshiong-tso, a man who might reasonably be described as the Nationalists' worst nightmare. Born in 1976, and hence growing up with no memory of the martial-law era, Lim ceased to follow the KMT party line during his school days, instead becoming an enthusiastic supporter of Taiwanese independence. He initially entered the public eye as the convenor of pro-independence rock concerts, and would eventually serve as the head of Taiwan's branch of Amnesty International, and become a key figure in the Sunflower movement. Throughout the late 1990s and the early years of the 21st century, he was also the lead singer of the death-metal band Chthonic, releasing a series of politically charged works, including a concept album about the 1930 Musha Incident (*Seediq Bale*, 2005), an album with allusions to the February 1947 unrest as an earthly manifestation of Hell (*Mirror of Retribution*, 2009), and an album dedicated to the conflicted loyalties of indigenous soldiers serving in the Japanese military in World War II (*Takasago Army*, 2011). Donning a suit instead of his habitual leathers and tribal face paint, Lim became one of the founders of the New Power Party, its emblem stark Sunflower-yellow, and he proved to be enough of a diplomat to shoo away other DPP-leaning candidates in a western Taipei suburban district, where he defeated the KMT incumbent. He then aligned his party broadly with the 'Green' policies of the victorious DPP.

Taiwan's new president, the DPP's Tsai Ing-wen, was just as emblematic of the vast transformations the island had undergone in the last century. She was highly educated — armed with a doctorate in law from the London School of Economics — and was also ideally connected to multiple groups within Taiwan, boasting a Hakka grandfather and a Paiwan grandmother. She was Taiwan's first female president, and the first with indigenous ancestry — her Paiwan name is Tjuku. She was also unmarried — a first for a Taiwanese leader — and prepared to stand up for a number of minority issues. One of her first acts was to deliver an official apology for 400 years of colonialism, followed by a pardon for Talum Sukluman, a high-profile defendant in a case of 'illegal' hunting on tribal lands. Her critics, however, decried this as a mere performance, designed to reinforce the image of the DPP at home and abroad as progressive and pro-indigenous, whereas it might be more reasonably described as anti-KMT. It was, for example, notable that indigenous solidarity was of little electoral value among Tsai's own Paiwan clansmen, many of whom continued to vote conservatively for the KMT rather than support one of 'their own' in a party that seemed determined to upset the status quo.[2]

Such criticism might seem unnecessarily harsh, although it does resurrect some of the old ideology of the 1970s, suggesting that the DPP in power was involved in a concerted effort to be as *not*-KMT as the *Dangwai* activists of old. But even if one believes such accusations of political opportunism, they did nevertheless create a safe space for numerous progressive *opportunities*. These included not only the legalisation of same-sex marriage, but the removal of Mandarin's unique status as Taiwan's national language — it now jostles for attention alongside 16 indigenous languages, sign language for the deaf, Hakka, and two forms of Hokkien. Tsai also proposed a long-term Bilingual Country Project, to make Taiwan's official second language English by 2030.

Unlike Chen Sui-bian, Tsai Ing-wen was returned to power with a majority in the government's legislative branch, allowing her a better leverage on reforms. Some of these included subtle digs at the old Nationalist ideology, such as her comments upon visiting a squalid army base in 2017. She asked the officers: 'How will the young boys and girls be willing to join the military if they know they will live in such ragged rooms?'[3]

Tsai Ing-wen, who served as president of the Republic of China
on Taiwan from 2016 to 2024.

Her sarcasm masked more wide-ranging concerns about Taiwan's ability to defend itself in a new era. The launch of the PRC's first aircraft carrier, the *Liaoning* in 2012, had completely upset the longstanding Strategic Sustainability doctrine of Hau Pei-tsun (see Chapter Ten). There was, after all, no point in having a mountain bastion on the east coast of Taiwan if the PRC could now attack the island from all sides at once. After spending years planning to fight the mainland Chinese in a 'Decisive Campaign at the Water's Edge', it was now argued that 21st-century deterrence required a more proactive ability to fight a 'Decisive Campaign Outside the Territory'. In the event of a Chinese attack on Taiwan, or the threat of a Chinese attack on Taiwan, the island's military would now apparently require the ability to strike back on the mainland, in order to neutralise long-range attacks or naval launches before they could happen. Tsai also personally ordered the creation of a Taiwanese cyberwarfare division in 2017, the Information, Communication, and Electronic Force Command (ICEFCOM).[4]

At the 19th Party Congress in Beijing in 2017, PRC president Xi Jinping put forward an unwavering policy regarding the attitude of the People's Republic towards the island he still regarded as a rogue province.

> We will resolutely uphold national sovereignty and territorial integrity and will never tolerate a repeat of the historical tragedy of a divided country. All activities of splitting the motherland will be resolutely opposed by all the Chinese people. We have firm will, full confidence and sufficient capability to defeat any form of Taiwan independence secession plot. We will never allow any person, any organisation or any political party to split any part of the Chinese territory from China at any time or in any form.[5]

On the surface, this might sound like a reiteration of the same position that has been in place since 1949, a form of 'don't ask, don't tell' regarding Taiwan's de facto independence. But rumblings elsewhere pointed to an escalation of the mainland's interest in resolving its Taiwan problem on a specific timetable. Xi Jinping has alluded to a 'China dream' that must be completed within his own lifetime — more specifically, complete reunification by 2049, the centenary of Mao's declaration of the People's Republic.[6]

Dwarfed by such large-scale geopolitical issues, political campaigners back in Taiwan continued to seek to attract attention through performative violence. The statue of the Japanese hydraulic engineer Hatta Yōichi, sequestered in 1949 but restored in 1981 to its original location overlooking his dam, had become an icon of goodwill and reconciliation between Taiwan and Japan, particularly at the turn of the 21st century, when the Japanese prime minister Mori Yoshirō hailed from the same birthplace. However, in 2017, the Hatta statue was beheaded. The culprit was soon revealed as a former Taipei city councillor, determined to score points on behalf of the China Unification Promotion Party.[7]

President Tsai Ing-wen also faced attention-seeking agitation within her own party. Peng Ming-min, the long-lived activist who had served as a political adviser to Chen Shui-bian, campaigned within the DPP for Tsai to push further towards independence, by holding a referendum on whether the people of Taiwan wanted it. Mere months after the disastrous Brexit vote in the United Kingdom, Tsai resisted a similar hot-button issue, liable to suffer comparable manipulations.[8]

At the start of the Chen Shui-bian era, the victorious DPP had commenced its efforts to remove many of the symbols of the KMT's old order. As president, Tsai presided over a continued removal of KMT symbols from public spaces, for which her Minister of Culture would receive a slap on the face from an angry singer, who accused her of 'de-Chiang Kai-shek-ising' Taiwan. Tsai-era assaults on the KMT's legacy included the suspension of the twice-daily playing of the 'Chiang Kai-shek Memorial Song' at the Generalissimo's Memorial Hall in Taipei, which some might regard as a mercy.

While the occasionally resurgent KMT might fight defensively over the Chiang Kai-shek Memorial, it remained relatively toothless in the face of the removal of multiple Chiang statues from DPP-dominated areas all around the 'fat Green doughnut'. By 2017, over 200 Chiang Kai-shek statues had been relocated to a park in Taoyuan, near his mausoleum. There, they lurk like a bunch of confused old men, reconceived as an art installation — a monument to monuments. Many thousands of statues of Chiang remain dotted around the country (47 still in place in Taipei alone, including the most massive, in the Memorial Hall itself), leading the DPP representative Pasuya Yao to make the modest proposal of removing *all* the Chiang statues to the same place, and while the government was at it, to scrub Chiang's face from Taiwanese coinage. Tsai Ing-wen, no doubt seeing this for the 'extreme-Green' dog whistle that it was, refused to comment on the issue. She, too, had to pick her battles.[9]

If the statues had a say in it, some might have preferred to be put out to pasture. In 2018, on the anniversary of the February 28 Incident, protestors hurled red paint at the statue of Chiang Kai-shek in his Memorial Hall. They did so as part of an ongoing movement demanding not merely an apology for the persecution of the KMT's enemies, but reparations and a more sensitive attitude towards the way in which the Taiwanese government tells its own story about itself. The KMT, it argued, was undoubtedly a major component in modern Chinese history, but so were the myriad victims of the KMT's clampdowns and killings. A few months later, the statue got another pelting, this time of eggs and paint thrown by independence activists. Far from presenting a focus of reflection and respect for the younger generation, Chiang's effigy had become more of a permanent target for dissidents.

After the relative détente of the Ma Ying-jeou years, Beijing renewed its arm-twisting in the international realm. The number of Chinese visitors, who formed a lucrative new tourist sector when Ma was president, plummeted to low levels that threatened to bankrupt many travel companies and sites.[10] The number of countries with which Taiwan enjoyed full diplomatic relations continued to dwindle in the Tsai era, after The Gambia opened a PRC embassy, followed by São Tomé and Príncipe (2016), Panama (2017), the Dominican Republic (2018), Burkina Faso (2018), El Salvador (2018), the Solomon Islands (2018), Kiribati (2019), Nicaragua (2021), and Honduras (2023). In a particularly cunning move, the PRC even claimed jurisdiction over Taiwanese *criminals*, demanding that Taiwanese citizens extradited from overseas had to be 'returned' to the People's Republic, rather than their birthplace.[11]

In the 2020 election, Tsai was able to point to Hong Kong as an example of what happened when China got what it wanted. Hong Kong had been offered in the 1990s as an illustration of how Taiwan might be reintegrated into the People's Republic as a Special Autonomous Region with its own laws and liberties secure for 50 years. Instead, the guarantees made to Hong Kong under its 1997 Basic Law were being ignored, suspended, or betrayed, adding fuel to the DPP's re-election campaign.

On Tsai Ing-wen's re-election, Xi Jinping sent a chilling warning from Beijing:

> Momentary reversals are but just bubbles left behind by the tides of history ... We want to directly warn Tsai Ing-wen and the DPP not to act wilfully and rashly because of a temporary fluke.[12]

Among the Strawberries, or at least their death-metal-loving faction, the most recent album from Chthonic offered a Buddhist analogy. *Battlefields of Asura* (2018) carried the alternate title *Politics*, and offered this assessment of the situation in 'A Crimson Sky's Command': 'Invade! Attack! Quell the foes and fiends / Destroy all enemies, / demon's blood streams'.[13]

It was all quite at odds with frontman Freddy Lim's earnest and nuanced approach to the issues offstage. Parting ways with his own New Power Party, he successfully ran for his district in 2020 as an independent with strong support for Tsai Ing-wen.

The Taiwanese themselves remained buoyant about the threat from the PRC. In a 2021 poll, 45 per cent of them regarded a war with China as unlikely, and 17 per cent regarded it as 'impossible'.[14] Such self-assurance should be balanced with the ominous wording of comments made from Beijing, but also with the inevitable fact that Taiwan and China have a symbiotic relationship that neither can really afford to jeopardise. Taiwan, in fact, is one of China's significant business partners, with annual bilateral trade topping $110 billion.

Tsai Ing-wen went so far as to call Taiwan's chip industry a 'silicon shield' that protected it from outside interference, although one might just have easily suggested that it was an asset that encouraged some states to interfere in order to prevent other states interfering *more*.[15]

Chris Miller's business history *Chip War*, for example, begins with a stirring account of US Navy build-up in the Taiwan Strait in 2020, which he relates not to Tsai's re-election, but to renewed cross-Strait tensions brought about by an embargo against selling US computer chips to the

Chinese mega-conglomerate Huawei. China, writes Miller, 'now spends more money each year importing chips than oil. These semi-conductors are plugged into all manner of devices, from smartphones to refrigerators, that China consumes at home or exports worldwide.'[16]

Miller points to a lethal choke point in modern geopolitics, the fact that entire economies and strategic considerations now rely not on commodities such as steel and oil, but on control of the market in integrated computer circuits — a market in which Taiwan is as crucial in the 21st century as it was to camphor in the 19th. As a case in point, Miller presents 2020's iPhone 12, a vital commodity for both Chinese manufacturers and American distributors, a device which could not function without the A14 processor chip, then made solely by a single factory at the Taiwan Semiconductor Manufacturing Company (TSMC). Amid tensions over the COVID-19 virus, itself causing substantial disruption to the global supply chain, the standoff over Huawei served to demonstrate the crucial strategic value of Taiwan. Computer chips are fundamental to so much in modern life, enabling the functioning not only of the computer on which I am writing this, but of the Kindle you might be reading it on, the programming settings on our washing machines and fridges, the dashboards of our cars, and the guidance systems of military hardware. After 2020, the realisation that TSMC's lone factory supplied 37 per cent of the world's annual computing power led to the swift set-up of fabrication units in other countries. At the time of writing, the 'Taiwan' Semiconductor Manufacturing Company now also makes chips in Japan and the United States, and hopes to open another facility in Germany. Nonetheless, Taiwan remains the world's major source of this crucial component.

As the 2024 presidential election neared, Tsai's DPP pushed through as many elements of 'Green' legislation as it could, while activists continued to point to many injustices and unresolved issues within the Taiwanese administration.

The dwindling Thao people of the shores of Sun-Moon Lake still faced an uphill struggle, with further expropriations of Thao territory being earmarked for development by a corporation that planned to put a massive resort hotel at Peacock Garden on the lake shore. The news could not have come at a worse time, since it came the day after a deliberately timed announcement by the Council of Indigenous Peoples (CIP), regarding the traditional territories of the Thao and Atayal peoples. According to the CIP's new guidelines, the Peacock Garden was on Thao lands, and consequently required the 'free, prior and informed consent' of Thao representatives before anyone could operate on it. The Thao, in fact, had been fighting the Peacock Garden project for years, but the CIP's announcement now added legislative buttresses to their complaints. Was the Taiwanese government going to honour its assurances to the Formosan indigenous peoples in its various new laws of the 2000s, or were they empty promises?[17]

In October 2022, Taiwan's constitutional court acknowledged the rights of the *pingpu* (plains) peoples' descendants to be recognised as 'indigenous' people, on the grounds that ignoring their status was tantamount to ethnic erasure. The news was greeted with elation, particularly among the Siraya people, whose tribal culture and language had been all but wiped out by centuries of Chinese, Dutch, and Japanese interactions in the Tainan plains area. But the decision was by no means welcomed by everybody — the court case had arisen from a dispute between representatives of the Siraya and the Council of Indigenous Peoples, which had repeatedly refused the Sirayan application for recognition. Reading between the lines of the court's statement, the CIP has merely been asked to *reconsider* its position by 2025, along parameters riddled with loopholes:

> For a tribe to be recognized, it has to continue to practice its ethnic languages, customs, traditions and culture, tribe members shall share a common sense of ethnic identity, and the tribe's ties to Austronesian peoples can be substantiated by historical data.[18]

The Siraya have a way to go before they can prove, for example, that they continue to practise a language that they themselves term 'dormant'. Should they be able to do so, they would qualify for a basket of indigenous concessions, including affirmative-action posts on various government bodies, and preferential access to certain scholarships and school admissions. But this is precisely why the CIP has presented such a stonewall, since its own officials regard the concessions to the 16 recognised tribes to be hard-won and justified, whereas the self-identified

Siraya are often indistinguishable from the Chinese population, and hence do not suffer the same sort of setbacks. Conversely, the Siraya have countered that they have been harder done by *because* they were exposed earlier to colonial influences, and that there is still a reparation to be addressed.

If the CIP acknowledges that the Siraya are 'indigenous', it opens the floodgates for a quarter of a million *pingpu* descendants to be similarly rebranded as indigenous people — Ketagalan, Taokas, Pazeh, Papora, Babuza, Hoanya, and Makatau. The recognition process is likely to create a degree of ethnic one-upmanship as the CIP argues that there is a world of difference between, say, a Chinese-speaking urban lawyer with a Babuza grandmother who wants his kids to have an easier ride in the university entrance exam, and a Paiwan girl who has grown up in rural poverty with limited access to amenities and education. Much as the KMT and then DPP turned on each other even as they won victories, progress for the indigenous peoples may induce factionalism and in-fighting.

This, however, is not the hottest of the hot-potato issues facing indigenous people in Taiwan in the 21st century. That's something yet to officially attract the notice of the People's Republic but must surely be a matter under consideration among the hawks who expect Taiwan to be assimilated within the People's Republic before the middle of the century.

The topic is one that, in theory, could have been placed in this book in Chapter One, since it relates to the prehistory of Taiwan and its inhabitants. I choose to place it here at the end of this book for historiographical reasons, because it is only in the 21st century that the idea has gained any traction.

It had been observed in academic circles, as early as the 1880s, that there were many words shared by various Austronesian languages, suggesting that all had a common ancestor, just as most European languages can be traced back to the theoretical Proto-Indo-European. In 1889, the Dutch linguist Hendrik Kern used the same sort of methodology to investigate Austronesian as had been used to investigate European linguistics, establishing a possible timeline to explain how some words remained the same and some became different. He observed that the languages shared many terms for marine life, suggesting a coastal affinity, but also that many shared the word for rice. Kern's theory helped feed into what is now the accepted belief — that people from somewhere in East Asia spread out across the Pacific, joining or sometimes supplanting the pre-existing inhabitants, not only in the Philippines, but further afield, in Indonesia, Micronesia, Malaysia, as far to the west as Madagascar, and over many centuries of island-hopping, eventually arriving in Hawaii and Easter Island around AD 800, and New Zealand around AD 1200.

It was not until a century later, armed with more information on Austronesian linguistics and other metadata, that Robert Blust of the University of Hawaii offered a more exacting theory. Blust condensed the 1,200 language variants of Austronesian — a polity so diverse as to encompass 20 per cent of all human languages — into ten subgroups, and then noted that nine of them were only found on Taiwan. It was possible, he argued, by applying forensic linguistics to the evolution of languages, that Taiwan had been the homeland of whatever sailors had set out on that long series of voyages across the Pacific. The key was the Taiwan Strait itself, which for much of human history had been uncrossable, until a 'eureka' moment 5,000 years ago, when proto-Dai people from what is now South China were able to make the crossing to Taiwan. From there, they spread out across the island, but now also developed the sea-faring technology to leave again a thousand years later, at first along the Batanes island chain that led to the Philippines, and thence out to the rest of the Pacific.

Blust offered multiple correlating data for such a hypothesis, including the fact that Austronesian languages had terms for many things found on Taiwan, including historical fauna and flora, but also for things that did not exist in those far-flung places, such as 'cold weather'. The word in Saisiyat for 'thank you' is *ma'alo* — a term that, according to this hypothesis, would be carried across the waves in successive migrations, across many centuries and thousands of miles, until it arrived in Hawaiian, where it endures as *mahalo*.[19]

The narrative presented by the 'Out of Taiwan' theory is potential catnip to the right wing, ready to use it as 'proof' that in ancient times Taiwan somehow *conquered* the Pacific Ocean, whereas all it really suggests is that today's indigenous Taiwanese have distant cousins far and wide. But it would only take one spurious paper in the right Chinese journal to suggest that this was indeed the case, that 'Chinese' people had settled in Taiwan, and that their descendants had settled across islands and distant lands that now constituted 37 sovereign states, thereby bringing a whole bunch of places — including the Solomon Islands, Guam, and Fiji, not to mention Myanmar and Cambodia — into a sphere of 'Chinese' interest.

The 'sphere of interest' of course, and Taiwan's location within it, remains the most visible element of modern Taiwanese politics, as Beijing and Taipei continue to argue over Taiwan's status. In many cases, the rhetoric is actually aimed at domestic populations, as politicians on both sides of the Strait try to cultivate a tough appearance. For Taipei, the issue is one of the 'Communist bandits' who have taken over the mainland. For Beijing, it is not Taiwan itself that presents a threat, but the very existence of a 'Republic of China' that offers an alternative to a Communist China.

The stresses and strains can take many forms, and manifest in many ways. In 2015, I was in Beijing when the US politician Nancy Pelosi visited for trade talks. Pelosi had been a vocal opponent of China's human-rights record since at least 1989 and the events in Tiananmen Square, but was obliged to be at least cordial with the PRC. I vividly remember the pearl-clutching horror among the mainland Chinese when, it was alleged, she finished a speech by throwing in a little bit of Mandarin.

'*Xiexie*,' she said — thank you.

Except she didn't. The word that came out of her mouth sounded more like *Siesie* — an easy mistake for a foreigner to make, but also, unfortunately, exactly the way that the word would sound if she had been coached by someone with a Taiwanese accent. It would come as no surprise to anyone that Pelosi had Taiwanese advisers, but it soured the mainlanders even more towards her. I myself never heard the speech, only the aghast reactions to it of the people around me ... many of whom had presumably not heard the speech, either, if it even happened at all.

Much of the mainland's behaviour towards Taiwan is regarded by the PRC as an entirely proportional response, designed to prevent its alleged 'rogue province' from slipping even further down the road to independence. Sometimes these acts are economic — sudden freezes on tourism, for example, or a brief boycott of Taiwanese pineapples, designed to make clear what a difference economic sanctions can make. Sometimes they are cultural — the cancellation or vilification of anyone who dares to wave a Taiwanese flag or refer to it as a nation in its own right, which sounds trivial until one considers the economic impact of a concert tour or movie release in the world's largest market.

But part of the PRC policy is to keep Taiwan guessing about the possibility of an actual military action. In 2017, Xi Jinping pointedly mentioned that 'complete national reunification is an inevitable requirement for realising the dream of the Chinese nation', implying that he wanted to see Taiwan back within China's authority by the 2049 centenary of the founding of the People's Republic.[20]

Taiwan's Minister of Defence took such proclamations seriously enough to suggest that the PRC would have evolved the military capacity to mount an invasion of Taiwan by 2025, but this, too, can be seen as a rhetoric designed for an unseen audience — in this case, the US government that continues to function as a deterrent, posting warships to the Taiwan Strait whenever things get particularly tense.

Taiwan's friends in the political sphere need to tiptoe around anything that risks 'provoking' Beijing. When US president Donald Trump answered a congratulatory phone call from Tsai Ing-wen after his election in 2016, it led to protests from the PRC that he was 'recognising' the leader of a rogue state. When Nancy Pelosi visited Taiwan in 2022, her trip was slammed by Beijing as a deliberate provocation. Simply by taking off for Taiwan in a plane, she managed to initiate mainland import restrictions on a hundred Taiwanese food products, as well as an export ban on mainland sand — the Taiwanese might be preparing to fight them on the beaches, but they would have to bring their own beach. Pelosi also caused a prolonged military exercise by the Chinese navy, not only within the Taiwan Strait, but to the island's north and south, as if to demonstrate the PRC's increasing competence in 'blue-water' operations, and hence its ability to come at Taiwan from all sides. The incursions were accompanied by live-fire artillery exercises in the Taiwan Strait, multiple airspace violations by PRC fighter jets, and the launch of a dozen ballistic missiles, five of which created an all-new issue by landing in Japanese waters.

Herself playing to her home constituency, Pelosi announced that the PRC had reacted 'like a scared bully'.

A significant number of armchair generals on PRC social media complained that Beijing had not gone far enough. They were advised by an official to be 'rational patriots', suggesting that Beijing and Taipei are both playing a carefully nuanced political game of proportional threats and proportional responses, each testing the other, each watching its own citizens to see how they react. The players, however, in this great game are constantly changing, not only within Taipei's party-political system, but behind the scenes of Beijing's monolithic façade. The PRC's most recent Five-Year-Plan, which ends in 2025, calls for a 'Made in China' initiative across multiple high-tech sectors, including crucial areas that influence military capability.[21]

It remains to be seen whether Taiwan will be the origin of a globally influential conflict in East Asia, or a masterclass in diplomacy, teaching an object lesson to the world. This small island off the coast of China has become the fulcrum of multiple issues in the history of the region, starting with the convenience its offshore position offered to pirates and foreign incursions. Its acquisition by the Qing dynasty marked the start of a century of imperial expansion that saw China turning into a multi-ethnic society. Its outlaw frontiers became a crucible of underground revolution and dissent, ultimately exported back to the mainland. Its treaty ports, chosen for their remoteness from the Chinese centre, fermented contacts with foreign powers. Its loss to the Japanese in 1895 turned it into a testing ground for Japan's own imperial expansion, soon exported throughout East Asia. After World War II, it became the last bastion of the Republic of China, and one of the vital preservers of traditions and artefacts that would have otherwise been lost in the Cultural Revolution. Its strategic commodities, from camphor to plastics to computer chips, have formed vital links in global economics for 200 years, and continue to do so. In our age, it could become a flashpoint of international tension, or an icon of how a Chinese democracy can function in the modern world. All these things, come out of Taiwan, that rebel island.

ACKNOWLEDGEMENTS

My thanks to Simon Wright at Scribe's London office for seeing the potential of this book; my readers, Sharon Gosling, Adam Newell, and Jenna Tang; and David Golding at Scribe Melbourne for a deft edit that improved even on the improvements of the others. Any remaining errors are sure to be mine. The library at London's School of Oriental and African Studies was a source of many obscure publications that have improved my citations. Thanks also to the Stefan R. Landsberger Collection at chineseposters.net for their invaluable curation of the propaganda images that appear in this book. My wife, Emily Carlson Clements, rashly boasted that my writing this book while she gave birth to our daughter Tara was not a problem, and graciously did not complain about it when it rather obviously became one.

NOTES ON NAMES

In the wake of the events in Tiananmen Square in June 1989, the authorities at the Department of East Asian Studies at the University of Leeds pulled their foreign exchange students out of institutions on the Chinese mainland. That year's sophomores were instead packed off to National Chengchi University in Taipei for their mandatory year abroad. I blundered along in their wake, getting on a plane for the first time in my adult life, for a 17-hour journey to a place I had barely heard of.

Back in Leeds, the students returning from Taiwan caused a stir in the department. To the ears of lecturers and classmates who had all previously existed in an entirely Beijing-oriented environment, we spoke Mandarin with odd, hissy accents, peppered with alien slang and snatches of Hokkien, Hakka, and Japanese. As if we had fallen through a timeslip from the 1930s, we wrote Chinese characters in complex, classical forms, and our bags and folders bore the forbidden flag of the Kuomintang. For good or ill, we represented a concept that mainland Chinese only occasionally embraced — what we would now call the prospect of *diversity* within China and the Chinese experience.

Over the years, particularly after my time in Xi'an in the 2010s, my own Taiwanese accent faded away almost completely. Every now and then, something still sneaks in, such as my habit of referring to *dalu* ('the mainland' or 'the continent'), which continues to give me away as someone who learned his Mandarin in Taipei. The term is so common on Taiwan because referring to the land across the Strait as 'China' would rather imply that Taiwan was *not*-China.

When it comes to writing about the history of Taiwan, there is a political dimension even to the transcription of Chinese that risks compromising any attempt at a readable narrative. The People's Republic asserts that everyone should speak standard Mandarin, even though it admits that 30 per cent of its citizenry do not meet this target. Instead, such people speak what Beijing describes as 'dialects' and what linguists insist are 'topolects', local variants so different as to be mutually unintelligible. Hokkien and Cantonese are as different from standard Mandarin as English is from Dutch, but such an assertion causes trouble with institutions on both sides of the Taiwan Strait that insist on a homogenous 'one China'.

When it comes to place names and personal names, the problems can evaporate in written Chinese, where the same characters are often used, even if a term *sounds* different in various topolects. However, the issues return when the foreign scholar tries to write out the story in English. I must state my own bias upfront — that I regard the Pinyin system introduced on the mainland in 1958 to be the most sensible and workable format for writing Chinese words in English, and have used it for all relevant terms and names in the pre-modern period. After 1949, it becomes increasingly difficult to square Pinyin Romanisation with the self-identification of people and places on Taiwan. For obvious reasons, the people of Taiwan long refused to use Pinyin, adhering instead to a mixture of contending spellings, drawing on the older Wade–Giles system, half-remembered Yale coinages, personal spellings that nod to Hokkien or Cantonese accents, and random guesses or fancies.

This is most obvious in the teaching of Chinese to elementary-school children and foreigners in Taiwan, where clarity of pronunciation is defeated by the mismatched policies in use in every street sign, book title, and business card. Teachers in Taiwan instead use yet another system, the Zhuyin Fuhao syllabary (also known as Bo Po Mo Fo, after its first four symbols). This predates Pinyin, having been developed in the early years of the Republic of China by the philologist Zhang Binglin (1868–1936), but frankly only makes life more difficult, and is of no help to the general reader unless the general reader feels like memorising 38 new symbols.[1]

The government of Taiwan recognised this issue in 2009, early in the Ma Ying-jeou era, when it decreed that it would henceforth be using the Pinyin system on official documents. However, it left personal names, and by implication, any place names already in use, to individual discretion, which has led to a predictably slow process of change, still ongoing and liable to afflict writing on Taiwanese issues for the foreseeable future. It does, at least, give me some justification for the choices I have made in this book.

Regardless, it still seems counterproductive to write the name of the Generalissimo as *Jiang Jieshi*, when he spelled it himself as Chiang Kai-shek, and would have surely regarded the use of his enemies' orthography as a hostile and dismissive imposition. Consequently, when writing about the modern period, I have been forced to juggle Pinyin readings that help Mandarin speakers make sense of what a word means, with local customs and popular usage more in keeping with how the people of Taiwan wish to define themselves. There were, in fact, almost *no* place names of standard Mandarin origin in Taiwan until the coming of the KMT in 1945 — modern pronunciations impose a Mandarin orthodoxy on nouns originally parsed in Hokkien, Hakka, or one of dozens of indigenous languages. Even acknowledging this on each occasion in the main text would send the reader down a rabbit hole of 'the town of *Tpdu*, which means "sugar palm" in the Truku language, transliterated by the Chinese as *Tabiduo*, but renamed *Tianxiang* in 1967 in commemoration of a Song dynasty hero. It was submitted for reversion to its original name in 2014, but was refused, on the grounds that *Tianxiang* had since become popular with tourists.'[2]

I hence write the name of the island's contemporary capital as Taipei, as it appears in most maps, rather than the *Taipeh* of late 19th-century European accounts, the *Taipak* of its Taiwanese-speaking residents, the *Taibei* of Pinyin and Yale, the *T'aipei* of Wade–Giles, or the *Taihoku* of its Japanese colonial years. The sacred lakeland of the Thao people, which they called *Zintun a Wazaqan*, and which the Chinese foresters called *Tutingzi*, and then *Sun-Moon Lakes* (*Riyue-tan*) after 1821, was christened *Lake Candidius* by European missionaries, named for one of their own, and *Nichigetsu-tan* by the Japanese in a straightforward transfer of the Chinese name. After the rising waters from Hatta Yōichi's hydroelectric dam flooded the shallows and wetlands, forever joining the 'Sun' and 'Moon', it is usually called Sun-Moon Lake, in the singular.

Taiwan's late-20th-century president is referred to as Lee Teng-hui, his own choice, and not *Li Denghui* (Pinyin) or *Li Denghwei* (Yale), or indeed *Iwasato Masao*, the name he used during his youth as a Japanese subject. Similarly, I refer to the writer Bo Yang by the pseudonym he chose to use, rather than his birth name, *Guo Dingsheng*, or the name to which he changed it later in life, *Kuo I-tung* or *Guo Yidong*. The political campaigner Peng Ming-min was *Hō Minmin* in his Japanese-ruled youth, and given the English name *Peter* by his associates, but this was originally more of a nom de guerre to allow them to talk about him without fear of triggering eavesdroppers. He signed his memoirs with his full Chinese name, and that is what I use here. In the case of Lu Hsiu-lien, the political prisoner and DPP activist who would ultimately become Taiwan's vice-president in 2000, I have deliberately used her English name, Annette Lu, in order to accentuate those moments when a woman's voice can be heard in a history that all too often is only told by men.

Sometimes it can become a bit convoluted. I have chosen to cite the author of the *General History of Taiwan* as Lien Heng, rather than *Lian Heng*, to reflect the usage of his surname by his later descendants, who are high-profile figures in modern Taiwan, and did not use the *Lian* spelling that I would have otherwise chosen.

As for the warlord born as *Zheng Sen*, ennobled as *Zheng Chenggong*, addressed as *Guoxingye* ['Knight of the Royal Surname'], but more likely to be known by his Hokkien-speaking subjects as *Koksengya*, my own biography of him calls him *Coxinga*, which 20 years ago was the most common spelling in English-language publications outside Taiwan. In the two decades since, the spelling Koxinga, favoured by Taiwan tourist documentation, has won out, and I reluctantly adopt it here. I have made hundreds of similar decisions behind the scenes in an attempt to avoid distractions in the text — all of them are sure to annoy somebody. Some involve nuances that are still playing out — repeatedly in accounts of Taiwan in the 19th century, foreign writers discuss dealings with 'the Chinese', unable or unwilling to differentiate between Hoklo and Hakka, which today is a distinction with political implications. In a 21st century where factional allegiances can have lasting effects on media attention and organisational funding, historical events and actors once claimed as 'Chinese' are now being more incisively rendered as, for example, moments in Hakka history.

Conversely, when writing about the indigenous history of Taiwan, I have deliberately applied a retroactive consistency in naming and spelling, since practically every observer seems to apply a different name — the mishmash of Koaluts, Botans, Kuskus, Tuliasok, Siaoliao, Sabaree, 'Peony people', and 'Ling Nuangs' of various contradictory sources, for example, are all references to subgroups of what is known today as the Paiwan, some, but not all, united in early modern times under the Seqalu confederacy. For the entire 20th century, even under the Republic of China, the authorities clung to the nine tribal categories recognised by the Japanese in the colonial period. It is only in this century that an increased awareness of tribal identities among politicians (i.e. with the rise to power of the DPP in 2000) has led to further diversification — the recognition of the Thao as a tenth tribe in 2001, soon followed by the Truku, Tavalan, and Akizaya by 2004, and then the calving off of the Seediq from the Truku in 2008.

I have had to make a judgement call in some cases, based purely on the need for clarity and readability in a popular history. The villages called *Paran* by the Tgdaya and *Busia* by their Seediq Atayal cousins were called *Wushe* by the Chinese, but Musha by the Japanese, and the rebellion there has been filed in subsequent historiography by the Japanese name. It seems pedantic to refer to it as the 'Paran Rebellion', when every source in the library has it filed under M. In other cases, there is such a tangle of contradictory names that I have ruled in favour of vagueness. The Musha survivors were exiled to *Chuanzhongdao* ('Midriver Island'), which was not actually an island, but a Mandarin transliteration of the Japanese *Kawanakajima*, a new-built town named after a famous samurai-era battle, but since renamed *Qingliu*, and called by exiles themselves by the indigenous name *Alang Gluban*. Rather than wade through such hyper-qualifications, my main text simply sands down the details to 'somewhere else'.

When it comes to indigenous names, the local languages employ a given name and the simple repeat of the father's name. Mona Rudao is hence Mona [son of] Rudao, and *his* son is called Dadao Mona. The second name is not a patronymic, but the actual name of the father, and so it is customary to use the given name when referring to someone, otherwise you are referring to their dad.

In a popular history such as this, we might also expect the reader to be less familiar than scholarly specialists with the Chinese language. As a result, I have sometimes sneaked glosses into the text to remind people what something actually is. To say 'Alishan mountains' is a tautology, since the term *shan* literally means mountain, but I strongly feel that non-Chinese speakers are struggling hard enough already, and that such infelicities make their reading experience a little easier.

REFERENCES AND FURTHER READING

The references of this book, intended for a reader who cannot easily access sources in Chinese or Japanese, are mainly cited in English, or in the first point of contact between an English-language source and a Chinese original. I have made a few exceptions, most notably for Lien Heng's landmark *Taiwan Tongshi* (*General History of Taiwan*) the first overview of Taiwanese history, written by an eyewitness to events of the short-lived Republic of Formosa and the years of Japanese occupation. Although not without its controversies, his book is of monumental importance to modern Taiwanese and preserves many moments of high drama or local colour.

As noted in the introduction, identity politics is a powerful influence on Taiwanese historiography, and sometimes even the titles of the books represent challenges to established premises, or attempts to establish new ones. Su Beng's title, *Taiwan's 400 Year History*, for example, is mounted as a direct claim for the rights of those *bensheng* Taiwanese who were living on the island before the arrival of the KMT. It is a product of its time, published in 1962, when political opposition to the KMT was still illegal, and is hence focused on Su's struggle. Were he to write the book anew in 2024, I suspect he would welcome the chance to draw upon the last two decades' boom in indigenous studies, which would allow him to establish an even more enduring provenance for a Taiwanese identity. However, as his book stands, it dismisses the indigenous peoples in its first two pages. Similarly, the Revised and Enlarged edition of Ong Iok-tek's

Taiwan: A History of Agonies carefully acknowledges the historicity of its own editions, the first appearing as a polemic so excoriating it could only be published overseas in 1964, and revised with additional materials in the author's later years when he came to appreciate that he had omitted due consideration of Taiwan's indigenous peoples.

Over the last 20 years, the emphasis within Taiwan Studies of an Austronesian or indigenous perspective has completely rewritten the Taiwanese history I learned in my youth. David Blundell's collection *Austronesian Taiwan* is a good place to start, as well as the archaeological focus of Kuo Su-chiu's *New Frontiers in the Neolithic Archaeology of Taiwan* and Richard Pearson's *Taiwan Archaeology*. I mention these latter two books because they are the most recent to appear as of time of writing, and make it all too clear how fast-moving archaeology can be. As they reveal, several truths held to be self-evident only four or five years ago have since been rewritten through better carbon-dating or data tabulation. Scott Simon's *Truly Human* takes the story out of archaeology and into anthropology, with priceless observations of indigenous culture drawn from many years of participant observation.

I have had to make brutal decisions when it comes to events and characters. José Eugenio Borao Mateo can write an entire book on *The Spanish Experience in Taiwan*, intricately contextualising the 16-year Spanish colony within global geopolitics and trade, but I have had to restrict myself to a few moments where his story interconnects with the grand narrative. There is, similarly, ample information available on the Dutch era, not the least William Campbell's sourcebook *Formosa Under the Dutch*, and Leonard Blussé and Natalie Everts' multivolume *The Formosan Encounter*, but I have had to be ruthless, even with stories that I cherish, such as the ridiculously tall tales of the *Taiwan Waiji* or the outrageous behaviour of Pieter Nuijts, covered in greater detail in my own *Coxinga and the Fall of the Ming Dynasty*. I have had to limit my coverage of the turbulent 17th century to little more than a single chapter, but the entire car crash of contending interest groups is covered in more comprehensive detail in Tonio Andrade's *How Taiwan Became Chinese* and *Lost Colony*, the latter of which makes use of new discoveries unavailable to me when I wrote my own book.

There is a similar embarrassment of riches when it comes to Taiwan's period as a Japanese colony, although I have deliberately made my own life difficult by concentrating elsewhere on several areas that are underrepresented in Anglophone scholarship. These include the Kingdom of Dongning, for which Hayashida's *Tei-shi Taiwan-shi* was particularly useful, the short-lived Republic of Formosa, for which Harry Lamley's 1968 article and Niki Alsford's 2018 book remain the most accessible sources, and the interregnum between 1945 and 1949 when Taiwan was, at least notionally, more directly integrated into a mainland Republic of China — ably covered in Steven Phillips' *Between Assimilation and Independence.* When it comes to the later 20th century, I have deliberately relied on accounts from prominent people in the *Dangwai* movement, such as Peng Ming-min and Annette Lu Hsiu-lien, who would not only go on to become prominent figures in the DPP, but unlike some of their colleagues, were not subsequently cancelled over criminal connections. If I seem overly interested in the opinions of the KMT's rivals, I plead in my defence that the DPP have been in power for 16 of the last 24 years, and the Nationalists' most progressive and liberal reformer, Lee Teng-hui, the man who steered Taiwan from one-party state to truly liberal democracy, was subsequently blamed by the KMT for ruining its legacy, and drummed out of his own party in 2001. When it comes to the chaotic ferment of politics beyond the bilateral KMT–DPP standoff of early free elections, the whirl of multiple political parties is almost impossible to adequately parse, and I direct the interested reader to the works of Dafydd Fell below.

Much Taiwan publishing is in the hands of small presses such as SMC or dedicated organisations like the Shung Ye Museum of Formosan Aborigines — in an odd off-shoot of modern geopolitics and trade, such works can prove difficult to obtain outside Taiwan itself. Camphor Press is not merely an excellent curator of worthy materials, but willing to release them in easily accessible electronic formats, a godsend to the hard-pressed author in COVID-era exile, unable to just hop on the MRT to the nearest Caves or Eslite bookshop. I am particularly indebted to Camphor's invaluable memoirs by some of Taiwan's modern movers and shakers, allowing me to lean on first-person accounts by some of Taiwan's leading historical actors in modern times. For further reading, I also recommend Han Cheung's endlessly inventive column 'Taiwan in Time', printed every

Sunday in the *Taipei Times* and often the sole credible Anglophone source on many a historical topic.

I hope the reader will indulge my interest in popular music, which has formed part of the background of Taiwanese life since the arrival of radio in the 1930s, if not before. This reflects an interest from my earlier books, particularly *Japan at War in the Pacific*, which often stops in the middle of a historical scene and wonders about the significance of *that tune* playing in the background. For this, Tsai Wen-ting's bilingual 'Taiwanese Pop Songs History' proved to be a crucial Rosetta Stone, allowing me to match references in multiple sources to their original song titles, and hence find their lyrics online.

References to the reports of the International Work Group for Indigenous Affairs (IGWA) are to their Taiwan publications, corralled year by year at: https://www.iwgia.org/en/taiwan.html

Alsford, Niki. *Transitions to Modernity in Taiwan: The Spirit of 1895 and the Cession of Formosa to Japan*. Abingdon, England: Routledge, 2018

Ambaras, David. *Japan's Imperial Underworlds: Intimate Encounters at the Borders of Empire*. New York: Cambridge University Press, 2018

Andrade, Tonio. *How Taiwan Became Chinese: Dutch, Spanish and Han Colonization in the Seventeenth Century*. New York: Columbia University Press, 2008

_____. *Lost Colony: The Untold Story of China's First Great Victory over the West*. Princeton, New Jersey: Princeton University Press, 2011

Ang, James Kaim. *Lishi jiyi yu lishi shishi — yuan zhumin shi yanjiu de yige changshi [Between Legend and Historical Facts: A Tentative Study on the Chinese Aborigines in Early Modern History]*. Taipei: Academia Sinica, 1996

Anon. 'The past and present of the tribes of Ami' in *Taiwan Today*, 1 October 1983. https://taiwantoday.tw/news.php?unit=20,29,35,45&post=25557

_____. 'Sparkling tears of the sun' in *Taiwan Today*, 1 March 2003. https://taiwantoday.tw/news.php?post=36610&unit=29,45

_____. 'Taiwanese Yasukuni Protest Foiled' at China.org, 15 June 2005. http://www.china.org.cn/english/2005/Jun/131970.htm

_____. 'Lanyu residents accused of abusing free electricity' at *Want China Times*, 16 July 2012. http://www.wantchinatimes.com/news-subclass-cnt.aspx?id=20120716000064&cid=1103

_____. '"Sword-lion" mail boxes become tourist attraction' in *Taipei Times*, 18 September 2016, p. 3

Antony, Robert J. *Rats, Cats, Rogues, and Heroes: Glimpses of China's Forbidden Past*. Lanham, Maryland: Rowman and Littlefield, 2023

Baldick, Julian. *Ancient Religions of the Austronesian World: From Australasia to Taiwan*. London, I.B. Tauris, 2013

Barclay, Paul. *Outcasts of Empire: Japan's Rule on Taiwan's 'Savage Border' 1874–1945*. Oakland, California: University of California Press, 2018

_____. 'The Musha Incident and the History of Tgdaya-Japanese Relations' in Michael Berry, op. cit., 2022, pp. 73–113

_____. *Kondo the Barbarian: A Japanese Adventurer and Indigenous Taiwan's Bloodiest Uprising*. Manchester: Eastbridge Books, 2023

Bax, Bonham Ward. *The Eastern Seas: Being a Narrative of the Voyage of HMS 'Dwarf' in China, Japan and Formosa*. London: John Murray, 1875

Bellwood, Paul. 'Formosan Prehistory and Austronesian Dispersal' in David Blundell (ed.) *Austronesian Taiwan: Linguistics, History, Ethnology, Prehistory*. Taipei / Berkeley, California: Shung Ye Museum of Formosan Aborigines / Phoebe A. Hearst Museum of Anthropology, 2009, pp. 336–64

Bennett, Terry. *Japan and the Illustrated London News: Complete Record of Reported Events 1853–1899*. Folkestone, England: Global Oriental, 2006

Berry, Michael (ed.). *The Musha Incident: A Reader on the Indigenous Uprising in Colonial Taiwan*. New York: Columbia University Press, 2022

Blundell, David (ed.). *Austronesian Taiwan: Linguistics, History, Ethnology, Prehistory* (Revised Edition). Taipei / Berkeley, California: Shung Ye Museum of Formosan Aborigines / Phoebe A. Hearst Museum of Anthropology, University of California, 2009

Blussé, Leonard and Natalie Everts (eds). *The Formosan Encounter: Notes on Formosa's Aboriginal Society, A Selection of Documents from Dutch Archival Sources*. Taipei: Shung Ye Museum of Formosan Aborigines, 1997–2010 (in four volumes)

Blussé, Leonard. 'Bull in a China Shop: Pieter Nuyts in China and Japan (1627–1636)' in Leonard Blussé (ed.) *Around and About Formosa: Essays in honor of Professor Ts'ao Yung-ho*. Taipei: Ts'ao Yung-ho Foundation for Culture and Education, 2003, pp. 95–110

Bo Yang. *The Ugly Chinaman and the Crisis of Chinese Culture*. St Leonards, New South Wales: Allen & Unwin, 1991

Borao Mateo, José Eugenio. *The Spanish Experience in Taiwan, 1626–1642: The Baroque Ending of a Renaissance Endeavour*. Hong Kong: Hong Kong University Press, 2009

Buckley, Chris and Austin Ramy. 'Singer's Apology for Waving Taiwan Flag Stirs Backlash of its Own' in *The New York Times*, 16 January 2016. https://www.nytimes.com/2016/01/17/world/asia/taiwan-china-singer-chou-tzu-yu.html

Bush, Richard C. 'Elections and the Challenges of Governing Under Tsai' in June Teufel Dreyer and Jacques deLisle (eds) *Taiwan in the Era of Tsai Ing-wen*. Abingdon, England: Routledge, 2021, pp. 19–38

Campbell, William. *Formosa Under the Dutch, described from Contemporary Records with Explanatory Notes and a Bibliography of the Island*. Taipei: Ch'eng-wen Publishing Company, 1803 [1967]

Carrington, George Williams. *Foreigners in Formosa 1841–1874*. San Francisco: Chinese Materials Center, 1977

Chaïkin, Nathan. *The Sino-Japanese War*. Martigny, Switzerland: Nathan Chaïkin, 1983

Chan, Minnie. 'Teen pop star Chou Tzu-yu's apology for waving Taiwan flag swayed young voters for DPP' in *South China Morning Post*, 17 March 2016. https://www.scmp.com/news/china/policies-politics/article/1902195/teen-pop-star-chou-tzu-yus-apology-waving-taiwan-flag

Chang Chiung-wen. '"Return to Innocence": In Search of Ethnic Identity in the Music of the Amis of Taiwan' in *College Music Symposium*, Vol. 49/50, 2009/2010, pp. 327–32

Chang Chung-shen. *Ts'ai Ch'ien, the Pirate King Who Dominates the Seas: A Study of Coastal Piracy in China, 1795–1810*. Unpublished PhD thesis, Department of Oriental Studies, University of Arizona, 1983

Chang, Kuang-chih. 'The Neolithic Taiwan Strait' in *Kaogu*, Vol. 6, 1989, pp. 541–50, 569. English translation repaginated to pp. 1–13

Charbonnier, Jean-Pierre. *Christians in China AD 600 to 2000*. San Francisco: Ignatius Press, 2007

Chen Kobo. 'Sun-Moon Lake: The Heart of Taiwan' at *Taiwan Panorama*, February 2014. https://www.taiwan-panorama.com.tw/Articles/Details?Guid=7f0ce287-e5e8-4699-b502-b5a38343da53&langId=3&CatId=7

Chen Kuo-tung. 'Chinese Knowledge of the Waters Around Taiwan' in Paola Calanca, Liu Yi-chang and Frank Muyard (eds) *Taiwan Maritime Landscapes from Neolithic to Early Modern Times*. Paris: École française d'Extrême-Orient, 2022, pp. 185–96

Chen Szu-wei. 'Producing Mandopop in 1960s Taiwan: When a Prolific Composer Met a Pioneering Entrepreneur' in Tsai et al., op cit., pp. 43–54

Chen Wei-han. 'Bill to propose CKS hall, statue moves' in *Taipei Times*, 24 April 2017, p. 1

Chen, York W. 'Constructive Build-up of Taiwan's Defense' in June Teufel Dreyer and Jacques deLisle (eds) *Taiwan in the Era of Tsai Ing-wen*. Abingdon, England: Routledge, 2021, pp. 108–28

Chen Yu-mei. 'The Austronesian Dispersal: A Lanyu Perspective' in Paola Calanca, Liu Yi-chang and Frank Muyard (eds) *Taiwan Maritime Landscapes from Neolithic to Early Modern Times*. Paris: École française d'Extrême-Orient, 2022, pp. 115–34

Cheng, Maria. 'Constructing a New Political Spectacle: Tactics of Chen Shui-bian's 2000 and 2004 Inaugural Speeches' in *Discourse & Society*, Vol. 17, No. 5, September 2006, pp. 583–608

Cheng, Wei-cheng. 'Emergence of Deerskin Exports from Taiwan Under VOC (1624–1642)' in *Taiwan Historical Research*, Vol. 24, No. 3, September 2017, pp. 1–48

Chin Ko-lin. *Heijin: Organized Crime, Business and Politics in Taiwan*. Abingdon, England: Routledge, 2015

Ching, Leo. *Becoming 'Japanese': Colonial Taiwan and the Politics of Identity Formation*. Berkeley, California: University of California Press, 2001

Chiu Hsin-hui. *The Colonial 'Civilizing Process' in Dutch Formosa, 1624–1662*. Leiden, Netherlands: Brill, 2008

Chiu Yu-kong. *The Triads as Business*. London: Routledge, 2000

Chong Wang. *Interpreting Zheng Chenggong: The Politics of Dramatizing a Historical Figure in Japan, China and Taiwan (1700–1963)*. Saarbrücken, Germany: VDM, 2008

Chou Wan-yao. *A New Illustrated History of Taiwan*. Taipei: SMC Publishing, 2020

Chu, Samuel C. 'Liu Ming-ch'uan and Modernization of Taiwan' in *Journal of Asian Studies*, Vol. 24, No. 1, November 1963, pp. 37–53

Chuang Fang-jung et al. (eds). *Historical Sites of the First Rank in Taiwan and Kinmen*. Taipei: Council for Cultural Planning and Development, Executive Yuan, 1987

Clements, Jonathan. *Coxinga and the Fall of the Ming Dynasty*. Stroud, England: Sutton Publishing, 2004

_____. *A Brief History of China: Dynasty, Revolution and Transformation*. Rutland, England: Tuttle, 2019

_____. *Japan at War in the Pacific: The Rise and Fall of the Japanese Empire in Asia 1868–1945*. Rutland, England: Tuttle, 2022

Craft, Stephen G. *American Justice in Taiwan: The 1957 Riots and Cold War Foreign Policy*. Lexington, Kentucky: University Press of Kentucky, 2016

Crook, Steven. 'Pingpu tribe: We have not disappeared!' at *Taiwan Culture Portal*, culture.tw, 26 September 2008

_____ and Katy Hung Hui-wen. *A Culinary History of Taipei: Beyond Pork and Ponlai*. Lanham, Maryland: Rowman and Littlefield, 2018 [Kindle]

Culver, John and Ryan Hass. 'Understanding Beijing's motives regarding Taiwan: a 35-year CIA officer's view' at *On the Record*, 30 March 2021. https://www.brookings.edu/on-the-record/understanding-beijings-motives-regarding-taiwan-and-americas-role/

Davidson, James W. *The Island of Formosa, Past and Present: History, People, Resources and Commercial Prospects*. London: Macmillan, 1903

Dawley, Evan N. 'Closing a Colony: The Meanings of Japanese Deportation from Taiwan After World War II' in Andrew D. Morris (ed.) *Japanese Taiwan: Colonial Rule and its Contested Legacy*. London: Bloomsbury Academic, 2015, pp. 115–32

deLisle, Jacques. 'Taiwan's Quest for International Space in the Tsai Era: Adapting Old Strategies to New Circumstances' in June Teufel Dreyer and Jacques deLisle (eds) *Taiwan in the Era of Tsai Ing-wen*. Abingdon, England: Routledge, 2021, pp. 239–83

Denton, Kirk. *The Landscape of Historical Memory: The Politics of Museums and Memorial Culture in Post-Martial Taiwan*. Hong Kong: Hong Kong University Press, 2021

der Haar, Barend. *Ritual and Mythology of the Chinese Triads: Creating an Identity*. Leiden, Netherlands: Brill, 1998

Dreyer, June Teufel. 'Taiwan-Japan Relations in the Tsai Era' in June Teufel Dreyer and Jacques deLisle (eds) *Taiwan in the Era of Tsai Ing-wen*. Abingdon, England: Routledge, 2021, pp. 208–38

Dudbridge, Glen (ed.). *Aborigines of South Taiwan in the 1880s: Papers by the South Cape Lightkeeper George Taylor*. Taipei: Shung Ye Museum of Formosan Aborigines, 1999

Eskildsen, Robert. 'Of Civilization and Savages: The Mimetic Imperialism of Japan's 1874 Expedition to Taiwan' in *The American Historical Review*, Vol. 107, No. 2, 2002, pp. 388–418

_____. 'An Army as Good and Efficient as Any in the World: James Wasson and Japan's 1874 Expedition to Formosa' in *Asian Cultural Studies*, Vol. 36, 2010, pp. 45–62

_____ (ed.). *Foreign Adventurers and the Aborigines of Southern Taiwan, 1867–1874*. Taipei: Academia Sinica, 2005

Everts, Natalie. 'Jacob Lamay van Taywan: An Indigenous Formosan Who Became an Amsterdam Citizen' in Blundell, David (ed.) *Austronesian Taiwan: Linguistics, History, Ethnology, Prehistory* (Revised Edition). Taipei / Berkeley, California: Shung Ye Museum of Formosan Aborigines / Phoebe A. Hearst Museum of Anthrolopology, University of California, 2009, pp. 153–8

Fell, Dafydd. *Party Politics in Taiwan: Party Change and the Democratic Evolution of Taiwan, 1991–2004*. Abingdon, England: Routledge, 2005

_____. *Government and Politics in Taiwan.* Abingdon, England: Routledge, 2011

_____. *Taiwan's Green Parties: Alternative Politics in Taiwan.* Abingdon, England: Routledge, 2021

_____ and Hsin-Huang Michael Hsiao (eds). *Taiwan Studies Revisited.* London: Routledge, 2015

Fenby, Jonathan. *Generalissimo: Chiang Kai-shek and the China He Lost.* London: Simon and Schuster, 2003

Goddard, W.G. *The Makers of Taiwan.* Taipei: China Publishing Company, 1963

Gordon, Leonard. *Confrontation over Taiwan: Nineteenth Century China and the Powers.* Lanham, Maryland: Lexington Books, 2007

_____ (ed.). *Taiwan: Studies in Chinese Local History.* New York: Columbia University Press, 1970

Guy, Nancy. "'Republic of China National Anthem" on Taiwan: One Anthem, One Performance, Multiple Realities' in *Ethnomusicology*, Vol. 46, No.1, 2002, pp. 96–119

_____ (ed.). *Resounding Taiwan: Musical Reverberations Across a Vibrant Island.* Abingdon, England: Routledge, 2022

Han Cheung. 'The drastic downfall of Wu Feng' in *Taipei Times*, 10 September 2017, p. 13

_____. 'Taiwan in Time: Brawls in the Legislature "Shame of Taiwan"' in *Taipei Times*, 3 April 2022, p. 13

Hao Yufan and Michael Johnston. 'Reform at the Crossroads: An Analysis of Chinese Corruption' in *Asia Perspective*, Vol. 19, No. 1, Spring–Summer 1995, pp. 117–49

Harris, Lane. *The Peking Gazette: A Reader in Nineteenth-Century Chinese History.* Leiden, Netherlands: Brill, 2018

Hayashida Yoshio. *Tei-shi Taiwan-shi: Tei Seikō Sanyo no Kobo Miki* [*A History of Zheng-clan Taiwan: A True Account of Zheng Chenggong and the Rise and Fall of Three Generations*]. Tokyo: Kyuko Shoin, 2003

Ho Ching-yao. *Taiwan no Yōkai Densetsu* [*Taiwan Ghost Legends*, a.k.a. *Yōkai Map of Taiwan*]. Tokyo: Hara Shobō, 2022

Ho Tin-jui. *A Comparative Study of Myths and Legends of Formosan Aborigines.* Taipei: Orient Cultural Service, 1971

House, Edward E. *The Japanese Expedition to Formosa.* Tokyo: no publisher given, 1875

Hsiao, L.C. Russell and H.H. Michael Hsiao. 'Cross-Straits Relations Under the Tsai Administration' in June Teufel Dreyer and Jacques deLisle (eds) *Taiwan in the Era of Tsai Ing-wen.* Abingdon, England: Routledge, 2021, pp. 129–60

Hu Tai-li. 'The Making of *Songs of Pasta'ay'.* Taipei: Taiwan Association of Visual Ethnology, 2007. https://www.tieff.org/en/reviews/review-songs-of-pastaay/

Huang Chih-huei. 'The *Yamatodamashii* of the Takasago volunteers of Taiwan' in Befu Harumi and Sylvie Guichard-Anguis (eds) *Globalizing Japan: Ethnography of the Japanese Presence in Asia, Europe, and America.* London: Routledge, 2001, pp. 222–50

Huang Kuo-chao. 'The Development of the Indigenous "Mountain Music" Industry and "Mountain Songs" (1960–1970s): Production and Competition' in Tsai et al., op. cit., pp. 55–72

Huang Yuyang. 'Cong minyan shengzhang chulai de jietou gequ: *Taiwan de Ge*' [Street songs grown from folk songs: *Songs of Taiwan*] at *Story Studio*, 29 July 2019. https://web.archive.org/web/20210225230504/https://storystudio.tw/article/gushi/qiu-chui-zhi-

and-his-musics-of-social-movement/

Hung Chien-chao. *Taiwan Under the Cheng Family 1662–1683: Sinicization after Dutch Rule.* Unpublished PhD thesis, Department of History, Georgetown University, 1981

Hung Hsiao-chun, Matsumura Hirofumi, Nguyen Lan Cuong, Hanihara Tsunehiko, Huang Shih-chiang, and Mike T. Clark, 'Negritos in Taiwan and the Wider History of South-East Asia: New Discovery from the Xiaoma Caves' in *World Archaeology*, October 2022, DOI: 10.1080/00438243.2022.2121315

Ishii Shinji. *The Island of Formosa and its Primitive Inhabitants.* London: China Society and Japan Society, 1916

Jacobs, J. Bruce. *The Kaohsiung Incident in Taiwan and Memoirs of a Foreign Big Beard.* Leiden, Netherlands: Brill, 2016

Jenco, Leigh K. 'Chen Di's *Record of Formosa* (1603) and an Alternative Chinese Image of Otherness' in *The Historical Journal*, Vol. 64, No. 1, pp. 17–42

Johnson, Robert. *Far China Station: The US Navy in Asian Waters 1800–1898.* Annapolis, Maryland: Naval Institute Press, 1979

Kagan, Richard C. *Taiwan's Statesman: Lee Teng-hui and Democracy in Asia.* Annapolis, Maryland: Naval Institute Press, 2007

Kaiteri, Sean. 'Behind the Legend of the Little Black People Ritual' in *The Wild East Magazine*, 29 June 2012. https://www.thewildeast.net/2012/06/the-story-of-the-legend-of-the-little-black-people/

Kan, Karoline. 'Friday Song: The Orphan of Asia, by the "idol's idol" Lo Ta-you' at *China Project*, 22 December 2018. https://thechinaproject.com/2018/12/22/friday-song-the-orphan-of-asia/

Kang, Peter. 'A Brief Note on the Possible Factors Contributing to the Large Village Size of the Siraya in the Early Seventeenth Century' in Leonard Blussé (ed.) *Around and About Formosa: Essays in honor of Professor Ts'ao Yung-ho.* Taipei: Ts'ao Yung-ho Foundation for Culture and Education, 2003, pp. 111–28

_____. 'Seeking "Roots" in Taiwan: "Red Hair" and the Dutch Princess of Eight Treasures' in J. Bruce Jacobs and Peter Kang (eds) *Changing Taiwanese Identities*. Abingdon, England: Routledge, 2018, pp. 27–38

_____. 'Indigenous Toponyms Under the State Policy of the Standardization of Geographical Names' in Scott E. Simon, Jolen Hsieh and Peter Kang (eds) *Indigenous Reconciliation in Contemporary Taiwan: From Stigma to Hope.* Abingdon, England: Routledge, 2023, pp. 61–76

Katz, Paul. 'Germs of Disaster: The Impact of Epidemics on Japanese Military Campaigns, 1874 and 1895' in *Annales de démographie historique, Morbidité, Mortalité, Santé.* 1996, pp. 195–220

_____. *When Valleys Turned Blood Red: The Ta-pa-ni Incident in Colonial Taiwan.* Honolulu: University of Hawaii Press, 2005

_____. 'Governmentality and Its Consequences in Colonial Taiwan: A Case Study of the Ta-pa-ni Incident of 1915' in *The Journal of Asian Studies*, Vol. 64, No. 2, May 2005, pp. 387–424

Keevak, Michael. *The Pretended Asian: George Psalmanazar's Eighteenth-Century Formosan Hoax.* Detroit: Wayne State University Press, 2004

Keliher, Macabe. *Out of China or Yu Yonghe's Tale of Formosa: A History of Seventeenth-Century Taiwan.* Taipei: SMC Publishing, 2003

Kerr, George. *Formosa Betrayed*. London: Eyre and Spottiswoode, 1966

_____. *Formosa: Licensed Revolution and the Home Rule Movement*. Honolulu: University of Hawaii Press, 1974

King, John W. *The China Pilot: The Coast of China, Korea and Tartary; the Sea of Japan, Gulfs of Tartary and Amur and Sea of Okhotsk*. London: Hydrographic Office, 1861

Kitamura Kae. 'Relistening to Her and His Stories: On Approaching "The Musha Incident" from an Indigenous Perspective' in Michael Berry, op. cit., 2022, pp. 114–42

Klöter, Henning. 'Language Policy in the KMT and DPP Era' in *China Perspectives*, No. 56, November–December 2004, pp. 1–12

Kuo Li-chuan. 'We're One Family — Songwriter Kao Tzu-yang' in *Taiwan Panorama*, July 2006. https://www.taiwan-panorama.com

Kuo Su-chiu. *New Frontiers in the Neolithic Archaeology of Taiwan (5600–1800 BP)*. Singapore: Springer, 2019

_____. *Tracing the History of Contemporary Taiwan's Aboriginal Groups: From the Periphery to the Centre*. New York: Routledge, 2023

Lai Tse-han et al. *A Tragic Beginning: The Taiwan Uprising of February 28, 1947*. Stanford, California: Stanford University Press, 1991

Lamley, Harry. 'The 1895 Taiwan Republic' in *The Journal of Asian Studies*, Vol. 27 No. 4, August 1968, pp. 739–62

_____. 'Subethnic Rivalry in the Ch'ing period' in Emily Martin Ahern and Hill Gates (eds) *The Anthropology of Taiwanese Society*. Stanford, California: University of California Press, 1981, pp. 284–91

Lan Shi-chi Mike. '"Crimes" of Interpreting: Taiwanese Interpreters as War Criminals of World War II' in Takeda Kayoko and Jesús Baigorri-Jalón (eds) *New Insights in the History of Interpreting*. Amsterdam: John Benjamins, 2016, pp. 193–223

Lancashire, Edel. 'Popeye and the Case of Guo Yidong, aka Bo Yang' in *China Quarterly*, Vol. 92, December 1982, pp. 663–86

Le Gendre, Charles W. *Notes of Travel in Formosa*. Tainan, Taiwan: National Museum of Taiwan History, 2012

Lee Ming-liang with Lee Yahwei. *Republic of Taiwan Postal History and Postage Stamps*. Hualien, Taiwan: Tiger Publishing, 1995

Leong Sow-theng. *Migration and Ethnicity in Chinese History: Hakkas, Pengmin and Their Neighbors*. Stanford, California: Stanford University Press, 1997

Li Kuang-ti. 'First Farmers and Their Coastal Adaptation in Prehistoric Taiwan' in Anne P. Underhill (ed.) *A Companion to Chinese Archaeology*. Oxford, England: Blackwell, 2013, pp. 1020–55

Li, Paul Jen-kuei. 'Time Perspective of Formosan Aborigines' in Alicia Sanchez-Mazas et al. (eds) *Past Human Migrations in East Asia: Matching Archaeology, Linguistics and Genetics*. Abingdon, England: Routledge, 2008, pp. 211–18

Li Yulan. 'Xu Zonggan dui Taiwan Yingwu Banbing zhi Zhengdun 1848–1853' [Xu Zonggan's Reorganisation of Taiwan's Battalion Squadrons 1848–1853] in *Taiwan Wenxian Jikan* [*Taiwan Literature Quarterly*], Vol. 52, No. 1, March 2001, pp. 539–64

Lien Heng. *Taiwan Tongshi* [*General History of Taiwan*]. 1927. Edition consulted is the ctext online version: https://ctext.org/wiki.pl?if=gb&res=798087

Lin, C.C. 'Geology and Ecology of Taiwan Prehistory' in *Asian Perspectives*, No. 7, 1963, pp. 203–13

Lin Chang-shun and Shih Hsiu-chuan. 'Court finds process for Indigenous recognition unconstitutional' in *Focus Taiwan*, 28 October 2022. https://focustaiwan.tw/politics/20221028002

Lin Hsiao-Ting. *Accidental State: Chiang Kai-shek, the United States, and the Making of Taiwan*. Cambridge, Massachusetts: Harvard University Press, 2016

_____. *Taiwan, The United States, and the Hidden History of the Cold War in Asia: Divided Allies*. London: Routledge, 2022

Lin, Nikky (ed.). *A Taiwanese Literature Reader*. Amherst, Massachusetts: Cambria Press, 2020

Lin Po-Hsien, Tseng Jao-Hsun, and Tsou Chih-yun. 'A Study of Applying Saisait Tribe's Tabaa Sang (Buttocks Bell) into Cultural Creative Industry from a Cross-Disciplinary Perspective' in Peter Vink (ed.) *Advances in Social and Organizational Factors*. Boca Raton: CRC Press, 2012, pp. 8488–99

Liu, Lucia Huwy-min. 'Substance, Masculinity, and Class: Betel Nut Consumption and Embarrassing Modernity in Taiwan' in Mark L. Moskowitz (ed.) *Popular Culture in Taiwan: Charismatic Modernity*. Abingdon, England: Routledge, 2011, pp. 131–48

Liu Shui-chi. 'Rebirth After the Flood' in *Indigenous Sight*, No. 20, September 2018, pp. 18–25

Long, Simon. *Taiwan: China's Last Frontier*. London: Macmillan, 1991

Lu Hsiu-lien and Ashley Esarey. *My Fight for a New Taiwan: One Woman's Journey from Prison to Power*. Seattle: University of Washington Press, 2014

Lu, Tasaw Hsin-chun. 'Experiencing the "Enchanting Golden Triangle" Through Music and Dance in a Yunnan Diasporic Community in Taiwan' in Nancy Guy (ed.) *Resounding Taiwan: Musical Reverberations Across a Vibrant Island*. Abingdon, England: Routledge, 2022, pp. 85–104

Mackay, George. *From Far Formosa: The Island, Its People and Missions*. New York: Fleming Revell, 1895

MacKay, Joseph. 'Pirate Nations: Maritime Pirates as Escape Societies in Late Imperial China' in *Social Science History*, Vol. 37, No. 4, Winter 2013, pp. 551–73

McGovern, Janet B. Montgomery. *Among the Head-Hunters of Formosa*. London: T.F. Unwin, 1922

Minorities at Risk Project. *Chronology for Aboriginal Taiwanese in Taiwan*, 2004. https://www.refworld.org/docid/469f38e4c.html

Morris, Andrew. *Defectors from the PRC to Taiwan, 1960–1989: The Anti-Communist Righteous Warriors*. Abingdon, England: Routledge, 2022

_____ (ed.). *Japanese Taiwan: Colonial Rule and its Contested Legacy*. London: Bloomsbury Academic, 2015

Murray, Diane with Qin Baoqi. *The Origins of the Tiandihui: The Chinese Triads in Legend and History*. Stanford, California: Stanford University Press, 1994

Ong Iok-tek. *Taiwan: A History of Agonies* (Revised and Enlarged Edition). No publisher given, undated. [Kindle]

Otness, Harold. *One Thousand Westerners in Taiwan, to 1945; A Biographical and Bibliographical Dictionary*. Taipei: Institute of Taiwan History, Preparatory Office,

Academia Sinica, 1999

Ouchterlony, John. *The Chinese War: An Account of All the Operations of the British Forces from the Commencement to the Treaty of Nanking.* London: Sanders and Otley, 1844

Pakula, Hannah. *The Last Empress: Madame Chiang Kai-shek and the Birth of Modern China.* New York: Simon & Schuster, 2009

Palameq, Yedda. *After All Ambivalence: The Situation of North Formosa and its Inhabitants in the Seventeenth Century.* Leiden, Netherlands: University of Leiden [MA thesis], 2012

Patridge, Dan. *British Captives in China: An Account of the Shipwreck on the Island of Formosa of the Brig Ann* [sic]. London: Wertheimer, Lea, and Co., 1876

Pearson, Richard. *Taiwan Archaeology: Local Development and Cultural Boundaries in the China Seas.* Honolulu: University of Hawaii, 2023

Pei, Kurtis. 'Hunting System of the Rukai Tribe in Taiwan, Republic of China'. Taipei: National Pingtung University of Science and Technology, 1999

Peiros, Ilia. 'The Formosan Language Family' in Alicia Sanchez-Mazas et al. (eds) *Past Human Migrations in East Asia: Matching Archaeology, Linguistics and Genetics.* Abingdon, England: Routledge, 2008, pp. 182–210

Phillips, Steven. *Between Assimilation and Independence: The Taiwanese Encounter Nationalist China, 1945–1950.* Stanford, California: Stanford University Press, 2003

Pickering, William Alexander. *Pioneering in Formosa: Recollections of Adventures Among Mandarins, Wreckers and Head-Hunting Savages.* London: Hurst and Blackett, 1898

Quo, F.C. 'British Diplomacy and the Cession of Formosa, 1894–5' in *Modern Asian Studies*, Vol. 2, No. 2, August 1968, pp. 739–62

Ramzy, Austin. 'Divisive Monuments? Put them all in a Taiwan park' in *The New York Times*, 22 August 2017. https://www.nytimes.com/2017/08/22/world/asia/taiwan-statues-chiang-kai-shek-park.html

Rauhala, Emily. 'The "Battle of Taipei" shows just how wary of China young Taiwanese are' in *Time*, 24 March 2014. https://time.com/35142/taiwan-protests-over-tisa-reveal-china-fears/

Rigger, Shelley. *The Tiger Leading the Dragon: How Taiwan Propelled China's Economic Rise.* Lanham, Maryland: Rowman & Littlefield, 2021

———. 'Kuomintang Agonistes: Party Politics in the Wake of Taiwan's 2016 and 2020 Elections' in June Teufel Dreyer and Jacques deLisle (eds) *Taiwan in the Era of Tsai Ing-wen.* Abingdon, England: Routledge, 2021, pp. 39–63

Rowen, Ian (ed.). *Transitions in Taiwan: Stories About the White Terror.* Amherst, Massachusetts: Cambria Press, 2021

———. *One China, Many Taiwans: The Geopolitics of Cross-Strait Tourism.* Ithaca, New York: Cornell University Press, 2022

Roy, Toulouse-Antonin. 'The Discourse and Practice of Colonial "Suppression" in the Making of the Musha Rebellion and its Aftermath' in Berry, op. cit., 2022, pp. 33–72

Rubinstein, Murray (ed.). *Taiwan: A New History* (Expanded Edition). London: Routledge, 2015

Saaler, Sven. *Men in Metal: A Topography of Public Bronze Statuary in Modern Japan.* Leiden, Netherlands: Brill, 2020

Sanchez-Mazas, Alicia et al. 'The GM Genetic Polymorphism in Taiwan Aborigines: New Data Revealing Remarkable Differentiation Patterns' in Alicia Sanchez-Mazas et al. (eds)

Past Human Migrations in East Asia: Matching Archaeology, Linguistics and Genetics. Abingdon, England: Routledge, 2008, pp. 313–33

Schubert, Gunther (ed.). *The Routledge Handbook of Contemporary Taiwan.* London: Routledge, 2016

Shackleton, Allan J. *Formosa Calling: An Eyewitness Account of the February 28th, 1947 Incident.* Manchester: Camphor Press, 1998 [Kindle]

Shepherd, John. 'The Island Frontier of the Ch'ing, 1684–1780' in Murray Rubinstein (ed.) *Taiwan: A New History.* Abingdon, England: Routledge, 2015, pp. 107–30

Shirane Seiji. *Imperial Gateway: Colonial Taiwan and Japan's Expansion in South China and Southeast Asia, 1895–1945.* Ithaca, New York: Cornell University Press, 2022

Simon, Scott E. *Truly Human: Indigeneity and Indigenous Resurgence on Formosa.* Toronto: University of Toronto Press, 2023

_____, Jolan Hsieh, and Peter Kang (eds). *Indigenous Reconciliation in Taiwan: From Stigma to Hope.* Abingdon, England: Routledge, 2023

Smits, Gregory. *Maritime Ryukyu 1050–1650.* Honolulu: University of Hawaii Press, 2019

So Kwan-wai. *Japanese Piracy in Ming China During the 16th Century.* East Lansing, Michigan: Michigan State University Press, 1975

Song Xiaokun. *Between Civic and Ethnic: The Transformation of Taiwanese Nationalistic Ideologies (1895–2000).* Brussels: Brussels University Press, 2009

Sterk, Darryl. *Indigenous Cultural Translation: A Thick Description of Seediq Bale.* Abingdon, England: Routledge, 2020

Su Beng. *Taiwan's 400 Year History* (Anniversary Edition). Taipei: Su Beng, 2017

Suenari Michio. 'Sinicization and Descent Systems: The Introduction of Ancestral Tablets among the Puyuma and Saisiyat in Taiwan' in Paul Jen-kuei Li et al. (eds) *Austronesian Studies Relating to Taiwan.* Taipei: Academia Sinica, 1995, pp. 141–59

Takekoshi Yosaburō. *Japanese Rule in Formosa.* London: Longmans, Green & Co., 1907

Tan Shzr Ee. *Beyond 'Innocence': Amis Aboriginal Song in Taiwan as an Ecosystem.* Farnham, England: Ashgate, 2012

Taylor, George. 'Formosa: Characteristic Traits of the Island and Its Original Inhabitants' in *Proceedings of the Royal Geographical Society*, Vol. 11, No. 4, April 1889, pp. 224–39

Taylor, Jay. *The Generalissimo's Son: Chiang Ching-kuo and the Revolutions in China and Taiwan.* Cambridge, Massachusetts: Harvard University Press, 2000

Teng, Emma Jinhua. 'Taiwan in the Chinese Imagination, 17th–19th Centuries' in *The Asia Pacific Journal*, Vol. 5, No. 6, 2007, Article ID 2450

Ter, Dana. 'Finding peace at Pasta'ay' in *Taipei Times*, 12 November 2014, p. 14

Thompson, Laurence. 'The Earliest Eye-Witness Accounts of the Formosan Aborigines' in *Monumenta Serica*, Vol. 23, 1964, pp. 163–204

Thornberry, Milo. *Fireproof Moth: A Missionary in Taiwan's White Terror.* Lemoyne, Pennsylvania: Sunbury Press, 2011

Tsai Chien-hsin. *A Passage to China: Literature, Loyalism and Colonial Taiwan.* Leiden, Netherlands: Brill, 2017 [2020]

Tsai, Eva et al. *Made in Taiwan: Studies in Popular Music.* Abingdon, England: Routledge, 2020

Tsai, Shih-Shan Henry. *Maritime Taiwan: Historical Encounters with the East and the West.* London: Routledge, 2009 [2015]

Tsai Wen-ting. 'Taiwanese Pop Songs History' in *Sinorama*, May 2022. https://web.archive. org/web/20120625164334/http://home.comcast.net/~tzeng2/TaiwanPopSongs/in_ english.htm

Tsang Cheng-hwa. 'New Archaeological Data from Both Sides of the Taiwan Straits and Their Implications for the Controversy About Austronesian Origins and Expansion' in Paul Jen-kuei Li et al. (eds) *Austronesian Studies Relating to Taiwan.* Taipei: Academica Sinica, 1995, pp. 185–225

Underhill, Ann (ed.). *A Companion to Chinese Archaeology.* Chichester, England: Wiley-Blackwell, 2013

Vermeer, E.B. (ed.). *Development and Decline of Fukien Province in the 17th and 18th Centuries.* Leiden, Netherlands: Brill, 1990

Wang, Dan. 'China's Hidden Tech Revolution: How Beijing Threatens U.S. Dominance' in *Foreign Affairs*, Vol. 102, No. 2, March/April 2023, pp. 65–77

Wang Fei-Hsien. *Pirates and Publishers: A Social History of Copyright in Modern China.* Princeton, New Jersey: Princeton University Press, 2019

Wang Kuan-wen et al. 'Glass Beads from Guishan in Iron Age Taiwan: Inter-Regional Bead Exchange Between Taiwan, South-East Asia and Beyond' in *Journal of Archaeological Science: Reports*, No. 35, February 2021. https://doi.org/10.1016/j.jasrep.2020.102737

Wang Yin-feng. 'Resounding Colonial Taiwan Through Historical Recordings: Some Methodological Reflections' in Nancy Guy (ed.) *Resounding Taiwan: Musical Reverberations Across a Vibrant Island.* Abingdon, England: Routledge, 2022, pp. 9–27

Watanabe Toshiaki. *Taiwan Risshiki Kenchiku Kikō [Travels in Taiwan's Japanese-style Architecture].* Tokyo: Kadokawa Shoten, 2022

Watanabe Toshio. *The Meiji Japanese Who Made Modern Taiwan.* Lanham, Maryland: Lexington Books, 2022

Wei Yuan. *Shengwuji [A Military History of the Holy Dynasty].* Chinese text at https:// ctext.org/wiki.pl?if=gb&res=329092

Wills, John. *Pepper, Guns and Parleys: The Dutch East India Company and China 1622–1681.* Cambridge, Massachusetts: Harvard University Press, 1974

Wong Young-tsu. *China's Conquest of Taiwan in the Seventeenth Century: Victory at Full Moon.* Singapore: Springer, 2017

Xing Hang. *Conflict and Commerce in Maritime East Asia: The Zheng Family and the Shaping of the Modern World c. 1620–1720.* Cambridge, England: Cambridge University Press, 2015

_____. 'Contradictory Contingencies: The Seventeenth-Century Zheng Family and Contested Cross-Strait Legacies' in *American Journal of Chinese Studies*, Vol. 23, July 2016, pp. 173–82

Xiong, Victor Xunrui. *Emperor Yang of the Sui Dynasty: His Life, Times and Legacy.* Albany, New York: State University of New York Press, 2006

Yang Ying. *Xian Wang Shilu Jiaozhu [Veritable Record of the Former Prince].* Fujian, China: Fujian Renmin Chubanshe, c. 1661 [1981, edited by Chen Bisheng]

Ye Shitao. *A History of Taiwan Literature.* Amherst, Massachusetts: Cambria Press, 2020

Yu Jinfu. 'Ai ling ji (paSta'ay) ji ge chengxian saixia-zu chuantong yinyue yu wenhua xianxiang'

[The paSta'ay: Presenting a Saisiyat Musical and Cultural Phenomenon] in *Yu-shan Theological Journal*, Vol. 24, June 2017, pp. 40–56

Yu Sen-lin. 'Home at Last' in *Taipei Times*, 25 October 1999, p. 2

Zhang Yueying. '228 Zhong de Ba Dakou: Jiang Jieshi song Yizuo Shan Yongyuan de Da Toumu — Mazhili' [The Eight Great Bandits of the 228 Incident: How Chiang Kai-shek Created an Eternal Mountain Headman in Matreli] in *Xin Xinwen Zhoukan*, No. 1043, 27 February 2007

NOTES

Preface

1 Smits, *Maritime Ryukyu*, p. 30.
2 Keliher, *Out of Formosa*, p. 39. Chen, 'Chinese Knowledge of the Waters Around Taiwan', p. 191, disagrees and equates the 'Black Ditch' not with the undersea canyon, but with the Kuroshio current itself.
3 Watanabe, *The Meiji Japanese Who Made Modern Taiwan*, p. 102.
4 Pearson, *Taiwan Archaeology*, p. 3.
5 Simon, *Truly Human*, p. 269.
6 See, for example, Lu, *My Fight for a New Taiwan*, p. 86; Klöter, 'Language Policy', p. 2. I was, in fact, the only person in the audience. Nobody else could be bothered to attend the press conference, held in the middle of a big media event that featured the launching of a replica of a Koxinga-era ship, but Hsu gave it his all in a passionate oration for the benefit of television, while the cameras discreetly avoided shooting the empty seats.
7 Klöter, 'Language Policy', p. 1.
8 Manthorpe, *Forbidden Nation*, p. 21; Ong, *Taiwan: A History of Agonies*, p. 34.

Introduction: The Rover Incident

1 King, *The China Pilot*, p. 279.
2 Pickering, *Pioneering in Formosa*, p. 179. Le Gendre and Davidson both claim that there was only one survivor, but I go with Pickering's first-hand account here.
3 Ishii, *Island of Formosa*, p. 18. McGovern, *Among the Head-Hunters of Formosa*, loc. 1316, points out that this is all very well, but the neighbouring Amis *also* have a taboo against eating chicken, and their reason is that the 'souls of good and gentle people' dwell in them. The practice of raising chickens for their eggs seems to have been introduced by Chinese settlers.
4 I cannot resist the term 'chivalrous promptitude' from Davidson, *Formosa, Past and Present*, p. 115, although the phrase is not his, but borrowed from William Makepeace Thackeray.
5 Le Gendre, *Notes of Travel in Formosa*, p. 253.
6 Ibid., p. 255.
7 This might have been true of the Koalut Paiwan, but not of all indigenous tribes. For the Favorlang, for example, women and children were fair game on head-hunting raids. See Chiu, *The Colonial 'Civilizing' Process in Dutch Formosa*, p. 20.
8 Pickering, *Pioneering in Formosa*, p. 185. Looking at Le Gendre's own maps of Seqalu territories, this claim appears to be true.
9 The Liangqiao Eighteen Societies (*Liangqiao Shiba-she*) was a tribal confederation from around 1630 to 1904, when it was disbanded by the Japanese colonial government. It is probably better known today by its indigenous name, Seqalu, following the release of a 2021 television series of the same name about the events surrounding the Rover Incident. This can throw

273

out some confusing returns in online searches, since the same characters in Chinese were previously used to write 'Skaro', the home planet of *Doctor Who*'s Daleks. I remain suspicious that the term 'Seqalu' has only come into public parlance in the 2020s, but use it here on the assumption that it was in wider use among indigenous people before coming to Chinese notice.

10 Le Gendre, *Notes of Travel in Formosa*, pp. 281–2.

11 Ibid., p. 281. The same speech is repeated, almost word for word, but without attribution, in House, *The Japanese Expedition to Formosa*, p. 5.

12 Pickering, *Pioneering in Formosa*, p. 188.

13 Ibid., p. 191.

14 See, for example, Ong, *Taiwan: A History of Agonies*, p. 139, which baldly states: 'It means Taiwan had two governments at that time.'

15 Davidson, *Formosa, Past and Present*, p. 122.

16 House, *The Japanese Expedition to Formosa*, p. 4.

17 Kang, 'Seeking "Roots" in Taiwan', pp. 30–3.

18 Not to be confused with *tanah tunux* ('red heads'), the Truku term for the Japanese, said to derive from the Rising Sun on soldiers' headbands. Simon, *Truly Human*, p. 365.

1. Songs of the Dead

1 Lin, 'Geology and Ecology of Taiwan Prehistory', p. 212.

2 Crook and Hung, *A Culinary History of Taipei*, loc. 204.

3 Peiros, 'The Formosan language family', p. 192.

4 Li, 'First Farmers', p. 1036.

5 Ibid., p. 1038. It is notable that the varieties of shellfish available to the people of Nan-kuan-li were substantially more diverse than can be found in modern times.

6 Li, 'First Farmers', p. 1034.

7 Chang, 'The Neolithic Taiwan Strait', p. 1; Pearson, *Taiwan Archaeology*, p. 4. The earliest and most impactful were the Beishi (roughly 7000 BC) and Longgang (c. 6500–5000 BC) inundations, by the end of which Taiwan had become an island far from the Chinese mainland. Later, lesser floods included the Tainan (c. 4500–3000 BC), Dahu (c. 2000–1500 BC), Guoshengpu (c. 700–600 BC), Zhanghua (AD 500–900), and Bin (AD 900).

8 Pearson, *Taiwan Archaeology*, pp. 120–1.

9 Taylor, 'Formosa', p. 227.

10 Simon, *Truly Human*, p. 142.

11 Ibid., pp. 33–4.

12 Ibid., pp. 45, 158. Note also Chen Di's comments in the 17th century (Chapter Two), that the indigenous people he encounters lived by the sea but appeared to ignore it.

13 Ho, *Taiwan no Yōkai Densetsu*, p. 126, says 1,100; Yu, 'Home at Last', p. 2, says 200.

14 Ibid., pp. 286–7.

15 Ibid., p. 130.

16 Pei, 'Hunting System of the Rukai Tribe', p. 4. I include the comments here on the husbandry required because, as noted in Simon's *Truly Human*, p. 196, a Formosan hunter's territory is so much more than merely an area on a map — a fact that eluded many 20th-century lawmakers, who expected indigenous men banished from national parks to simply take up hunting elsewhere.

17 Pei, 'Hunting System of the Rukai Tribe', pp. 7–10.

18 Chiu, *The Colonial 'Civilizing' Process in Dutch Formosa*, p. 16. See also Chapter One, for discussion of the nature of rice-growing in Taiwan's varied climate.

19 Huang, 'The Development of the Indigenous "Mountain Music" Industry', p. 63.

20 Lu, *My Fight for a New Taiwan*, p. 185.

21 Wang Yin-feng, 'Resounding colonial Taiwan', p. 13.

22 Tsai, 'Taiwanese Pop Songs History'.

23 Ang, *Lishi jiyi yu lishi shishi*, p. 9.
24 Bax, *The Eastern Seas*, pp. 261–2.
25 Yu, 'Ai ling ji (paSta'ay)', p. 42.
26 Kaiteri, 'Behind the Legend of the Little Black People Ritual'. See also Ho, *Myths and Legends*, p. 144.
27 Lin, 'A Study of Applying Saisait Tribe's Tabaa Sang', p. 8490.
28 Yu, 'Ai jing ji (paSta'ay)', pp. 51–2.
29 Hu, 'The Making of *Songs of Pasta'ay*'; Yu, 'Ai ling ji (paSta'ay)', pp. 46–7, reports considerable academic infighting over just how many songs there are. Depending on how you count it, between 12 and 16.
30 Hung, 'Negritos in Taiwan', p. 10.
31 Yu, 'Ai jing ji (paSta'ay)', p. 44; 'Dui yuan zhumin de zhengfa' at https://www.taiwanus.net/history/2/31.htm
32 Dudbridge, *Aborigines of South Taiwan*, p. 140. It is listed as a 'Botan' folktale, but I have glossed it as Paiwan in my main text. See Simon, *Truly Human*, p. 300, for a similar tale among the Truku.
33 Hung, 'Negritos in Taiwan', p. 4.
34 Thompson, 'The Earliest Chinese Eyewitness Accounts', pp. 182–3.
35 Both the Republic of China and the People's Republic of China can be reluctant to discuss 'wandering' peoples, preferring their ethnic minorities to be fenced off in whichever place they were first registered as resident. I certainly found many resonances with the Taiwanese indigenous peoples when I was sent by National Geographic to make films among the Miao of southern China — in customs, attitudes, and legends. But the Miao themselves have an origin myth that starts far to the north in China.
36 Liu, 'Rebirth After the Flood', pp. 20–1.
37 McGovern, *Among the Head-Hunters of Formosa*, locs 1350, 1581.
38 Ishii, *Island of Formosa*, p. 8.
39 Crook and Hung, *A Culinary History of Taipei*, loc. 230.
40 Pickering, *Pioneering in Formosa*, p. 148.
41 Crook and Hung, *A Culinary History of Taipei*, locs 351–9.
42 Ishii, *Island of Formosa*, p. 2.
43 Xiong, *Emperor Yang of the Sui Dynasty*, p. 201. The precise identity of the *Book of Sui*'s 'Liuqiu' remains hotly contested among scholars, fraught as it is with implications for pre-modern Chinese territorial limits. Xiong's index diplomatically glosses it as 'Taiwan [?]'. George Kerr in *Formosa Betrayed*, p. 57, observes that as late as the 1940s, Chinese intelligence reports were asserting that China had 'discovered' Taiwan in AD 607, and that it had hence been part of China thereafter.
44 McGovern, *Among the Head-Hunters of Formosa*, loc. 442. Gordon, *Confrontation Over Taiwan*, p. 2, reports a criminally free translation of the name of these invaders that terms their territory 'the land of the vampire demons'. Sadly, that is a story too incredible even for me.
45 Anon, 'Sparkling Tears of the Sun'.
46 Wang, 'Glass Beads from Guishan'.
47 Sanchez-Mazas, 'The GM Genetic Polymorphism in Taiwan Aborigines', p. 313.
48 These words are carefully chosen, and relate to the Expanded Graded Intergenerational Disruption Scale, a tabulation for the degree to which a language might be considered to be in use. 'Dormant' is level nine of ten, defined as 'a reminder of heritage identity for an ethnic community'. A language is only officially 'Extinct' when 'no one retains a sense of ethnic identity associated with the language, even for symbolic purposes'.
49 Crook, 'Pingpun Tribe'. Even my ability to tell you this is a matter of scholarly brinksmanship — the 2008 article I am quoting has already disappeared, and can only be found in the Internet Archive Wayback Machine.
50 Chiu, *The Colonial 'Civilizing' Process in Dutch Formosa*, p. 18. Chiu notes that while Basai was the name of their territory, they were technically the Basayo people in their own language.
51 Barclay, 'The Musha Incident', p. 86. The nature of head-hunting among the

Tsou would become a major factor in querying the veracity of the story of the martyrdom of Wu Feng — see Chapter Four.

52 Ishii, *Island of Formosa*, p. 19.

53 Suenari, 'Sinicization and Descent Systems', p. 141.

54 Ishii, *Island of Formosa*, p. 17.

55 Ho, *Myths and Legends*, pp. 120–3.

2. The Beautiful Island

1 Thompson, 'Earliest Chinese Eyewitness Accounts', p. 168.

2 Ibid., pp. 168–9.

3 Chiu, *The Colonial 'Civilizing' Process in Dutch Formosa*, p. 1.

4 Thompson, 'The Earliest Chinese Eyewitness Accounts', pp. 169–70.

5 So, *Japanese Piracy in Ming China*, p. 52; see also Thompson, 'The Earliest Chinese Eyewitness Accounts', p. 176

6 Andrade, *How Taiwan Became Chinese*, Chapter 6, Section 5. Andrade notes that the coastal prohibitions were lifted again a generation later in 1567, but that 'the Ming still only tolerated overseas adventurism; they did not support it.'

7 There is some argument over who the Portuguese sailors were, reliant on a number of doubtful sources, which is why I don't attempt to name names in my main text. See Manthorpe, *Forbidden Nation*, p. 21, for a run-down of the suspects.

8 Ong, *Taiwan: A History of Agonies*, p. 37.

9 Chiu, *The Colonial 'Civilizing' Process in Dutch Formosa*, p. 13, p. 26.

10 Borao Mateo, *The Spanish Experience in Formosa*, pp. 207–8.

11 Chiu, *The Colonial 'Civilizing' Process in Dutch Formosa*, p. 25.

12 Jenco, 'Chen Di's *Record of Formosa*', p. 29.

13 Thompson, 'The Earliest Chinese Eyewitness Accounts', p. 175.

14 Chiu, *The Colonial 'Civilizing' Process in Dutch Formosa*, p. 17.

15 Thompson, 'The Earliest Chinese Eyewitness Accounts', pp. 175–6.

16 I know this because I had to learn how to cook with it when I was filming *Route Awakening* with National Geographic. The Kam people of Guizhou call it *niubie*. Yu Yonghe, when he visited Taiwan in 1696, would specifically observe that many of the Formosan customs he witnessed seemed analogous to descriptions of ancient Chinese peoples, which *I* note here are similar to many customs of south China's ethnic minority groups.

17 Thompson, 'The Earliest Chinese Eyewitness Accounts', p. 172.

18 Smits, *Maritime Ryukyu*, p. 320.

19 Ibid., pp. 206, 204 n40.

20 Campbell, *Formosa Under the Dutch*, p. 26. Campbell retains the pronunciation *Pehoe* for Penghu from François Valentyn's original *Oud en Niuew Oost-Indien* (1724). Clearly, Warwyk's contacts were solely with Hokkien speakers, which is to say: fishermen from Fujian.

21 Campbell, *Formosa Under the Dutch*, p. 27.

22 Keliher, *Out of Formosa*, p. 47.

23 Ibid., p. 51.

24 Chiu, *The Colonial 'Civilizing' Process in Dutch Formosa*, p. 6.

25 Ibid., p. 7, quoting the Taiwanese anthropologist Huang Ying-kuei. She adds, p. 9, that in ultimately swamping the indigenous people by forming 98 per cent of the population, Taiwan is also the first and most successful historical event in what would be known as the 'Chinese diaspora' — a different 'Out of Taiwan' hypothesis, for which see Chapter Twelve.

26 Blussé and Everts, *The Formosan Encounter*, Vol. I, p. 20.

27 Nuijts' colourful career was forgotten in China, Japan, and his native Netherlands, until it was resurrected in Japanese colonial-era schoolbooks as an example of Western predations. See Blussé, 'Bull in a China Shop', pp. 95–6.

28 Borao, *The Spanish Experience in Taiwan*, p. 47.

29 Ibid., p. 60.

30 Chiu, *The Colonial 'Civilizing' Process in Dutch Formosa*, pp. 99–101, 245 n90. was referred to by the Chinese as the 'King of the Barbarians', a title mangled through Hokkien into Dutch as *Quataong*.

31 Campbell, *Formosa Under the Dutch*, p. 6.

32 Chiu, *The Colonial 'Civilizing' Process in Dutch Formosa*, p. 25.

33 Campbell, *Formosa Under the Dutch*, p. 20. Twins were also regarded as taboo, and one would usually be killed at birth.

34 Chiu, *The Colonial 'Civilizing' Process in Dutch Formosa*, p. 26.

35 Peter Kang, in 'A Brief Note', p. 123, raises the topic. Chiu, *The Colonial 'Civilizing' Process in Dutch Formosa*, p. 26, more boldly links this directly to Chinese incursions since the 1560s. The deeds of Candidius among the indigenous people would become legendary — in particular, a number of paramedical 'miracles' in which he used rudimentary skills to treat ailing tribespeople. Three centuries later, there would still be folktales among the Amis of his magical healing powers. McGovern, *Among the Head-Hunters of Formosa*, loc. 3737.

36 Andrade, *How Taiwan Became Chinese*, Chapter 6, Section 7.

37 See, for example, Smits' *Maritime Ryukyu*; MacKay's 'Pirate Nations'.

38 Campbell, *Formosa Under the Dutch*, p. 39. Wong, *China's Conquest of Taiwan*, p. 57, suggests that Iquan actually rose to power in the organisation as the catamite of its former leader, a queering of history yet to be fully investigated.

39 Andrade, *How Taiwan Became Chinese*, Chapter 6, Section 9, cautions that there are not yet enough available sources to confirm that Zheng Zhilong was in full collaboration with the Dutch, and that it is unwise to speculate too much. Then again, *someone* had to move thousands of Chinese settlers across the Strait, and since it couldn't have been the Dutch

alone, the most obvious candidate is the master of the region's largest shipping fleet.

40 Chiu, *The Colonial 'Civilizing' Process in Dutch Formosa*, p. 29.

41 Again, this is a matter that historians are sure to revisit. For now, we can surely admit that the VOC and the Zheng organisation formed a mutually beneficial and unstoppable synergy in the 1620s. Chinese historians are increasingly asserting the agency of the Chinese themselves in what was an overwhelmingly ethnic-Chinese operation, with a handful of VOC officials claiming the credit for it at the top.

42 Blussé and Everts, *The Formosan Encounter*, Vol. I, p. 18.

43 Campbell, *Formosa Under the Dutch*, p. 12.

44 Chiu, *The Colonial 'Civilizing' Process in Dutch Formosa*, p. 21.

45 I lack the space to really go into all the machinations of the Dutch in a single chapter, but recommend the works of Tonio Andrade and Chiu Hsin-hui to anyone seeking to delve further.

46 The reader may enjoy a longer appraisal of Nicholas Iquan's achievements to be found in Clements, *Coxinga and the Fall of the Ming Dynasty*, pp. 51–89.

47 Blussé, 'The Cave of the Black Spirits', pp. 147–8.

48 Ibid., p. 149. Blussé revisits the original Dutch accounts of the extermination, but also notes that modern-day tourist signage on Lamey (Xiao Liuqiu) completely bodges the story behind the 'Black Spirit Cave', claiming instead that it was occupied by 'fugitive Negroes' [sic] from the entourage of Koxinga who were killed by the men of a British warship after attacking some of its crew on land.

49 Chiu, *The Colonial 'Civilizing' Process in Dutch Formosa*, p. 69.

50 Ibid., p. 100. The fact that Chiu takes 40 pages to cover a single paragraph of events should tell you how much drama I am missing out for space.

51 Everts, 'Jacob Lamay van Taywan', pp. 145–7.

3. Rebel Base

1   Clements, *Coxinga and the Fall of the Ming Dynasty*, p. 127.
2   Wong, *China's Conquest of Taiwan*, p. 89. I have substituted my own translation, since Wong's is rather free.
3   Ibid., p. 108.
4   Ong, *Taiwan: A History of Agonies*, p. 79.
5   Campbell, *Formosa Under the Dutch*, pp. 63–4.
6   Ibid., p. 65.
7   Ibid., p. 459.
8   Clements, *Coxinga and the Fall of the Ming Dynasty*, p. 182. Purportedly, the idea was suggested to the Qing by Huang Wu, a defector from Koxinga's army, who realised it would present a severe blow.
9   Ibid., pp. 145–68; see also Wong, *China's Conquest of Taiwan*, p. 102.
10 Ong, *Taiwan: A History of Agonies*, p. 86.
11 Clements, *Coxinga and the Fall of the Ming Dynasty*, p. 191.
12 Yang, *Xian Wang Shilu Jiaozhu*, pp. 202–3.
13 Campbell, *Formosa Under the Dutch*, p. 416. When Frederick Coyett was put on trial for his alleged mismanagement of the defence of Taiwan, he wrote an impassioned account of his superiors' incompetence and his men's devoted defence, much of which is reprinted in Campbell.
14 Clements, *Coxinga and the Fall of the Ming Dynasty*, p. 200.
15 Andrade, *Lost Colony*, p. 186.
16 Watanabe, *The Meiji Japanese Who Made Modern Taiwan*, p. 54.
17 Ong, *Taiwan: A History of Agonies*, p. 91. Ong's figures seem to refer solely to the *Chinese* population of Taiwan, an exclusion of the indigenous population that he would himself later acknowledge.
18 Andrade, *Lost Colony*, pp. 188–9. I restore 'on the Eastern Expedition' for the term that Andrade glosses as 'in Taiwan'.
19 Campbell, *Formosa Under the Dutch*, p. 421.
20 Chiu, *The Colonial 'Civilizing' Process in Dutch Formosa*, p. 222.
21 Andrade, *Lost Colony*, pp. 279–80. Andrade uncovers Dutch claims that argue Radis was a double agent, sent by Coyett to infiltrate the enemy camp and assassinate Koxinga, a mission that seems to have been news to Coyett.
22 Ibid., p. 285. This evocative image is one of many from the diary of the interpreter Philip Meij, only published in 2003, and rightly described by Andrade as containing 'the finest first-hand descriptions of Koxinga ever discovered'.
23 Tsai, *Passage to China*, p. 118.
24 Ong, *Taiwan: A History of Agonies*, p. 93. Xing, *Conflict and Commerce*, p. 146, notes it is a paraphrase of a similar line from the Bronze Age *Spring and Autumn Annals*.
25 Xing, *Conflict and Commerce*, pp. 146, 155.
26 Ibid., p. 160.
27 Hung, *Taiwan Under the Cheng Family*, p. 148, for example, states that the entire regime 'passed from incipient crisis to near collapse' on Koxinga's death. Zheng Jing's achievement in simply holding it together is one of the matters often overlooked. If some of Koxinga's relatives had their way, a falsified will would have testified that he died desiring accommodation with the Manchus, and history would have looked very different.
28 Ho, *Taiwan no Yōkai Densetsu*, pp. 22, 42, 78.
29 Ong, *Taiwan: A History of Agonies*, p. 88, states that a brief military parade past the villages in the immediate area around Fort Provintia was the 'only time' Koxinga ever left his residence there.
30 Ho, *Taiwan no Yōkai Densetsu*, p. 184. The original carving on the rock, now lost, referred to Koxinga's mother not by her Japanese surname, Tagawa, but by the supposed surname of her Chinese father or stepfather, Weng,

suggesting that whoever carved it was intimately familiar with the complexities of her origins, for which see Clements, *Coxinga and the Fall of the Ming Dynasty*, p. 281 n26. The statue in the modern temple looks suspiciously like a repurposed image of the sea goddess Mazu. I can well imagine a Formosan cult of a 'mother stone' eventually leading to the question 'Whose mother?' and the consequent evolution of the most obvious and alluring answer.

31 Thompson, 'Earliest Chinese Eyewitness Accounts', p. 201. The identification of the textual 'Douweilongan' people with the Atayal is made in 'Dui yuan zhumin de zhengfa' at https://www.taiwanus.net/history/2/31.htm

32 Xing, *Conflict and Commerce*, p. 162.

33 Ho, *Taiwan no Yōkai Densetsu*, p. 140.

34 Anon., 'Sword-lion mail boxes become public attraction'. Some accounts place the origin of the sword-lions as an affectation of Chinese troops stationed in Tainan during the Qing era, after 1683, but I repeat the version of the legend as it was told to me repeatedly by Tainan residents.

35 Chinese Wikipedia confidently claims that this was actually a reference to Anping Bridge, a fondly remembered landmark back in Quanzhou. I have not seen this assertion anywhere else.

36 Ong, *Taiwan: A History of Agonies*, p. 34, notes that many of these name changes were initiated by Koxinga himself, who was deeply superstitious, and hated the idea of a place called Taiwan, as to him it sounded like a homonym for 'burial afterwards'.

37 Xing, 'Contradictory Contingencies', p. 179.

38 Ibid., p. 180. Xing, *Conflict and Commerce*, p. 179, records that this was no private comment, but a term used by commoners abroad.

39 Xing, *Conflict and Commerce*, p. 163.

40 Xing, 'Contradictory Contingencies', p. 175, observes that this split, between Zheng Jing as either a Ming loyalist focused on the mainland, and as the ruler of a thriving island kingdom, is also reflected in modern historiography, with 'Blue' Nationalist historians focusing on the former, and 'Green' historians on the latter.

41 Xing, *Conflict and Commerce*, p. 178.

42 Hung, *Taiwan Under the Cheng Family*, p. 296: 'none of the [Zheng] rulers on Taiwan proclaimed a new state.' The term *wang* has been so devalued within imperial protocols that it is perfectly reasonable these days to translate it as 'prince'.

43 Wong, *China's Conquest of Taiwan*, p. 164. I have polished Wong's prose a bit, as his editors don't seem to have bothered.

44 Xing, *Conflict and Commerce*, p. 182.

45 Ibid., p. 190.

46 Ibid., p. 211.

47 Ong, *Taiwan: A History of Agonies*, p. 101. Wong, *China's Conquest of Taiwan*, p. 191, regards such assurances as 'utterly detestable' to the Manchus, and liable to be bogus.

48 Xing, *Conflict and Commerce*, p. 223.

49 Clements, *Coxinga and the Fall of the Ming Dynasty*, p. 256.

50 Xing, *Conflict and Commerce*, p. 229.

51 Hung, *Taiwan Under the Cheng Family*, p. 228, mentions that Keshuang's advisers briefly dusted off the old plan to invade the Philippines as a new redoubt, only for Liu Guoxuan to talk them out of it, as his defeated troops were in no mood for yet another venture.

52 Chuang, *Historical Sites of the First Rank*, p. 128. Hung, *Taiwan Under the Cheng Family*, p. 274, notes that 17 other lower-ranking Ming princes on Taiwan accepted Qing terms and journeyed to the mainland.

53 Xing, *Conflict and Commerce*, p. 234.

4. Beyond the Sea

1 Teng, 'Taiwan in the Chinese Imagination', p. 1. The quote is from the *Veritable Record of the Kangxi Emperor* for 27 November 1683. Hung, *Taiwan Under the Cheng Family*, p. 292, observes that the Qing administration retained 'practically all' of the institutions and boundaries established by the Kingdom of Dongning, doing little more than changing the signage.

2 Keliher, *Out of China*, p. 71.

3 Teng, 'Taiwan in the Chinese Imagination', p. 7.

4 Crook and Hung, *A Culinary History of Taipei*, loc. 432.

5 One would be forgiven for thinking that, just as the word Fujian becomes *Hokkien* in its native pronunciation, a *Hoklo* would be a twist on the Mandarin *Fu-lao* — 'folk from Fujian'. The topic has been a matter of considerable dispute among the Hoklo themselves, and the other language groups that talk about them. In the Hakka language, 'folk from Fujian' is a perfectly reasonable translation, but the Cantonese-speakers on their borders often assume it is a different *Hok*, meaning 'learned folk'. The Hoklo themselves insist it should be translated as 'river venerable', while Mandarin-speakers have created a trend, repeated in some modern dictionaries, for assuming that Hok and Lo actually refer to ancestral homes somewhere near the Yellow and Luo rivers.

6 Both the Republic of China and the People's Republic of China insist that their national language is Mandarin Chinese, and then act surprised when huge swathes of their citizenry don't speak it. Cantonese and Hokkien are bullishly filed as 'dialects'. The word 'Hokkien' is actually the Hokkien pronunciation of the word 'Fujian' — see Notes on Names.

7 Ong, *Taiwan: A History of Agonies*, p. 106, notes that Shi Lang himself held a number of grievances against the

Hakka, and did his best to limit their migration to Taiwan during his period in office.

8 Thompson, 'Earliest Chinese Eyewitness Accounts', p. 186.

9 Ibid., p. 186.

10 Ibid., p. 186.

11 Ibid., p. 180.

12 Ishii, *Island of Formosa*, p. 4. Lin's observations were published in 1685, and based on his observations made during the previous decade. I include them here for the sake of concision.

13 Thompson, 'Earliest Chinese Eyewitness Accounts', p. 197.

14 Alsford, *Transitions to Modernity in Taiwan*, p. 87.

15 Thompson, 'Earliest Chinese Eyewitness Accounts', p. 198.

16 Ong, *Taiwan: A History of Agonies*, p. 112. Ong dates the song's first inclusion in a compendium to the Daoguang era (1820–1850).

17 Thompson, 'Earliest Chinese Eyewitness Accounts', p. 187. Alsford, *Transitions to Modernity in Taiwan*, p. 77, translates the same quote as: 'Since the Chaos of Creation, no axe has entered here.'

18 Ibid., p. 188.

19 Ibid., p. 188.

20 Davidson, *Formosa, Past and Present*, p. 70.

21 Shepherd, 'Island Frontier of the Ch'ing', p. 114.

22 The term given in Chinese is '*qiang qu*' which is 'forced marriage' but I feel that we might as well call a spade a spade.

23 Murray, *Origins of the Tiandihui*, p. 14.

24 Davidson, *Formosa, Past and Present*, pp. 71–2.

25 Lamley, 'Subethnic Rivalry', p. 296.

26 Antony, *Rats, Cats, Rogues, and Heroes*, pp. 1–2.

27 Leong, *Migration and Ethnicity in Chinese History*, p. 54. A more obvious spike in Hakka migration to Taiwan might be placed after the prominent contribution of Hakkas towards the suppression of the Lin Shuangwen rebellion.

28 Chou, *A New Illustrated History of Taiwan*, p. 73. It would drop again to today's 12 per cent when the influx of *waisheng* refugees in the 1940s overwhelmed the country with other Chinese.

29 Ho, *Taiwan no Yōkai Densetsu*, pp. 123–4. The name Guzong only exists in Chinese sources, and may merely be an approximation of the original Thao. The date is not available, but the earliest Chinese gravestone was recently revealed by low-level waters in a drought, and dates the first burial of a Chinese colonist to 1746.

30 Harris, *Peking Gazette*, p. 228.

31 Goddard, *The Makers of Taiwan*, pp. 50–1. Goddard's breathless account reflects the KMT textbooks of the 1960s, long before the backlash against the Wu Feng legend began.

32 Chou, *A New Illustrated History of Taiwan*, pp. 72–3.

33 Chu, *The Triads as Business*, p. 71.

34 der Haar, *Ritual and Mythology of the Chinese Triads*, p. 29. It was the seizure of Triad materials and the interrogation of rebels in 1767–1768 that provided the first glimpses of Triad lore in the historical record. It had arguably already been evolving for several generations by that point. The story about the Shaolin Temple is nonsense; see Murray, *The Origins of the Tiandihui*, p. 162. The common claim in Triad lore, that the mother organisation first developed in 1674, makes me suspect that some elements of it arose during the Revolt of the Three Feudatories (1673–1681), when Chinese on Taiwan were briefly drawn into an irredentist Ming uprising. Manthorpe, *Forbidden Nation*, p. 118, tells the tantalising yarn that Ming loyalists, including Koxinga's nephew, 'Cheng Kuan Tat' hid out at the Shaolin Temple and founded the Triads. He offers no citation for this, the use of Cantonese romanisation in which betrays it as a Hong Kong fantasy.

35 der Haar, *Ritual and Mythology of the Chinese Triads*, p. 338.

36 Ho, *Taiwan no Yōkai Densetsu*, pp. 96–7. The location of the tomb today is a mere plot of land in an otherwise unremarkable suburban street.

37 der Haar, *Rituals and Mythology of the Chinese Triads*, p. 362.

38 Murray, *Origins of the Tiandihui*, pp. 26–7. I use the term 'Triads' hereafter for brevity's sake, but most documentation in Chinese in this period calls them the Heaven and Earth Society (*Tiandihui*).

39 Keliher, *Out of Formosa*, p. 47.

5. Warlike Enterprise

1 Clements, *Brief History of China*, p. 230.

2 Li, 'Xu Zonggan dui Taiwan Yingwu Banbing zhi Zhengdun', pp. 539–40.

3 Tsai, *Maritime Taiwan*, p. 66.

4 Ouchterlony, *The Chinese War*, pp. 501–2. Some sources claim that the Indians onboard were Sepoy soldiers, not non-combatants.

5 Pickering, *Pioneering in Formosa*, p. 46.

6 Tsai, *Maritime Taiwan*, p. 67.

7 Davidson, *Formosa, Past and Present*, p. 108.

8 Tsai, *Maritime Taiwan*, p. 68; but compare to Gordon, *Confrontation Over Taiwan*, p. 181, who reports on the '*poor* quality' of the coal. Dan Patridge, a survivor of the *Anne*, wrote bitterly in *British Captives in China*, p. 63, of his annoyance with the British ambassador and his minions, 'none of whom took any notice of us afterwards, or as far as I know, represented our case of cruel captivity in China to the Government'.

9 Otness, *One Thousand Westerners*, p. 1.

10 Tsai, *Maritime Taiwan*, p. 72.

11 Ibid., p. 78.

12 Ibid., p. 82.

13 Otness, *One Thousand Westerners*, p. 2.

14 Davidson, *Formosa, Past and Present*, p. 181. I cover only a selection of the incidents he lists. Not every one was a murderous disaster. The men of the

Susan Douglas, wrecked in 1864 in indigenous territory, were 'kindly treated and supported by the natives for over a month'.

15 Harris, *Peking Gazette*, p. 232 (1886).

16 Tsai, *Maritime Taiwan*, pp. 83–4.

17 Ibid., p. 80.

18 Pickering, *Pioneering in Formosa*, p. 39. In 1893, shortly before the island was annexed by Japan, Pickering estimated that the European trading houses operating on Taiwan made an annual turnover of £4.5 million — about £562 million in today's money. The price of camphor on the international market would double by the 1880s, but collapsed after 1903, when the Finnish scientist Gustaf Komppa perfected a method of synthesising it.

19 Ibid., p. 206.

20 Ibid., p. 216. It seems likely that it was this bombardment that also finally destroyed the old Dutch base at Fort Zeelandia, which was left in a ruined state thereafter and was further dilapidated by locals in search of building materials. The stepped pyramid that is on the site today was built from the rubble during the Japanese era, and in no way reflects the size and shape of the original fort.

21 House, *The Japanese Expedition to Formosa*, p. 10.

22 Le Gendre, *Notes of Travel in Formosa*, p. 329.

23 Bax, *The Eastern Seas*, p. 249.

24 Chaïkin, *The Sino-Japanese War*, p. 31.

25 For details of the machinations over the Taiwan expedition, which was itself an extrusion of local politics back in Japan, see Clements, *Japan at War in the Pacific*, pp. 42–4.

26 House, *The Japanese Expedition to Formosa*, pp. 16–17. The *New York* was successfully prevented from leaving on

the expedition, which led to the bizarre sight of the Japanese unsuccessfully suing its owners in a California court for failing to fulfil their contract. Gordon, *Confrontation Over Taiwan*, p. 100.

27 Bax, *The Eastern Seas*, pp. 261–2.

28 Eskildsen, 'An Army as Good and Efficient', p. 55.

29 Such confusions would continue throughout the Japanese colonial period. See, for example, Simon, *Truly Human*, p. 96.

30 Bax, *The Eastern Seas*, pp. 265–6.

31 Ibid., pp. 273–4.

32 He resigned soon after, claiming to be facing an incompetent bureaucracy with little support from Beijing.

33 The term 'warlike enterprise' shows up in the *Peking Gazette* for 5 December 1874, but was a classical allusion by its author, reaching back to Suetonius through Shakespeare. Harris, *Peking Gazette*, p. 226.

34 Harris, *Peking Gazette*, p. 227.

35 Taylor, 'Formosa', p. 224.

36 Tsai, *Maritime Taiwan*, p. 96.

37 Tsai, *Passage to China*, p. 56.

38 Davidson, *The Island of Formosa*, p. 254.

39 Ibid., p. 255, substituting today's Daxi for Davidson's Tokoham, which is actually the Atayal name for the river that flows through it.

40 Mackay, *From Far Formosa*, pp. 275–6.

41 Teng, 'Taiwan in the Chinese Imagination', p. 22.

42 Chaïkin, *The Sino-Japanese War*, p. 31. Or so he claimed. The Japanese minutes of his meeting with Marquis Itō Hirobumi instead show Li making veiled threats of foreign intervention, including the pointed statement: 'I don't think Britain will be happy to see any country except China in possession of Formosa.' Quo, 'British Diplomacy and the Cession of Formosa', p. 142.

6. Perfect Panic

1 Lien, *Taiwan Tongshi*, 4.6.

2 Ibid., 4.3.

3 Alsford, *Transitions to Modernity in Taiwan*, pp. 5–6.

4 Ibid., p. 65.

5 Ibid., p. 44.

6 Davidson, *Formosa, Past and Present*, pp. 279–80. See also Lee, *Republic*

of Taiwan Postal History and Postage Stamps, p. 406.

7   Lamley, 'The 1895 Taiwan Republic', p. 739.

8   Pickering, *Pioneering in Formosa*, p. 48.

9   *North China Herald*, No. 1453, 6 June 1895, p. 863. The report had been delayed two weeks by the cutting of telegraph lines during the invasion.

10 Alsford, *Transitions to Modernity in Taiwan*, p. 157.

11 Lamley, 'The 1895 Taiwan Republic', p. 758.

12 Ibid., p. 740n.

13 Lien, *Taiwan Tongshi*, 4.4.

14 Chou, *A New Illustrated History of Taiwan*, p. 151.

15 Ibid., p. 152.

16 Takekoshi, *Japanese Rule in Formosa*, p. 84.

17 Lamley, 'The 1895 Taiwan Republic', p. 753.

18 Clements, *Japan at War in the Pacific*, p. 80. It's this fact, coupled with Tang's unlikely claims of secret foreign deals, that is likely to have provoked Qiu Fengjia into writing to the Emperor that 'various countries' were blocking the terms of the treaty; see Tsai, *Passage to China*, p. 75.

19 Alsford, *Transitions to Modernity in Taiwan*, p. 45.

20 Lamley, 'The 1895 Taiwan Republic', p. 751; Alsford, *Transitions to Modernity in Taiwan*, p. 156. A vague nod from a passing French sailor strikes me as a risky thing to base a republic on, but Tang was clutching at straws.

21 Davidson, *Formosa, Past and Present*, p. 285.

22 Alsford, *Transitions to Modernity in Taiwan*, p. 171.

23 Davidson, *Formosa, Past and Present*, p. 282.

24 Tsai, *Passage to China*, p. 55.

25 Ibid., p. 58. This was not merely a case of the same animal sign, but of the same elemental *and* animal sign (in this case, *jiazi*, or Wood/Rat) — a conjunction that occurs once every sixty years.

26 *North China Herald*, No. 1451, 24 May 1895, p. 779.

27 Lamley, 'The 1895 Taiwan Republic', p. 746, points to a meeting on 16 May in which Qiu and a delegation of Hakkas met with Tang and demanded that he form an independent 'island state' (*dao guo*). When he refused, they telegraphed the mainland to announce that he was a mere figurehead, and that they would pursue independence of their own accord. A week later, left out in the cold by his contacts on the mainland, Tang appeared to answer their request with the declaration of independence, although as Lamley observes, it wasn't that much of a 'request'.

28 Alsford, *Transitions to Modernity in Taiwan*, p. 65. 'Bribe' seems a trifle unfair — one might equally argue that he just wanted to get paid.

29 Davidson, *Formosa, Past and Present*, p. 297.

30 Lien, *Taiwan Tongshi*, 4.12. I resisted the 'disguised as a woman' phrase for many days while writing this book, but its appearance in Alsford, *Transitions to Modernity in Modern Taiwan*, p. 163, convinced me that it was not random sensationalist gossip after all.

31 *North China Herald*, No. 1453, 7 June 1895, p. 851. Davidson, *Formosa, Past and Present*, pp. 307–9, gives a blow-by-blow account of the incident, in which unpaid shore-based troops reacted with understandable annoyance to the sight of the president's paymaster bringing money aboard the *Arthur* to pay its crew.

32 Davidson, *Formosa, Past and Present*, pp. 301–2.

33 Davidson may have been repeating a commonplace elision in Chinese, which was to call Hakkas *Yue*, i.e. Cantonese. Many of them did come from Canton (Guangdong province), but so did many non-Hakkas. See Chou, *A New Illustrated History of Taiwan*, p. 72.

34 Davidson, *Formosa, Past and Present*, p. 305.

35 Bennett, *Japan and the London Illustrated News*, p. 386 (8 June 1895).

36 *North China Herald*, No. 1457, 5 July 1895, p. 16.

37 Davidson, *Formosa, Past and Present*, p. 291. Prince Kitashirakawa was a German-trained officer in Japan's modern army, but also a figure of some embarrassment to the Japanese, since he had previously been a pretender to the imperial throne. For details of his past, see Clements, *Japan at War in the Pacific*, p. 29.

38 Davidson, *Formosa, Past and Present*, p. 311.

39 Ibid., pp. 319–20. Davidson calls it Teckcham; I've switched it to Hsinchu because life is hard enough.

40 Ibid., p. 323. Takekoshi, *Japanese Rule in Formosa*, p. 88, makes very similar observations, but is more forgiving of the principles of guerrilla warfare, at which, he concedes, the Chinese are 'adept'.

41 Alsford, *Transitions to Modernity in Taiwan*, p. 172.

42 Lee, *Republic of Taiwan Postal History and Postage Stamps*, p. 108. McCallum had tried to flee Taiwan with his colleagues, but had been 'prevented from boarding the *Spartan*' that had spirited most of the foreigners out of Tainan, and was marooned on the island to supervise the ongoing exports of 'sugar, camphor and others', even in the midst of the Japanese invasion.

43 Lee, *Republic of Taiwan Postal History and Postage Stamps*, p. 124.

44 Ibid., p. 96.

45 Ibid., p. 78.

46 Lamley, 'The 1895 Taiwan Republic', p. 755.

47 Davidson, *Formosa, Past and Present*, p. 325.

48 Ibid., pp. 327–9. I have replaced Davidson's place names with those in use today.

49 Katz, 'Germs of Disaster', pp. 209–12.

50 Lien, *Taiwan Tongshi*, 4.19.

51 Tsai, *A Passage to China*, p. 80.

52 Ibid., p. 67, which he translates more exactly with extensive commentary on the classical allusions in the third line, which I have glossed for brevity. See also Hummel, *Eminent Chinese of the Ch'ing Period*, pp. 171–2. Qiu's role in the defence of Taiwan and the establishment of the Republic of China made him a dual hero in the eyes of the KMT, and his Hakka connections did him no harm in the ROC political economy. He lends his name to a modern-day university, as well as a frigate, the former USS *Gary*, officially commissioned into the Taiwanese navy in 2018. It's not clear precisely when Qiu left Taiwan. Hummel's text restricts itself to 'that year'. Goddard, *Makers of Taiwan*, p. 82, suggests it was not until October, possibly misreading the text in Hummel. I follow Tsai, *Passage to China*, p. 61, which states he left Taiwan 'two months' after Tang's flight on 6 June.

53 Bennett, *Japan and the London Illustrated News*, p. 384 (20 April 1895). The *News* claimed that the ship was crewed and captained by Chinese, which does not explain why it was flying a British flag. Possibly this is the same 'treasure' mentioned by Davidson in *Formosa, Part and Present*, p. 283, ferried to Taiwan by Billy Waters, a former barkeep and winner of a Montana boxing competition. Waters told Davidson that he was now the Formosan 'Minister of War', which would have been news to the Formosan Minister of War. Otness, *One Thousand Westerners*, p. 165, more accurately rates him as the 'chief artillery officer' in Tamsui.

54 Bennett, *Japan and the Illustrated London News*, p. 387 (8 June 1895).

55 Lien, *Taiwan Tongshi*, 4.17. Alsford, *Transitions to Modernity in Taiwan*, p. 181, has Liu offering a conditional surrender calling for a pardon for all Chinese forces, which the Japanese refused. Clearly, the different sides had a different concept of what constituted 'clemency'. Kinder readers might regard Liu's subsequent flight in this context, not as the exit of a coward, but of a

defeated general sure he would be executed.

56 Davidson, *Formosa, Past and Present*, p. 349.

57 Lee, *Republic of Taiwan Postal History and Postage Stamps*, p. 110. As for the stamps, they would indeed become valuable commodities in the expat community. As late as 1917, there were reports of sheets being traded on the Chinese market by would-be speculators, sometimes clearly trading in fakes (p. 230).

58 Lien, *Taiwan Tongshi*, 4.23.

59 Takekoshi, *Japanese Rule in Formosa*, p. 90; Davidson, *Formosa, Past and Present*, p. 363.

60 McGovern, *Among the Head-Hunters of Formosa*, loc. 3628.

7. Takasago

1 Sterk, *Indigenous Cultural Translation*, p. 29.

2 Takekoshi, *Japanese Rule in Formosa*, p. 86. I remain amazed at the historiographical acrobatics required to make such a claim, particularly considering the likelihood that Koxinga's mother was half-Chinese herself. The possibility that he only had one Japanese grandparent is liable to have been a contributing factor for him leaving Japan in the first place during Tokugawa purges of foreigners, whereas his half-brother Shichizaemon, who would have had three Japanese grandparents, remained in Japan for his whole life. See Clements, *Coxinga and the Fall of the Ming Dynasty*, p. 26.

3 Pickering, *Pioneering in Formosa*, p. vii.

4 Ibid., p. 49.

5 Wu Zhuoliu, quoted by Phillips, *Between Assimilation and Independence*, p. 19.

6 Watanabe, *The Meiji Japanese Who Made Taiwan*, p. 200.

7 Takekoshi, *Japanese Rule in Formosa*, p. 4. Takekoshi is able to devote an entire chapter to the 'brigand uprisings' that characterised the official Japanese victory over the Republic of Formosa. I gloss it all in a couple of sentences here merely for space.

8 Ibid., p. 5.

9 Roy, 'The Discourse and Practice of Colonial "Suppression"', p. 44. My thanks to Katy Hui-wen Hung, for pointing out that the term for 'savage' here was retconned into the name by the Japanese, who changed the term 番 to 蕃. The transition from 'barbarians' to 'savages' in the eyes of the administration might appear minor, but goes to the state of mind of the aforesaid administration. Barclay, *Kondo the Barbarian*, p. 13, notes that the electrified fence was operated from a central guardhouse, and hence often killed unwary Japanese guards as well.

10 Watanabe, *The Meiji Japanese Who Made Taiwan*, p. 96.

11 Ibid., p. 215. The tiger flag's unlikely fate was pointed out to me by Katy Hui-wen Hung, who found it in the Academia Sinica archives: https://www.ith.sinica.edu.tw/archives/collections_con2_en.php?no=177

12 Ibid., pp. 226–8. Japan did have the capability to grow sugar cane on Kyushu and sugar beets on Hokkaido, but the acquisition of Taiwan vastly increased the available quantity, causing a drop in local prices and a willingness to experiment at both industrial and domestic levels.

13 Phillips, *Between Assimilation and Independence*, p. 19.

14 Roy, 'The Discourse and Practice of Colonial "Suppression"', p. 48.

15 Kitamura, 'Relistening to Her and His Stories', p. 119, characterises the 1903 massacre as a critical turning point in both attitudes and demographics, pushing some Seediq towards resistance and others towards resignation, and leading ultimately to the Musha Incident a generation later.

16 Roy, 'The Discourse and Practice of Colonial "Suppression"', p. 51.

17 Tsai, *Passage to China*, p. 109.

18 Ibid., p. 122.

19 Katz, 'Governmentality and its Consequences', pp. 404–5.

20 McGovern, *Among the Head-Hunters of Formosa*, loc. 1336.

21 Ibid., loc. 1255.

22 See, for example, Watanabe, *Taiwan Risshiki Kenchiku Kikō*.

23 Ho, *Taiwan no Yōkai Densetsu*, p. 111.

24 Shackleton, *Formosa Calling*, loc. 154.

25 Watanabe, *The Meiji Japanese Who Made Modern Taiwan*, p. 24. The 'prosperous century' claim from the Hōrai Rice song turned out to be a little on-the-nose. As early as 1934, hydrologists were warning the authorities that the damming and canal scheme throughout Taiwan was subject to severe silting issues, and might only remain operational until the 2030s.

26 Ibid., pp. 128–68.

27 Barclay, *Outcasts of Empire*, p. 43.

28 Barclay, *Kondo the Barbarian*, p. 102, has an evocative scene in which Seediq tribesmen, planning a war party, are obliged to go to the local Japanese subprefect and request 'a little over a kilo of gunpowder ... and some matchlock fuses'.

29 Barclay, 'The Musha Incident', p. 81.

30 Berry, *The Musha Incident*, p. 18.

31 Sterk, *Indigenous Cultural Translation*, p. 3.

32 Ching, *Becoming 'Japanese'*, p. 138. Many accounts of the Musha Incident draw a discreet veil over the incident itself, preferring to focus with postmodern concision on the events before and after. Barclay, *Kondo the Barbarian*, p. 33, notes that the school massacre was preceded by several dawn raids on police stations to acquire the necessary weapons.

33 Berry, *The Musha Incident*, p. 26.

34 Ching, *Becoming 'Japanese'*, pp. 141–2. Barclay, *Kondo the Barbarian*, p. 33, observes that 'Japanese overseers were fussy about gouges and cuts on the felled timber', insisting that the logs be physically carried out of the forests instead of rolled or dragged. This only added to the Seediq's annoyance.

35 Simon, *Truly Human*, p. 261.

36 Sterk, *Indigenous Cultural Translation*, p. 36.

37 Barclay, *Kondo the Barbarian*, pp. 42–3; Sterk, *Indigenous Cultural Translation*, p. 26.

38 I give the Mandarin here for ease of identification, but the song is better known through its Taiwanese pronunciation 'Bang Chhun Hong'. The author was a Hakka, Ten Yu-hsien.

39 Lu, *My Fight for a New Taiwan*, p. 115, writes of it being used to calm demonstrators at the confrontation over *Formosa* magazine — see Chapter Nine.

40 Tsai, 'Taiwan Music History'. The banned song was voted the nation's favourite a generation later in 1965 by readers of the *Taiwan Daily*, see Huang, 'Cultural Hybridization of Taiyu Pop Songs', p. 97.

41 See Clements, *Japan at War in the Pacific*, pp. 89–90, for an example, the Amoy Incident of 1901. Such events are not strictly speaking part of the history of 'Taiwan', at least not in a necessarily concise book as this.

42 Ibid., pp. 190–1.

43 Huang, 'The Cultural Hybridization of Taiyu Pop Songs', p. 95. The use of the term 'five-coloured flag' implies that the Chinese song was appropriated by the Japanese to refer to Manchukuo, the Japanese puppet state in north-east China.

44 Huang, 'The *Yamatodamashii* of the Takasago Volunteers of Taiwan', p. 224.

45 Ibid., p. 226.

46 Ibid., p. 228.

47 Ibid., p. 231.

48 Watanabe, *The Meiji Japanese Who Made Modern Taiwan*, p. 196.

8. The Law of Squeeze

1   Fenby, *Generalissimo*, loc. 6647.

2   Ibid., loc. 7388. See also Lin, *Accidental State*, for a fuller account of the politicking around Cairo and the many might-have-beens of history.

3   Fenby, *Generalissimo*, loc. 7390.

4   George Kerr, *Formosa Betrayed*, p. 72.

5   Ibid., p. 74.

6   Phillips, *Between Assimilation and Independence*, pp. 41–2. There is little comment in the historical record about this new republican scheme. George Kerr, *Formosa Betrayed*, p. 112, claims that it was proposed by Japanese officers, and was an idea that even their commander General Andō Rikichi, dismissed as 'mischievous and dangerous.'

7   Wu, quoted in Dawley, 'Closing a Colony', p. 117.

8   I translate the literal meaning here, not the more poetic version put about by the Republic of China with singable English lyrics that inadvertently mirror 'One Vision' by Queen: 'One heart, one soul / One mind, one goal'.

9   Shackleton, *Formosa Calling*, loc. 1494. The scholar Darryl Sterk notes the deep irony at the heart of Kuomintang policy, that 'the Kuomintang had no intention of protecting ethnic minority cultures except to legitimate claims to territory that was now out of reach, on the other side of the Taiwan Strait'. The Kuomintang were ready to rattle sabres and wag fingers at the People's Republic regarding the rights of, say, Tibetans, Mongols, or Uighurs, but not to acknowledge the ethnic communities in Taiwan itself. Not that the Formosans would have fared any better under the People's Republic, which acknowledged the existence of Formosans in 'Taiwan province', but describes them not as a patchwork of different societies, but simply as the *Gaoshanzu*, literally 'High Mountain People', a source of some annoyance, particularly to coastal tribes like the Amis, who do not actually live

on mountains. See Sterk, *Indigenous Cultural Translation*, pp. 17, 26.

10 Phillips, *Between Assimilation and Independence*, pp. 39, 53.

11 Kerr, *Formosa Betrayed*, p. 124.

12 Phillips, *Between Assimilation and Independence*, p. 57. See also Kerr, *Formosa Betrayed*, p. 119.

13 Phillips, *Between Assimilation and Independence*, pp. 59–60.

14 Peng, *Taste of Freedom*, p. 66. George Kerr, *Formosa Betrayed*, p. 64, notes that Taiwan in the 1940s 'was many years in advance of mainland China in terms of technological organization'.

15 Peng, *Taste of Freedom*, pp. 68–9.

16 Kerr, *Formosa Betrayed*, p. 148.

17 Peng, *Taste of Freedom*, p. 70.

18 Kerr, *Formosa Betrayed*, p. 123.

19 Peng, *Taste of Freedom*, pp. 79–80.

20 Kerr, *Formosa Betrayed*, pp. 148–51, mentions many other incidents, including Chinese soldiers gawping in amazement at department store elevators, and the Nationalist signals corps stringing their telecoms wires across an operational railway line into the path of passing trains.

21 Shackleton, *Formosa Calling*, loc. 894.

22 Kerr, *Formosa Betrayed*, p. 159.

23 Ibid., p. xiv.

24 Dawley, 'Closing a Colony', pp. 116, 122.

25 In Taiwanese: 'Bang Li Tsakui'. The Cowherd and the Weaver Girl are the stars Altair and Vega, said to be lovers that can only meet once a year, across a bridge of birds.

26 Kerr, *Formosa Betrayed*, p. 137.

27 Huang, 'The *Yamatodamashii* of the Takasago Volunteers of Taiwan', pp. 233–4.

28 Shackleton, *Formosa Calling*, loc. 552.

29 Ibid., loc. 273.

30 Phillips, *Between Assimilation and Independence*, p. 67.

31 Kerr, *Formosa Betrayed*, p. 317.

32 Lai, *A Tragic Beginning*, pp. 102–4.

33 Ibid., p. 106; Kerr, *Formosa Betrayed*, p. 320.

34 Shackleton, *Formosa Calling*, loc. 277.

35 Wang Kang, quoted in Lai, *A Tragic Beginning*, pp. 106–7.
36 Lai, *A Tragic Beginning*, p. 129.
37 Phillips, *Between Assimilation and Independence*, pp. 38, 99.
38 Kerr, *Formosa Betrayed*, p. 369.
39 21 January 1947 was the last day of the Year of the Dog, followed by the Year of the Pig, which is why I presume the famous epithet 'Dogs leave; Pigs come' dates to this period, and not, as some sources imply, immediately after the arrival of the KMT in 1945. The use of the 'pig' epithet for the Chinese does seem to have been in more general and prosaic use beforehand. See, for example, Kerr, *Formosa Betrayed*, p. 343.
40 Lu, *My Struggle for a New Taiwan*, p. 6.
41 Phillips, *Between Assimilation and Independence*, p. 83.
42 Lu, *My Fight for a New Taiwan*, p. 192.
43 Phillips, *Between Assimilation and Independence*, pp. 95–6.
44 Taylor, *The Generalissimo's Son*, loc. 2056. Chen has since been lionised on the mainland as something of a Communist hero for his attempted defection, but considering his clear approval of private enterprise, one suspects that his career as a Communist would have been very short.
45 Ibid., loc. 2309.
46 Ibid., loc. 2030.
47 Peng, *A Taste of Freedom*, p. 138.
48 Pakula, *The Last Empress*, p. 592.

9. Cold Peace

1 Kerr, *Formosa*, p. xv.
2 Fenby, *Generalissimo*, locs 8962–9075. If I were writing this book in the 1980s or before, Chiang Kai-shek and his entourage would have occupied a far larger component of it. But the political ferment of the last 30 years, particularly Taiwan's split into two-party and then multi-party politics, has substantially diluted the part of Chiang Kai-shek in Taiwanese history, and surely will continue to do so.
3 I knew an ex-soldier in Taipei who told me of periodic incursions on Matsu and the Kinmen islands by 'water ghosts' (*suigui*) — commandos who would swim ashore, often as a bet or a dare, to conduct sabotage or mischief. He told me of his own encounter with one, who swam ashore to face a lone ROC guardsman who was carrying an unloaded rifle. The commando sat on a rock, took out a packet of cigarettes, and asked the trembling rookie for a light. My friend believed that this was a regular occurrence, and served as a sort of hazing prank on both sides.
4 Ong, *Taiwan: A History of Agonies*, p. 254.
5 Peng, *A Taste of Freedom*, p. 146. The political uses of Matsu and the Kinmen islands, as pillars of the KMT's extraordinary powers, was one of the early contentions of *Dangwai* activists.
6 Taylor, *The Generalissimo's Son*, loc. 2547.
7 Denton, *The Landscape of Historical Memory*, pp. 126–33; Crook and Hung, *A Culinary History of Taipei*, locs 1331–64.
8 Chin, *Heijin*, p. 7.
9 Zhang, '228 Zhong de Ba Dakou'.
10 Taylor, *The Generalissimo's Son*, locs 2581 and 2566. The 'military paradises', or 'Unit 831', would remain open on Matsu and the Kinmen islands even after prostitution was declared illegal in the 1960s. The last would not close until 1991. The 21st century has seen a series of flip-flopping on decriminalising prostitution by various Taiwanese administrations, and an attempt by apologists to declare Unit 831 as a necessary evil, in order to protect the womenfolk of the islands from rapacious soldiers. An off-duty soldier in Kenting in 1991 told me that the 'volunteers' in the brothels were often female convicts given a choice between a six-month tour of duty at a military paradise, or prison. Rumours persisted that some of these 'convicts' were actually the daughters

of political dissidents, imprisoned on trumped-up charges as a form of sexual intimidation.

11 Taylor, *The Generalissimo's Son*, loc. 2458.
12 Ibid., loc. 2471.
13 Ibid., locs 2482–4.
14 Ibid., loc. 2617.
15 Taylor, *The Generalissimo's Son*, locs 2619–25.
16 Lu, 'Experiencing the "Enchanting Golden Triangle"', p. 86.
17 Peng, *A Taste of Freedom*, p. 211.
18 Lu, *My Fight for a New Taiwan*, p. 26; Kagan, *Taiwan's Statesman*, p. 50.
19 Lu, *My Fight for a New Taiwan*, p. 25.
20 Chen, 'Producing Mandopop', p. 45.
21 Huang, 'Cultural Hybridization of Taiyu Pop Songs', pp. 97–9.
22 Ibid., p. 102.
23 Craft, *American Justice in Taiwan*, pp. 35, 46.
24 The events of 'Black Friday' and its consequences are covered in detail in Craft, *American Justice in Taiwan*, pp. 101ff.
25 Taylor, *The Generalissimo's Son*, loc. 2832, does not go quite so far as Craft, but does note that the protestors would have had to seek approval from Chiang Ching-kuo's office before assembling, and suggests that he allowed the embassy attack to happen on the grounds that he would have otherwise been forced to authorise opening fire on his own people.
26 Rigger, *The Tiger Leads the Dragon*, p. 26.
27 Miller, *Chip War*, p. 63.
28 Kagan, *Taiwan's Statesman*, p. 180. The young Cornell graduate Lee Teng-hui was accused by the KMT secret police of having co-authored the letter, but would later admit that it was the work of his friend David Tsai (p. 66).

29 Su, *Taiwan's 400 Year History*, pp. 157–79. The book was banned in Taiwan for many years.
30 Taylor, *The Generalissimo's Son*, loc. 3223. This event happened in 1964.
31 Peng, *A Taste of Freedom*, p. 138.
32 Kagan, *Taiwan's Statesman*, p. 59.
33 Peng, *A Taste of Freedom*, pp. 149–52.
34 Ibid., p. 157.
35 Lancashire, 'Popeye and the Case of Guo Yidong aka Bo Yang', pp. 671–2.
36 Peng, *A Taste of Freedom*, p. 240, is frustratingly discreet about the whole affair, and refuses to name names or give details in order to protect his associates and their methods. Milo Thornberry, the Christian missionary-turned-passport-forger, has no such qualms and offers a thrilling blow-by-blow account in his own *Fireproof Moth*, pp. 109–17.
37 Thornberry, *Fireproof Moth*, pp. 124–5; Peng, *A Taste of Freedom*, pp. 246–7.
38 Peng, *A Taste of Freedom*, pp. 266–7.
39 Ibid., p. 279.
40 Ibid., p. 269.
41 Taylor, *The Generalissimo's Son*, loc. 3547. See also Kagan, *Taiwan's Statesman*, p. 68.
42 Jacobs, *The Kaohsiung Incident*, p. 5.
43 Ibid., p. 6.
44 Kuo, 'We're One Family'.
45 Fenby, *Generalissimo*, loc. 9068. It should be noted that formal burial for his remains also ran into partisan trouble during the DPP era, when the incumbent administration baulked at according funereal honours to a man they regarded as a dictator.
46 Jacobs, *The Kaohsiung Incident*, p. 5.
47 Taylor, *The Generalissimo's Son*, locs 2772–7. South Africa only rescinded its recognition of the Republic of China in 1998.
48 Jacobs, *The Kaohsiung Incident*, p. 8.
49 Taylor, *The Generalissimo's Son*, loc. 4090.

10. Black Gold and Wild Lilies

1 Ching, *Becoming 'Japanese'*, pp. 1–4.
2 Dreyer, 'Taiwan-Japan Relations', p. 238. Who knew?

3 Manthorpe, *Forbidden Nation*, p. 209, ably covers the contradictions of Chiang Ching-kuo's chaotic behaviour

in the late 1970s and early 1980s, when he would both call for reforms and attack reformers. Jacobs, *The Kaohsiung Incident*, p. 3, stresses that Chiang Ching-kuo was never an advocate for democracy, and that his actions to protect his own position should not be misinterpreted as such. This was also the claim of Lee Teng-hui, who would say in 2002 that Chiang's hiring of Taiwanese consultants in the 1970s was merely an attempt to 'buy people's hearts' — Kagan, *Taiwan's Statesman*, p. 75.

4 The magazine's Mandarin name was *Meilidao*, 'Beautiful Island', a calque of the Portuguese 'Ilha Formosa' and hence only a rebellious term in historical context.

5 Jacobs, *The Kaohsiung Incident*, pp. 18–20.

6 The song is riddled with political dog whistles — not only 'beautiful island' (Formosa), and the pointed exclusion of new arrivals whose grandfathers *weren't* part of it all (i.e. the *waisheng* refugees), but also the use of *zanmen*, an inclusive form of the more usual *women* for 'us', which includes the listener in the community of the singer, as if recruiting them already.

7 Lu, *My Fight for a New Taiwan*, pp. 115, 185. Huang, 'Cong minyan shengzhang ...' observes that this was no idle phrasing, as Lu had herself appointed Chiu to her election campaign team, specifically to lead crowds in singing activities. He was arrested on the charge of being the 'Formosa [Magazine] Recreation Officer'. 'Come Home Soon' was first sung as a protest song *at* the December event, by the wife of an imprisoned *Dangwai* dissident.

8 Chen, 'Constructive Build-up', p. 120.

9 Ibid., p. 119.

10 Morris, *Defectors from the PRC to Taiwan*, p. 205.

11 Ibid., pp. 167–73.

12 Ibid., p. 175.

13 Chin, *Heijin*, p. 7. See also Rigger, 'Kuomintang Agonistes', p. 61, for the

suggestion that the KMT had since the 1950s, been sitting on a 'war chest' of funds appropriated from the mainland evacuation and seizures among the deported Japanese, which it used to fund many of its off-the-books campaigns and ventures.

14 Chin, *Heijin*, p. 3.

15 Kagan, *Taiwan's Statesman*, p. 11.

16 Ibid., p. 83.

17 Ibid., p. 49.

18 Ibid., p. 87.

19 Anon, 'The past and present of the tribes of Ami'. They had been at loggerheads over a conflict with a third tribe, the Tsikajoman, which the Vat'an had defeated with some difficulty, having mistakenly counted on Tavalong assistance. A punitive Vat'an assault led to the ceding of some Tavalong lands, only for the Tavalong to make a counter-attack some years later. Oral histories, using the four-yearly generation-name system of the Amis, referred to the long-term rivalry commencing 'in the time of Okak and Komod', which meant that it had only been ongoing for a century. It had, it seems, been relatively fresh in 1895 when the Japanese took over the island, but had become part of the fabric of tribal existence by the time Taiwan was retroceded to the Republic of China in 1945.

20 Klöter, 'Language Policy', p. 3.

21 Miller, *Chip War*, p. 167.

22 https://www.nytimes.com/1985/12/26/world/taiwan-chief-rules-out-chance-family-member-will-succeed-him.html

23 Chiang's children, of course, did find their way into high-profile positions, but were edged out of the main race by their own father's actions. Later in the century, covered here in Chapter Eleven, his illegitimate son John Chiang would reclaim his paternity and fashion it into a run for office that was at least partly dynastic. Taylor, *The Generalissimo's Son*, loc. 4513.

24 The record would subsequently be broken by Syria, 1964–2011.

25 Thornberry, *Fireproof Moth*, p. 87.
26 Kagan, *Taiwan's Statesman*, p. 121. Lee is directly alluding to the work of Benedict Anderson, whose book *Imagined Communities* (1983) examined the development worldwide of nationalism.
27 Ibid., p. 120.
28 Kuo, 'We're One Family'.
29 Taylor, *The Generalissimo's Son*, loc. 5006.
30 Han, 'Brawls in the Legislature'.
31 Han, 'The drastic downfall of Wu Feng'.
32 Chin, *Heijin*, pp. 88–90. I picked just one; Chin's book has dozens.
33 Kagan, *Taiwan's Statesman*, p. 143.

34 Rigger, *The Tiger Leading the Dragon*, pp. 31, 40.
35 Ibid., p. 141.
36 Minorities at Risk Project, *Chronology for Aboriginal Taiwanese in Taiwan*.
37 Chang, 'Return to Innocence', p. 331. Musicologists later observed that the 'traditional' tribal song showed traces of a musical scale liable to have been incorporated from Japanese contacts during the colonial period, and that the singers had made modifications of their own to it.
38 Chin, *Heijin*, p. 91.
39 Cheng, 'Conducting a New Political Spectacle', p. 587.

11. Wild Strawberries

1 Cheng, 'Conducting a New Political Spectacle', p. 596.
2 Guy, '"Republic of China National Anthem" on Taiwan', p. 104.
3 Miller, *Chip War*, p. 200.
4 Ibid., pp. 147, 177.
5 Bush, 'Elections and the Challenges of Governing', p. 19.
6 Kagan, *Taiwan's Statesman*, p. 111. These ideas were first mooted at Lee Teng-hui's National Affairs Conference in 1990.
7 Lu, *My Fight for a New Taiwan*, p. 233.
8 IWGIA, Taiwan 2019.
9 Yu, 'Home at Last'.
10 Morris, *Defectors from the PRC to Taiwan*, p. 248.
11 Manthorpe, *Forbidden Nation*, p. 237.
12 Ibid., pp. 240–1.
13 Lu, *My Fight for a New Taiwan*, p. 269.
14 Anon., 'Taiwanese Yasukuni Protest Foiled'.
15 Han, 'Brawls in the Legislature'.
16 https://www.taipeitimes.com/News/front/archives/2006/01/27/2003290901 He claimed that he respectfully waited

until after the 2004 death of Chiang Ching-kuo's widow, Faina, before going public.
17 https://www.coolloud.org.tw/node/30105
18 Anon., 'Lanyu residents accused of abusing free electricity'.
19 Rauhala, 'The "Battle of Taipei"'.
20 deLisle, 'Taiwan's Quest for International Space', p. 240.
21 Buckley and Ramza, 'Singer's Apology' claims that the effect on voters was liable to be only marginal, but that the KMT might lean on it as an excuse for their defeat. Chan, 'Teen pop star', cites an online survey that points to a huge uptick in pro-DPP young voter turnout after the apology, swamping the older voters who were voting for the KMT. She does not disclose whether the 'survey' was a representative sample or a random selection of aggrieved tweets.
22 Rowen, *One China, Many Taiwans*, p. 32.

12. The Tides of History

1 Rigger, 'Kuomintang Agonistes', p. 39.
2 Simon, *Truly Human*, pp. 379–80.
3 Chen, 'Constructive Build-up', p. 108.

4 Ibid., p. 121. Popular myth held that the original plan was to call the aircraft carrier the *Shi Lang*, after the admiral who defeated the Zheng regime (see

Chapter Three). But the convention for Chinese aircraft carriers was to name them after provinces, hence the *Liaoning* and later the *Shandong* and the *Fujian*.

5   Hsiao and Hsiao, 'Cross-Strait relations', p. 138.

6   Ibid., p. 151. Hsiao and Hsiao allude to a timetable of 'two one-hundreds' and claim this represents the centenary of the founding of the Chinese Communist Party (2021) and of the People's Republic (2049). I suspect they have misread the original, and that the 'two centenaries' is actually two *centuries* — the Century of Humiliation that ended in 1949, and the China Dream that is expected to reach its fulfilment in 2049.

7   Saaler, *Men in Metal*, pp. 237, 322.

8   Bush, 'Elections and the Challenges of Governing', p. 30. Tsai Ing-wen never called Brexit a disaster; that was me. She did, in fact, over-optimistically seize upon it as an opportunity for Taiwan to form new trade agreements with a Britain that was doing its best to become the Taiwan of Europe.

9   Ramzy, 'Divisive Monuments'; Chen, 'Bill to propose CKS Hall, statue moves'.

10 Rowen, *One China, Many Taiwans*, p. 118.

11 Hsiao and Hsiao, 'Cross-Strait relations', p. 134.

12 Ibid., p. 149.

13 https://www.musixmatch.com/lyrics/ CHTHONIC-3/A-Crimson-Sky-s-Command

14 Miller, *Chip War*, p. 341.

15 Ibid., p. 341.

16 Ibid., p. xviii.

17 IWGIA, Taiwan 2019.

18 Lin and Shih, 'Court finds process for Indigenous recognition unconstitutional'.

19 See, for example, Bellwood, 'Formosan Prehistory and Austronesian Dispersal', pp. 342–4. The 'Out of Taiwan' hypothesis remains one of the most contentious issues in Taiwan Studies, not the least for the fuel it offers to a number of modern political fires. I choose to discuss it here, not as established fact in Chapter One, because academia is still scuffling over proving it. The arguments in comparative linguistics are compelling, but do not sway *all* comparative linguists, nor are all archaeologists persuaded that the migrations went in a single direction — there may have been a degree of back-and-forth, such that Taiwan might have been *re*-settled by arrivals from the Philippines. More recent research in the Philippines suggests that the Batanes Islands and Luzon were indeed settled by people from Taiwan, but this, too, has been challenged. See Chen, 'The Austronesian Dispersal', pp. 115–6, 131.

20 Culver and Hass, 'Understanding Beijing's Motives'.

21 Wang, 'China's Hidden Tech Revolution', p. 71.

Notes on Names

1   I once made the mistake of asking one of my teachers in Taipei, Ms Zhu, why the Republic of China didn't use Bo Po Mo Fo for transcribing non-Chinese words like 'McDonald's'. You know, like the Japanese. 'Because,' she hissed vehemently, 'we are *not* Japanese!'

2   Kang, 'Indigenous toponyms', p. 67.

INDEX